# Egypt Under the Stars

Astral Religion and Cosmogonic Myth in Ancient Egypt

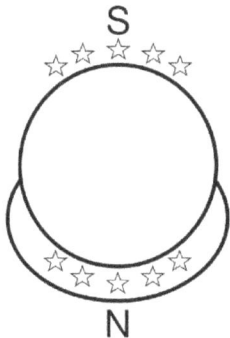

# Ev Cochrane

Zanzara Press

Zanzara Press
PO Box 5069
Madison, WI 53705-5069
USA
zanzarapress.com
editor@zanzarapress.com

EGYPT UNDER THE STARS: ASTRAL RELIGION
AND COSMOGONIC MYTH IN ANCIENT EGYPT
2025 © Ev Cochrane

All rights reserved. No part of this work covered by the copyright hereon may be reproduced or used in any form or by any means—graphic, electronic, or mechanical, including photocopying, recording, taping, or information storage and retrieval systems—without written permission of the publisher. Neither the author nor the publisher make any representation, express or implied, with regard to the accuracy of the information contained in this book and cannot accept any legal responsibility or liability for any errors or omissions that may be made.

ISBN: 978-1-68315-156-2

Our books may be purchased in bulk for promotional, educational, and/or business use. Please contact your local bookseller or the Culicidae Press Sales Department at +1-515-462-0278 or by email at sales@culicidaepress.com

twitter.com/culicidaepress – facebook.com/culicidaepress
threads.net/culicidaepress -– instagram.com/culicidaepress

Book layout and design by polytekton.com

# Table of Contents

Preface ............................................................................................................. 5
Introduction ..................................................................................................... 6

**The Horus-Star** ............................................................................................. 9
    Lord of the Netherworld ........................................................................... 16
    Horus and Nergal ..................................................................................... 19

**The Cataclysmic Context of the King's Ascent to Heaven** ............................ 23

**The Eye of Horus** ........................................................................................ 30

**Horus: Lord of Appearances** ........................................................................ 53

**The Greening of the Cosmos** ....................................................................... 67

**The Return of the Eye of Horus** ................................................................... 74

**Horus in the *Akhet*** ..................................................................................... 86

**Return to the Motherland** ........................................................................... 95

**Horus *spd*** ................................................................................................. 101
    Spd Wr ..................................................................................................... 106

**Sothis, Sirius, and the Astronomical Foundations of Egyptian Chronology** 113

**Lifting the Veil on Sothis/Spdt** .................................................................... 126
    Sothis as Year .......................................................................................... 134
    Summary ................................................................................................. 142

**The Imperishable Stars** .............................................................................. 144

**The Boats of the Sun** .................................................................................. 153

**Localizing the Imperishable Stars in the Egyptian Cosmos** ......................... 164

**Horus and the Ship of Heaven** .................................................................... 170

**Horus of the Daybreak** ................................................................................ 174
    The Doors of Heaven .............................................................................. 176
    Horus in utero ......................................................................................... 182

Horus: Star of the Corporation .................................................................. 184
The Star at the Front of the Sky ................................................................ 189
The Horus-pillar ............................................................................................. 195
The Horus-Bull ............................................................................................... 199
The Separation of Heaven and Earth ..................................................... 204
Identifying Thoth ........................................................................................... 211
The Bull of the Stars .................................................................................... 220
Creation Ideology in Ancient Egypt ........................................................ 225
Conclusion ....................................................................................................... 237

Acknowledgments ........................................................................................ 241
Bibliography .................................................................................................... 242

# Preface

On December 16th, 1993, the world-renowned Egyptologist James Allen mailed me a computer disk containing a complete transliteration of the Pyramid Texts. I was a complete nobody at the time as, in fact, I remain to this very day. Allen's generous gesture launched me upon an odyssey of learning and discovery that has continued unabated for some 30 years now and, I like to think, produced a number of important insights into the astronomical origins of Egyptian religion and cosmogonic myth. Try as I might, I will never be able to repay this singular act of kindness. I dedicate this book to Jim Allen, a gentleman and a scholar and a mentor to this would-be Odysseus, drifter to distant shores.

# Introduction

"The earliest home of the gods that we can discern is the sky."[1]

"Royal ideology and ideas about the Hereafter seem to have had cosmological and stellar foundations which may well go back to predynastic times."[2]

"On the day the young ruler Tutankhamun was placed in his tomb in the Valley of Kings for eternal rest, the people of ancient Egypt had already spent more than 3000 years thinking about what the sky and the sun represented and what they meant."[3]

The towering pyramids and magnificent architectural monuments created by the ancient Egyptians continue to elicit wonder and speculation some five thousand years after they were first constructed. What on earth could have inspired the early pharaohs to commission such colossal structures in the first place?

The conventional story, agreed upon by nearly every Egyptologist, holds that the pyramids were an enduring testament to a seemingly obsessive worship of the Sun.[4] Egyptian pharaohs, according to this narrative, were so impressed by the miracle of sunrise that they rallied thousands of workers to build a mountain-sized burial chamber intended to ensure their eternal life. In the pages to follow, we will enumerate reasons for questioning this oft-told tale.

---

[1] E. Hornung, *Conceptions of God in Ancient Egypt* (Ithaca, 1982), p. 227.
[2] R. Krauss, "The Eye of Horus and the Planet Venus," in J. Steele & A. Imhausen eds., *Under One Sky* (Munster, 2002), p. 205.
[3] M. Barta, "The Ancient Egyptian Sky," in S. Vannini ed., *King Tut: The Journey Through the Underworld* (New York, 2020), p. 247.
[4] M. Lehner, *The Complete Pyramids* (London, 1997), p. 34 and throughout. See also K. Goebs, "Kingship," in T. Wilkinson ed., *The Egyptian World* (New York, 2007), p. 285: "The pyramids, preferred funerary monuments of kings in the Old and Middle Kingdoms, are commonly accepted to represent replicas of the primeval mound, the location of the first sunrise out of the aquatic pre-creation universe, and 'stairways' to the heavens."

Although an aura of mystery continues to surround the religious beliefs of the ancient Egyptians this much is certain: They were fixated on the sky and its manifold stellar inhabitants and structures. The principal Egyptian gods were identified with the most prominent celestial bodies; the pyramid, their most enduring architectural achievement, was purposefully patterned after a celestial prototype (the *akhet*) and copiously decorated with stars; and the pharoah's single-minded goal, upon dying, was to return to a celestial Hereafter wherein he hoped to be reunited with the "Imperishable Stars" and great mother goddess. In the face of this incontrovertible testimony attesting to the Egyptians' profound interest in astronomical phenomena, it stands to reason that their religious beliefs are fated to remain elusive until we gain additional insight into their core beliefs regarding the stars and the celestial landscape. The purpose of the present monograph is to summarize the data at hand and attempt a reconstruction of the astronomical information encoded in Egyptian cosmogonic myth and funerary beliefs.

In addition to their architectural grandeur, the Egyptian pyramids were also inscribed with the world's oldest body of religious texts. To judge by the formulaic language and exquisitely detailed imagery employed, the so-called Pyramid Texts represent the culmination of a long period of deep thinking about cosmogony, presumably preserved for untold centuries by oral tradition. While the primary theme is the deceased king's ascent to the celestial Hereafter, there is also a rich vein of material on the momentous events recalled as Creation. Indeed, the Egyptian texts offer us the earliest and, in many respects, the most comprehensive commentary on the subject. For this reason alone, the Pyramid Texts represent an invaluable treasure trove of historical testimony.

In attempting to rediscover and reconstruct the natural history behind a religious system over five thousand years old, it would appear only logical to proceed from the known to the less well known or opaque. With this strategy in mind, we begin with the stellar god Horus. For if there is one thing that all Egyptologists can agree on, it is that Horus represented the very epitome of Egyptian ideas of divinity and kingship. Toby Wilkinson pointed out the obvious when he summarized the god's cult as follows:

"The most fundamental aspect of kingship was the ruler's embodiment of Horus, the supreme celestial deity. The king's principal title was the Horus title, 'the simplest and most direct statement regarding the king's nature' (Frankfort 1948: 46). It expressed the notion that Horus was incarnate in the reigning monarch…The identification of the ruler with Horus, represented by a falcon, is apparent from late Predynastic times, and is given expression on royal monuments and in the serekhs of kings from the period of state formation."[5]

Who or what, then, was Horus?

---

[5] T. Wilkinson, *Early Dynastic Egypt* (London, 1999), p. 184.

## The Horus-Star

> "Pharaoh is Horus, and of this god little enough is known."[6]

> "Horus was the power of kingship. To the Egyptians this was as much a force of nature as those embodied in the other gods. It was manifest in two phenomena: the sun, the most powerful force in nature; and the pharaoh, the most powerful force in human society. Horus's role as the king of nature is probably the origin of his name: *ḥrw* seems to mean 'the one above' or 'the one far off'…This is apparently a reference to the sun, which is 'above' and 'far off' in the sky, like the falcon with which Horus is regularly associated (and with which his name is usually written)."[7]

The great gods confront us already at the dawn of history. The Egyptian Horus is a case in point, his cult being paramount already in predynastic times. Well before the unification of Egypt, rulers from the Naqada I period (circa 4000-3500 BCE) worshipped the falcon-god.[8]

The pharaoh himself was considered to be the earthly embodiment of the god. This archaic belief-system is reflected in the so-called Horus names borne by Egyptian rulers from the First Dynasty on.[9]

Yet if it is commonly acknowledged that Horus represents the quintessential Egyptian god, there is little agreement as to his origins or fundamental nature. That he was a celestial power all authorities concur. The question, however, is what celestial body best explains Horus's manifold functions in Egyptian religion?

---

[6] H. Frankfort, *Kingship and the Gods* (Chicago, 1948), p. 37.
[7] J. Allen, *Middle Egyptian* (Cambridge, 2010), p. 148.
[8] J. Assmann, *The Mind of Egypt* (Cambridge, 1996), p. 33.
[9] H. Frankfort, *op. cit.*, p. 39.

A survey of the relevant scholarship on the matter reveals that Horus has typically been identified with the Sun.[10] That said, leading Egyptologists have advanced arguments that the god is to be identified with the planet Venus;[11] with the star Sirius;[12] and with the amorphous sky itself.[13] The following statement from Rudolf Anthes aptly illustrates the fuzzy thinking that has often characterized modern Egyptology's attempt to decipher the multiform traditions surrounding the Horus-star:

"The heavenly Horus was a star as well as the sun, and perhaps also the moon. It seems as if he was that celestial body which appeared conspicuous either at day or at night."[14]

In order to bring some clarity to the all-important question of Horus's original celestial identification, it is instructive to review the evidence that has survived from the very dawn of Egyptian history. In the Early Dynastic Period (ca. 3000-2600 BCE), Horus is explicitly identified as a star. An annal from the First Dynasty reign of King Aha bears the name "Festival of the Horus-Star-of-the-Gods."[15] Royal domain names from the first three dynasties likewise reference the stellar god. The domain established by Anedjib (First Dynasty) was called *Ḥr-sbꜣ-ḫt*, "Horus, star of the corporation (of gods)."[16] Hetepsekhemwy (Second Dynasty) founded a domain called *Ḥr-ḫꜥ-sbꜣ*, "Horus risen as a star."[17] Khasekhemwy's domain was called *Ḥr-sbꜣ-bꜣw*, "Horus, the star of

---

[10] J. Assmann, "Sonnengott," *Lexikon der Ägyptologie VI* (Wiesbaden, 1984), col. 1087. T. Allen, *Horus in the Pyramid Texts* (Chicago, 1916), p. 11, writes: "The solar element in Horus clearly predominates."

[11] R. Krauss, *Astronomische Konzepte und Jenseitsvorstellungen in den Pyramidentexten* (Wiesbaden, 1997), pp. 216-234.

[12] R. Anthes, "Horus als Sirius in den Pyramidentexten," *ZÄS* 102 (1975), pp. 1-10.

[13] W. Schenkel, "Horus," *Lexikon der Ägyptologie* III (Wiesbaden, 1977), col. 14, writes: "The oldest function of Horus may have been that of a Heaven-god." See also L. Lesko, "Ancient Egyptian Cosmogonies and Cosmology," in B. Shafer ed., *Religion in Ancient Egypt* (Ithaca, 1991), p. 93.

[14] R. Anthes, "Egyptian Theology in the Third Millennium B.C.," *JNES* 18 (1959), p. 171.

[15] E. Hornung, *Idea Into Image* (Princeton, 1992), p. 158.

[16] T. Wilkinson, *Early Dynastic Egypt* (London, 1999), p. 121.

[17] *Ibid.*, p. 121.

souls."[18] A domain established by Djoser at the beginning of the Third Dynasty was named *Ḥr-sbꜣ-ḫnti-pt*, "Horus-star at the front of the sky."[19] To judge by the evidence of these names, Horus was conceptualized as a stellar power—indeed, as a prominent star "at the front of the sky." Yet as valuable as these epithets are, they are not sufficiently detailed or informative in nature to pinpoint exactly which particular celestial body Horus was identified with during this period.

In addition to his status as a conspicuous star, there is also abundant evidence that Horus was conceptualized as a powerful warrior very early on. This idea is evident in the so-called Horus-names of early pharaohs which bear witness to the god's warrior-prowess. Toby Wilkinson emphasized this point:

"The Horus names of several First Dynasty kings expressed the aggressive authority of Horus, perhaps reflecting the coercive power of kingship at this stage of Egyptian statehood. Names like 'Horus the fighter' (Aha), 'Horus the strong' (Djer) or 'arm-raising Horus' (Qaa) call to mind the warlike iconography of the earliest royal monuments from the period of state formation."[20]

Additional information attesting to the war-like nature of the star-god Horus is to be found in the Pyramid Texts dating from roughly a half millennium later (ca. 2300 BCE). The following spell from Queen Neith's pyramid is a case in point:

"So, ascend to the sky amongst the stars in the sky, and those before you shall hide and those after you shall be afraid of you, because of this your identity of Horus of the Duat…of the one who strikes them, of the one who spews them out, and wipes them out, and you will strike them, spew them out, and wipe them out at the lake, at the Great Green. You

---

[18] *Ibid.*, p. 121.
[19] Toby Wilkinson, *op. cit.*, p. 122, translates this name as "foremost star of the sky."
[20] *Ibid.*, p. 202.

shall come to stand at the fore of the Imperishable Stars and sit on your metal throne from which the dead are far away."[21]

In the Coffin Texts, the Horus-star is described as warring against the other gods. The following text is representative: "I have smitten the gods with my hands…because my strength [is greater] than theirs in my avatar as Horus great of strength."[22]

The Horus-star is elsewhere described as warring against the powers of chaos at the time of creation. Witness the following passage from Papyrus Berlin:

"The sky jubilates, the earth is joyful, the gods and goddesses are in festival, giving praise to Re-Harakhte, when they see him arisen in his barque after he has felled the rebels with his striking power."[23]

Such traditions are of untold antiquity and remained in vogue for well over three thousand years, as evidenced by the fact that they were still a central subject of the inscriptions adorning the god's Edfu temple constructed during the Ptolemaic period. A common theme alluded to an apocalyptic "rebellion" at the time of the First Occasion. It was the Horus-star that put down this rebellion, according to several ancient sources: "The warrior hero wastes no time…he massacres the miscreants."[24]

This testimony, considered alongside that of the Horus-names, confirms that the stellar Horus was envisaged as a formidable warrior. As we intend to document, this portrait of the god constitutes a decisive clue with regards to his original stellar identification.

That Horus is not to be identified with the current solar orb, as per the conventional opinion, is suggested by various hymns wherein the god is explicitly distinguished from the ancient sun god Re. In the following

---

[21] *PT* 1925-1927 as translated in J. Allen, *The Ancient Egyptian Pyramid Texts* (Atlanta, 2005), p. 323.
[22] *CT* IV:92 as translated in R. Faulkner, *The Ancient Egyptian Coffin Texts* (Oxford, 1973), p. 235. Hereafter *CT*.
[23] 3050 II, 7 III, 3 as translated in K. Goebs, *Crowns in Egyptian Funerary Literature* (Oxford, 2008), p. 47.
[24] D. Meeks & C. Favard-Meeks, *Daily Life of the Egyptian Gods* (Ithaca, 1996), p. 24.

passage, for example, Horus (as the deceased king) is implored to ascend to heaven and join Re:

"Reᶜ summons you into the zenith (?) of the sky as the Jackal, the Governor of the Two Enneads, and as Horus *Ḫnty-mnit.f*; may he set you as the Morning Star in the midst of the Field of Rushes."[25]

Here, as elsewhere in these archaic texts, Horus is identified with the "Morning Star" (*nṯr dwꜣ*). In this guise Horus is described as the "son" of Re and thus he would appear to represent a distinct celestial body altogether—presumably a particularly brilliant planet or star.

In order to clarify the origins of Horus's cult it is necessary to identify the celestial body signified by the epithet "Morning Star." Yet this is easier said than done insofar as the earliest Egyptian texts, such as the Pyramid and Coffin Texts, never describe the Horus-star in a sufficiently clear astronomical context that would enable a secure identification with a particular star. Instead we read that the Morning Star—as Horus—ascended to heaven in order to command the Imperishable Stars in the celestial Hereafter.

Raymond Faulkner considered it a foregone conclusion that Venus must be the stellar body referenced by the phrase "Morning Star." Thus, in a survey of Egyptian star-lore Faulkner wrote as follows: "As regards the identification of the Morning Star and the Lone Star with actual celestial bodies, there can be little doubt that, as elsewhere, the Morning Star is Phosphorus, Venus as seen at dawn."[26]

The most systematic and informed study of Egyptian star-religion to date is that produced by Rolf Krauss.[27] He, too, would identify the Horus-star with the planet Venus, citing as evidence various passages in the Pyramid Texts that purportedly describe it as shining in the "eastern"

---

[25] *PT* 1719d as translated by R. Faulkner, *The Ancient Egyptian Pyramid Texts* (Oxford, 1969). Hereafter *PT*.
[26] R. Faulkner, "The King and the Star-Religion in the Pyramid Texts," *JNES* 25 (1966), p. 161.
[27] *Astronomische Konzepte und Jenseitsvorstellungen in den Pyramidentexten* (Wiesbaden, 1997).

portion of the morning sky while moving with respect to other stars, a characteristic of planets rather than stars.[28] Krauss points to Utterance 437 as being especially decisive with regards to Horus's Venusian identification. The relevant section from this long hymn is as follows:

"Seth is brotherly toward you as the Great One of On, for you have traversed the Winding Waterway in the north of the sky as a star crossing the sea which is beneath the sky. The Netherworld has grasped your hand at the place where Orion is, the Bull of the Sky has given you his hand, and you eat of the food of the gods whereof they eat… Rēʿ has summoned you from the zenith(?) of the sky as Horus who presides over his thigh-offerings…He sets you as the Morning Star in the middle of the Field of Rushes, you being seated on your throne."[29]

Krauss's pronouncements notwithstanding, it seems perfectly obvious that there is nothing here that serves to securely identify the "Morning Star" in question. And so it is with every other passage cited by this distinguished scholar. Krauss summarized his findings as follows:

"As early as the beginning of dynastic times Horus seems to be identified with the planet Venus. The names of the so-called royal vineyards describe Horus as a star. The name of Djoser's vineyard reveals that Horus is a particular star 'at the front of the sky'. The identification of Horus with Venus as known from the Pyramid Texts suggests itself."[30]

Yet the identification of Horus with the planet Venus *is not known* from the Pyramid Texts—quite to the contrary, as we intend to show. Indeed, Krauss has simply assumed what has yet to be proven—that early references to Horus as the "Morning Star" have reference to Venus—and argued in a wholly circular fashion.

---

[28] *Ibid.*, pp. 216-234. Krauss repeats this identification in "Stellar Power and Solar Components in Ancient Egyptian Mythology and Royal Ideology," in M. Rappenglück et al eds., *Astronomy and Power* (Oxford, 2016), pp. 137-138 but offers no new compelling arguments.
[29] *PT* 802-805.
[30] R. Krauss, "The Eye of Horus and the Planet Venus: Astronomical and Mythological References," in J. Steele & A. Imhausen eds., *Under One Sky* (Münster, 2002), p. 205.

In a more recent study, Krauss returned to the problem. There he claimed that the Early Dynastic names also point to Venus:

"The identification of the early dynastic Horus as the planet Venus in particular and not just any star is confirmed by his epithet 'foremost star of the sky' which applies first and foremost to Venus among all the stars."[31]

Once again, however, there is nothing in these domain names that warrants Krauss's conclusion.

---

[31] R. Krauss, "Stellar Power and Solar Components in Ancient Egyptian Mythology and Royal Ideology," in M. Rappenglück et al eds., *Astronomy and Power* (Oxford, 2016), p. 138. See also the more recent study, "The morning star of PT and CT on the move, up or down the arcs of the ecliptic," *Studien zur Altägyptischen Kultur* 51 (2022), pp. 65ff where many of the same claims are repeated.

## Lord of the Netherworld

Horus's earliest epithets offer additional insight into his astral identity. A recurring epithet of the god in the Pyramid Texts is *Duat*, conventionally translated as "Netherworld." The word *Duat*, written with the following determinative—⊗—is derived from the root *dwȝ*, "morning," whence comes Horus's epithet *Neter Dua* signifying "Morning Star (or Morning God)."[32] The etymology in question suggests that Horus's identity as the Morning Star is indissolubly connected to his role as Lord of the "Netherworld." Indeed, a passage from the Pyramid Texts sets the two epithets in apposition: "O Morning Star, Horus of the Netherworld, divine Falcon, *wȝdȝd*-bird whom the sky bore…"[33]

Although often sought for underground, the earliest texts indicate that the Duat was celestial in nature.[34] The following passage is especially telling:

"Make the sky clear and shine on them as a god; may you be enduring at the head of the sky as Horus of the Netherworld."[35]

Horus is described here as standing at the "head" or front *(ḫnt)* of the sky as Lord of the Duat. This epithet, together with the fact that the Horus-star is said to shine and "clear" the sky, would appear to confirm that the Duat was located in a prominent place in the visible sky overhead.

Other spells implying that the Duat is to be found in close proximity to the ancient sun-god point to the same conclusion. Especially relevant here is the following passage from the Pyramid Texts, wherein the deceased king ascends to the Duat in order to be near Re:

"Lift up your faces, you gods who are in the Netherworld [Duat], for the King has come that you may see him, he having become the great god.

---

[32] J. Allen, "The Cosmology of the Pyramid Texts," in J. Allen et al eds., *Religion and Philosophy in Ancient Egypt* (New Haven, 1989), p. 23.
[33] *PT* 1207.
[34] E. Hornung, "Dat*,*" *Lexikon der Ägyptologie 1* (Wiesbaden, 1975), col. 994. See also L. Lesko, "Ancient Egyptian Cosmogonies and Cosmology," in B. Shafer ed., *Religion in Ancient Egypt* (Ithaca, 1991), pp. 119-120.
[35] *PT* 1948.

The king is ushered in with trembling, the King is robed. Guard yourselves, all of you, for the King governs men, the King judges the living within the domain of Rēʿ…The King sits with those who row the bark of Rēʿ, the King commands what is good and he does it, for the King is the great god."[36]

As Samuel Mercer pointed out in his commentary on this particular passage, it offers compelling testimony that the Duat is associated with the domain of Re: "The *Dwꜣ.t* here is heaven, identical with the 'land of Rēʿ' (273b), which is heaven, where the king becomes a great god, 272b."[37]

The intimate association between Horus Duat and the region of the sky occupied by the ancient sun god is also evident in the following passage, wherein Horus is said to illuminate the sky from his station in the Duat near Re:

"Rēʿ has [taken (?)] me to himself, to the sky, to the eastern side of the sky; As this Horus, as the dweller in the Netherworld, As this star which illumines the sky."[38]

In apparent contradiction to its intimate association with the ancient sun-god, the Pyramid Texts elsewhere describe the Horus-star as standing in close proximity to the Imperishable Stars—the latter conventionally identified with the circumpolar stars.[39] In the following passage, for example, the deceased king is identified with Horus Duat and set amongst the Imperishable Stars:

"May you go up as Horus of the Netherworld who is at the head of the Imperishable Stars."[40]

---

[36] *PT* 272-274.
[37] S. Mercer, *The Pyramid Texts, Vol. 2* (New York, 1952), p. 126. R. Krauss, *op. cit.*, pp. 212-214 offered a similar opinion.
[38] *PT* 362.
[39] J. Allen, "The Cosmology of the Pyramid Texts," in W. Simpson ed., *Religion and Philosophy in Ancient Egypt* (New Haven, 1989), p. 4. P. Wallin, *Celestial Cycles* (Uppsala, 2002), p. 94 observes: "The astronomical identification of the *iḥmw-sk* as the circumpolar stars of the northern sky is generally accepted."
[40] *PT* 1301.

Horus Duat is here described with the epithet *ḫntj jḫmw-skjw*, translated alternately as "head" or "front" of the Imperishable Stars.[41] Taken literally this passage poses a seemingly insurmountable problem for the view that Horus is to be identified with the planet Venus, insofar as that planet can hardly be said to stand at the "front" of the circumpolar stars (In its current orbit, Venus never moves more than 45 degrees from the ecliptic and is thus far removed from the northern circumpolar region at all times).[42]

---

[41] J. Allen, *The Ancient Egyptian Pyramid Texts* (Atlanta, 2005), p. 117, translates as "at the fore of the Imperishable [Stars]." R. Krauss, *Astronomische Konzepte und Jenseitsvorstellungen in den Pyramidentexten* (Wiesbaden, 1997), p. 229 translates: "Mögest du herausgehen als Datischer Horus, 'befindlich an der Spitze' der 'Unvergänglichen Sterne'."

[42] R. Krauss, *op. cit.*, p. 129 concedes this point.

### Horus and Nergal

Important clues with regards to Horus's stellar identification can be gleaned by comparing the Egyptian astral traditions with those from other ancient astronomies. The evidence from Mesopotamia is especially instructive insofar as it was the provenance of the world's earliest systematic observations of the primary celestial bodies—hence its proverbial status as the birthplace of scientific astronomy. In early texts from ancient Egypt, as we have seen, Horus was represented as a prominent star and warrior. In Babylonian astronomical texts it is the planet Mars—conceptualized as the god Nergal—that was regarded as the warrior-star par excellence.[43] There is much reason to believe, in fact, that the two gods share a fundamental affinity.

Horus, as we have seen, was known as "Lord of the Netherworld" (*Duat*). This epithet finds a precise parallel in the cult of Nergal, who was invoked as $^d$*umun-úrugal*, "Lord of the Netherworld."[44] The epithet "en of the Kur" attests to the same general idea.[45] The fact that the planet-god Nergal was described simultaneously as a god of the Netherworld *and* as a denizen of heaven has long presented a puzzle to Sumerologists and yet it forms a close parallel with respect to the Egyptian traditions identifying Horus Duat as the "Morning Star."[46] An Old Babylonian hymn is relevant in this regard: "You are manifest in the bright heavens, your station is exalted, You are great in the netherworld, you have no rival."[47]

---

[43] D. Brown, *Mesopotamian Planetary Astronomy-Astrology* (Groningen, 2000), p. 56. See also the extensive discussion in E. Cochrane, *Martian Metamorphoses* (Ames, 1997), pp. 15-26.

[44] D. Katz, *The Image of the Netherworld in the Sumerian Sources* (Bethesda, 2003), p. 404.

[45] F. Wiggermann, "Nergal," *RlA* 9 (Berlin, 1999), p. 218. See also D. Frayne, *Old Babylonian Period* (2003-1595 BC) (Toronto, 1990), p. 246: "[Nergal] powerful lord of the underworld," translating en-ir₉-kur a-gal.

[46] E. von Weiher, *Der babylonische Gott Nergal* (Berlin, 1971), p. 73 remarks: "In den sumerischen Texten der altbabylonischen Zeit war schon andeutungsweise zu erkennen gewesen, daß Nergal nicht nur 'Herr der Unterwelt' ist, sondern auch gleichzeitig (!) am Himmel herrscht."

[47] Lines 5-6 from Nergal 2 as translated in T. Abusch, *Essays on Babylonian and Biblical Literature and Religion* (Leiden, 2020), p. 165.

Nergal is elsewhere described by the epithet *Lugal-IGI.DU-anna*, "king at the front of heaven."[48] This epithet offers a semantic analogue to Horus's epithet *sbꜣ-ḫnti-pt*, "star at the front of the sky," cited earlier.

A recurring epithet for Horus in the Pyramid Texts and elsewhere is *nḏ jt.f*, "avenger of his father."[49] Nergal, too, was invoked as "avenger of his father."[50] Such epithets are of great antiquity and, although their original significance is unknown, likely reflect some memorable astronomical event, subsequently mythologized.

In the Pyramid Texts, the Horus-star was described with the epithet *nb wꜣḏ*, literally "Lord of the green."[51] The epithet *wꜣḏ*, "green," also describes the Horus-star in a First Dynasty domain name, thereby attesting to its antiquity.[52] Nergal shares an analogous epithet: *ᵈLugal-sig₇-a*, "The green lord."[53]

In the Pyramid and Coffin Texts Horus is intimately associated with the *akhet*, an all-important Egyptian cosmological concept conventionally translated as "horizon"—hence the epithet *Harakhte* ("Horus-of-the-horizon"). As its hieroglyph suggests—⌂—the *akhet* came to denote the twin-peaked celestial mountain associated with the sun-god's daily appearance.[54]

The planet-god Nergal is likewise associated with the mountain of sunrise. Thus an early Sumerian temple hymn says of the god that he

---

[48] W. Lambert, "Lugal-IGI.DU-anna," *RlA* 7 (Berlin, 1983), p. 142.

[49] *PT* 1685a. S. Mercer, *op. cit.*, p. 311: "The assertion that Horus avenged his father is very common in these texts, e.g. 634, 636, 1637, 1685, 1753, 2191."

[50] Line 42 in "A tigi to Nergal (Nergal C)," in J. Black et al., *The Electronic Text Corpus of Sumerian Literature* (http://www-etcsl.orient.ox.ac.uk/) (Oxford, 1998). Hereafter *ETCSL*.

[51] *PT* 457, for example. So translated by T. Allen, *op. cit.*, p. 17. James Allen, *op. cit.*, p. 56 translates as "Horus lord of malachite."

[52] T. Wilkinson, *Early Dynastic Egypt* (London, 2001), p. 121 translates as *Wꜣḏ-Ḥr*, "Horus flourishes."

[53] W. Lambert, "Lugal-sig₇-a," *RlA* 7 (Berlin, 1983), p. 151.

[54] J. Assmann, "Horizont," *Lexikon der Ägyptologie III* (Wiesbaden, 1977), cols. 3-7.

"rises in the mountain where the sun rises."[55] According to the Sumerian hymn *Enlil and Ninlil*, the newly born Nergal was assigned the mountain of sunrise (*Ḫursag*) at the time of creation.[56] This Sumerian tradition, in turn, finds a close parallel in Egyptian texts, wherein the newly born Horus was installed within the *akhet* during the formative events of creation: "My flight aloft has reached the horizon, I have overpassed the gods of the sky, I have made my position more prominent than that of the Primaeval Ones."[57] Such evidence, considered together with the fact that Egyptian astronomical texts from the New Kingdom identified "Horus in the Akhet" (*Horakhti*) with the planet Mars, strongly suggests that it was the red planet—not Venus—which formed the subject of Egyptian traditions testifying to Horus's intimate association with the *akhet*.[58]

To summarize our findings in this chapter: As a warrior-star, Lord of the Netherworld, the star "at the front of the sky," "Lord of the green," and avenger of his father—not to mention his intimate association with the mountain of sunrise—the Egyptian star-god Horus shares a set of diverse epithets and attributes with the Sumerian Nergal. This is unlikely to be a matter of cultural borrowing, much less coincidence. On the contrary, these analogous epithets and mythological attributes suggest that the two gods share a fundamental affinity and likely trace to a common celestial prototype—namely, the planet Mars.

Horus's identification with the planet Mars constitutes a cornerstone of the present study. If this finding can be substantiated, it stands to reason that it will revolutionize Egyptology as we know it while shedding some

---

[55] Å. Sjöberg & E. Bergmann, *The Collection of the Sumerian Temple Hymns* (Locust Valley, 1969), p. 106.
[56] *Ibid.*, pp. 51, 88. See also line 12 in "A tigi to Nergal (Nergal C)," *ETCSL*.
[57] *CT* II:223.
[58] As in Senmut's tomb (TT 353), for example. See also O. Neugebauer & R. Parker, *Egyptian Astronomical Texts, Vol. 3* (London, 1960), p. 179. Witness also R. Krauss, "Stellar Power and Solar Components in Ancient Egyptian Mythology and Royal Ideology," in M. Rappenglück et al eds., *Astronomy and Power* (London, 2016), p. 140: "It is noteworthy that in the sky diagrams Harakhty is a name of the planet Mars, also known as Horus *deser* (red Horus)."

much-needed light on the stellar identifications of other deities mentioned in the Pyramid Texts.

# The Cataclysmic Context of the King's Ascent to Heaven

> "Cataclysm, marked by thunder, earth- and sky-quake, is a standard motif, that greets the appearance of the god and defines the king's progression to heaven as a cataclysmic return to the pre-created state."[59]

> "[Ideas of global catastrophe] are not specifically Late Period conceptions, but very old and very real anxieties based on multifarious historical and personal experiences (famine, epidemic, revolution, foreign rule etc.). The persistence of this theme in quite diverse areas of Egyptian literature reveals the obsessional nature of these anxieties."[60]

> "In the traceable early history of language the concrete usually precedes the abstract—'first the natural and then the spiritual'."[61]

A number of spells in the Pyramid Texts describe the king's post-mortem journey and ensuing transfiguration as an occasion of apocalyptic cosmic catastrophe, marked by the shaking of heaven and earth amid a profound disturbance or dislocation of the stars. Raymond Faulkner, with good reason, spoke of the "cataclysm of the King's ascension."[62] Why the king's ascent to heaven should involve cosmic upheaval, or what historical events might have inspired this particular belief-system, Faulkner never bothered to explain.

In the so-called "Cannibal Hymn," generally considered to be among the most archaic Utterances in the Pyramid Texts, the king's post-mortem

---

[59] C. Eyre, *The Cannibal Hymn* (Liverpool, 2002), pp. 76-77.
[60] J. Assmann, *Egyptian Solar Religion in the New Kingdom* (London, 1995), p. 54.
[61] R. Onians, *The Origins of European Thought* (Cambridge, 1954), p. 313.
[62] R. Faulkner, "The King and the Star-Religion in the Pyramid Texts," *JNES* 25 (1966), p. 153.

ascent to heaven occurs in the midst of a world-convulsing cataclysm. The hymn in question begins as follows:

"The sky is overcast, The stars are darkened, The celestial expanses quiver, The bones of the earth-gods tremble, The planets(?) are stilled, For they have seen the King appearing in power."[63]

Given the fact that the terminology and imagery employed in this hymn is far from transparent in meaning, it is understandable that translations have differed rather markedly. Joris Borghouts, for example, asked: "Could the Pyramid passage be translated as 'the stars are driven away'?"[64] Erik Hornung offered a similar conclusion, translating the passage in question as follows:

"The sky is clouded, the stars disturbed, the 'bows' quake, the bones of the earth god tremble. But those who move are still when they have seen the King with (his) soul manifest."[65]

How are we to interpret the explicit cataclysmic imagery and language attested here and elsewhere? What does it mean that the stars are disturbed or somehow displaced or "shaken up"?[66] Are the striking images of celestial upheaval to be interpreted as figurative in nature, or as relatively faithful descriptions of cataclysmic astronomical and geological events as witnessed by the Egyptian skywatchers firsthand?

Stephen Quirke doubtless speaks for the majority of Egyptologists when he dismisses the imagery in the "Cannibal Hymn" as primarily metaphorical in nature: "It requires little imagination to realize that the descriptions of chaos, like the descriptions of order at the accession of a

---

[63] *PT* 393-394.
[64] *The Magical Texts of Papyrus Leiden I 348* (Leiden, 1971), p. 192.
[65] *PT* 393-394 as translated by E. Hornung, *Conceptions of God in Ancient Egypt* (Ithaca, 1996), p. 131. In his commentary to this passage, Hornung points out that, while many scholars follow Faulkner in rendering *jhj* as "to become dark(?)," the word actually has a more forceful or cataclysmic meaning: "the word is a passive participle of *ḥwj* 'to strike, drive, heave'; compare also the writing with the 'striking man' in *CT* VI, 177b. Roeder's translation 'quake'…is also possible."
[66] K. Goebs, *Crowns in Egyptian Funerary Literature* (Oxford, 2008), p. 213 translates this passage as follows: "The stars are shaken up."

king, present in exaggerated style the world we live in, not historical catastrophe nor in the case of the hymns to the accession of a king, cosmic miracle."[67] We beg to differ. Virtually every scholar who has devoted serious study to archaic Egyptian religion has called attention to the Egyptians' penchant for concrete imagery and matter-of-fact language. Writing at the turn of the last century (1912), James Breasted offered the following observation:

"One characteristic of Egyptian thinking should be borne in mind from the outset: it was always in graphic form. The Egyptian did not possess the terminology for the expression of a system of abstract thought; neither did he develop the capacity to create the necessary terminology as did the Greek. He thought in concrete pictures, he moved along tangible material channels, and the material world about him furnished nearly all of the terms which he used. While this is probably ultimately true of all terms in any early language, such terms for the most part remained concrete for the Egyptian."[68]

In his monumental *Egyptian Grammar*, Alan Gardiner likewise emphasized the concrete nature of the Egyptian language. There he wrote as follows:

"The most striking feature of Egyptian in all its stages is its concrete **realism**, its preoccupation with exterior objects and occurrences to the neglect of those more subjective distinctions which play so prominent a part in modern, and even in the classical, languages. Subtleties of thought such as are implied in 'might', 'should', 'can', 'hardly', as well as such abstractions as 'cause', 'motive', 'duty', belong to a later stage of linguistic development; possibly they would have been repugnant to the Egyptian temperament. Despite the reputation for philosophic wisdom attributed to the Egyptians by the Greeks, no people has ever shown itself

---

[67] S. Quirke, *Ancient Egyptian Religion* (London, 1992), p. 131.
[68] J. Breasted, *Development of Religion and Thought in Ancient Egypt* (Philadelphia, 1912), pp. 7-8.

more averse from speculation or more wholeheartedly devoted to material interests."[69]

Raymond Faulkner, the esteemed translator of the Pyramid and Coffin Texts, arrived at much the same opinion. With specific reference to the "Cannibal Hymn," Faulkner underscored the literal nature of the language employed by the Egyptian scribes: "The Egyptian, so far as his writings reveal him to us, was a literal person, whose attempts at metaphor were usually commonplace and often clumsy, and a piece of sustained symbolism such as this [the imagery within the Cannibal Hymn] would be quite beyond his powers."[70]

Given that the record is so clear on the Egyptians' decided preference for literal language and concrete imagery, it is disconcerting to see how often Egyptologists resort to figurative language and abstraction in their endeavor to make sense of the earliest Egyptian descriptions of the celestial landscape and attendant astronomical phenomena. Louis Lesko, for example, wrote as follows of early accounts of the deceased king's ascent to heaven: "Conceptualizing both an ascent to the sky to join the gods and how to accomplish it required the Egyptians to engage in considerable speculation."[71]

Rather than attempting to understand the Egyptian cosmological ideas as firmly rooted in the natural world and thus reality-based, Egyptologists have all-too-often interpreted them as metaphorical or speculative in nature.[72] In this sense the whole tendency of modern Egyptology is away

---

[69] A. Gardiner, *Egyptian Grammar* (Oxford, 1957), p. 4.
[70] R. Faulkner, "The 'Cannibal Hymn' from the Pyramid Texts," *JEA* 10 (1924), p. 103.
[71] L. Lesko, "Ancient Egyptian Cosmogonies and Cosmology," in B. Shafer ed., *Religion in Ancient Egypt* (Ithaca, 1991), p. 121.
[72] Typical are the comments of Alicia Maravelia, "The Function and Importance of Some Special Categories of Stars in the Ancient Egyptian Funerary Texts, 2," in A. Maravelia & N. Guilhou eds., *Environment and Religion in Ancient & Coptic Egypt* (Oxford, 2020), p. 244: "Ancient Egyptian priests-astronomers and theologians were using a rich variety of cosmographic allegories and metaphors, in order to describe in a pre- or perhaps (sometimes) proto-scientific way the heavenly phenomena and the periodicities of the surrounding firmament. These very allegoric schemes must not be taken literally most of the times…"

from concreteness, to paraphrase George Orwell.[73] A few additional examples will suffice to illustrate this point.

For James Allen, as for most Egyptologists, the myth of the deceased king's ascension to heaven and transfiguration constitutes an imaginative interpretation of the daily sunrise.[74] With specific reference to the opening lines from the "Cannibal Hymn," quoted above, Allen opines that the imagery in question is to be explained by reference to the familiar skies: "The image is that of the night sky, thrown into a paroxysm of fear at the arrival of the king."[75] Remarkably, Allen would have his readers believe that the ancient Egyptians were so impressed by the reappearance of the Sun from the clutches of night that they would make this wholly mundane and ever-recurring phenomenon the cornerstone of their creation myth, not to mention the subject of their funerary religion's central mystery—i.e., the deceased king's ascent to heaven and his glorious transfiguration within the *akhet*. This seems most unlikely, to put it mildly. Were the ancient Egyptians so naïve as to believe that nightfall was accompanied by a cataclysmic disturbance of stars and the shaking of heaven and earth?[76]

It is our opinion, in contrast, that the dramatic events mythologized as the king's ascension to heaven have nothing whatsoever to do with the familiar sun or regularly occurring celestial phenomena. Rather, Egyptian traditions describing the pharaoh's post-mortem ascent to heaven and concomitant transfiguration into a glorious Imperishable Star have their

---

[73] Orwell's phrase was "The whole tendency of modern prose is away from concreteness." See George Orwell, "Politics and the English Language," *The Orwell Reader* (New York, 1984), p. 360.
[74] W. Westendorf, "Sonnenlauf," *Lexikon der Ägyptologie VI* (Wiesbaden, 1984), col. 1103: "Das Wunder des täglich neu einsetzenden Sonne war Vorbild und Garant für die Jenseitserwartungen der Menschen (zunächst wahrscheinlich für den König)."
[75] J. Allen, "Reading a Pyramid," in C. Berger et al eds., *Hommages à Jean Leclant I* (Cairo, 1994), p. 22.
[76] K. Goebs, *Crowns in Egyptian Funerary Literature* (Oxford, 2008), p. 294 concurs with Allen in this regard: "Such a description [the disturbance of cosmic order associated with the deceased king's ascent to heaven] suggests a major cosmic event like the sunrise."

origin in singular and decidedly catastrophic natural events—specifically, the nova-like appearance of the primordial sun (Horus) amidst cosmic upheaval *in illo tempore*.[77] It was these catastrophic events which formed the primary subject matter of Egyptian cosmogonic myth.

Compelling support for this hypothesis is provided by the fact that ancient descriptions of sunrise are frequently said to be accompanied by terrifying sights and sounds, including the shaking of heaven and earth and prodigious bouts of thunder and lightning. The roughly contemporaneous Sumerian hymns describing the epiphany of the sun-god Utu are instructive: "As my king [Utu] comes forth, the heavens tremble before him and the earth shakes before him."[78] Elsewhere in the same hymn Utu is described as follows: "The lord, the son of Ningal…thunders over the mountains like a storm."[79] Now I ask: Does this sound like a realistic description of the modern experience of sunrise? In what sense is the solar epiphany ever accompanied by thunder or the shaking of heaven and earth? And yet these are the very same meteorological phenomena said to accompany the deceased king's ascent to the sky in the Pyramid Texts:

"Geb laughs, Nut shouts for joy before me when I ascend to the sky. The sky thunders for me, the earth quakes for me, the hail-storm is burst apart for me, and I roar as does Seth."[80]

Here, much as in the Sumerian hymn recounting Utu's epiphany, the deceased king's ascent to heaven is marked by earthquake, thunder, and the bursting apart of *šnjt*, translated as "hailstorm" by Faulkner and as

---

[77] This interpretation is supported by the fact that analogous traditions from around the globe also emphasize cataclysms of an extraterrestrial nature. See the discussion in E. Cochrane, *The Case of the Turquoise Sun* (Ames, 2024), pp. 21-63.
[78] Lines 13-14 from "A hymn to Utu (Utu B)," *ETCSL*.
[79] Line 28. See also lines 3-4 in "An adab (?) to Utu for Shulgi (Shulgi Q)," *ETCSL*: "Hero emerging from the holy interior of heaven, storm whose splendour covers the Land and is laden with great awesomeness."
[80] *PT* 1149-1150.

"stormclouds" by Allen (as we will discover, the word *šnjt* has nothing whatsoever to do with hail or cumulonimbus clouds).[81]

The remainder of this volume will be devoted to outlining and bolstering this novel hypothesis. We begin with a forensic analysis of the manifold traditions surrounding the Eye of Horus, wherein cataclysmic imagery is both ubiquitous and explicit. Yet strange to say, such imagery has been thoroughly misinterpreted by multiple generations of Egyptologists.

---

[81] Note also that the word translated as "shout" by Allen—*nhm*—as in the sky will "shout," also denotes "shake, quake," and thus we likely have another reference to the cosmic upheaval attending the king's ascent to heaven (=primordial sunrise). See R. Hannig, *Ägyptisches Wörterbuch I* (Mainz, 2003), p. 641.

## The Eye of Horus

> "The symbolism of the eye was the most important thing in the mythological and religious notions in ancient Egypt."[82]

> "The departure of the Eye, or Hathor, results in a series of natural disasters in Egypt, where perpetual night prevails."[83]

Of all the astral agents in Egyptian cosmogonic mythology, the Eye of Horus remains the most enigmatic and misunderstood. This is only to be expected given the fact that the original celestial referent for Horus himself continues to elude Egyptologists.

A number of leading scholars have identified the Eye of Horus with the Sun.[84] Others have pointed to Sirius as the star behind the goddess.[85] Katya Goebs, on the other hand, observed: "Scholars have traditionally associated it with the moon."[86] In short, there is no consensus on the astral identification of one of the most important symbols in all of Egyptian religion.[87]

---

[82] T. Sherkova, "Solar Notions, Rituals and Images in Pre-Dynastic Egypt," in A. Maravelia ed., *In Quest of Light* (Montpellier, 2009), p. 134.

[83] M. Rikala, "Sacred Marriage in the New Kingdom of Ancient Egypt," in M. Nissinen & R. Uro eds., *Sacred Marriages* (Winona Lake, 2008), p. 122.

[84] J. Allen, *The Ancient Egyptian Pyramid Texts* (Atlanta, 2005), p. 6: "Originally an explanation of the daily disappearance and reappearance of the sun, 'Horus's eye' became a symbol of permanent soundness and was evidently adopted in rituals to signify the eternal viability of the offering."

[85] J. Quack, "A Goddess Rising 10,000 Cubits into the Air," in J. Steele ed., *Under One Sky* (Münster, 2002), pp. 287ff.

[86] "A Functional Approach to Egyptian Myth and Mythemes," *JANER* 2 (2002), p. 45. See also R. Wilkinson, *Reading Egyptian Art* (London, 1992), p. 43: "A mythological story which tells how the Eye of Horus was damaged and then healed reflects the waning and waxing of the moon."

[87] The most authoritative discussion of the Eye of Horus known to me is that by Samantha Edwards, *The Symbolism of the Eye of Horus in the Pyramid Texts* (1995). After some 200 pages of analysis, she concludes, p. 232: "There seems to me no clear reference that proves an identification of the Eye of Horus with a specific celestial body." Note: This is a Dissertation for the University of Swansea.

In order to make sense of the manifold symbolism attached to the Eye of Horus, it is essential at the outset of our investigation to come to grips with the Egyptian traditions telling of its incendiary rampage at the Time of Beginning that purportedly brought the world to the very brink of extinction. This tradition is most familiar, perhaps, from a text known as the *Destruction of Mankind*, inscribed on the tomb-walls of various kings from the 18th Dynasty and, as such, one of the oldest mythological narratives to survive from ancient Egypt.[88] There we read that the Eye, as the goddess Hathor, was dispatched by Re to punish mankind, who had evidently rebelled against his rule:

"Then mankind plotted something in the (very) presence of Re…Then they [Re's advisors] said in the presence of his majesty: 'May thy Eye be sent, that it may catch for thee them who scheme with evil things…It should go down as Hathor.' So then this goddess came and slew mankind in the desert."[89]

The destructive campaign against mankind was commonly mythologized as a "bloodbath" (*ḥrt, šbbw, šʿt*) waged by the warrior-goddess Hathor or her alter ego Sakhmet. Indeed, in that same text we read: "Hathor will wade in the blood of mankind as Sakhmet."[90]

Although the *Destruction of Mankind* dates to the New Kingdom,[91] memory of the raging Eye-goddess is attested already in the pyramid of Unis (circa 2350 BCE) and hence was of untold antiquity. In Unis's

---

[88] E. Hornung, *Der ägyptische Mythos von der Himmelskuh* (Freiburg, 1982). See also J. G. Griffiths, "Remarks on the Mythology of the Eyes of Horus," *Chronique d'Égypte* 33 (1958), pp. 182-193; K. Sethe, *Zur Sage vom Sonnenauge* (Leipzig, 1912); G. Rudnitzky, *Die Aussage über 'Das Auge des Horus'* (Copenhagen, 1956); R. Anthes, "Das Sonnenauge in den Pyramidentexten," *ZÄS* 86 (1961), pp. 1-21.
[89] J. Wilson, "Deliverance of Mankind from Destruction," in J. Pritchard ed., *The Ancient Near East* (Princeton, 1958), p. 4.
[90] Lines 58-59 as translated in A. Spalinger, "The Destruction of Mankind…," *Studien zur Altägyptischen Kultur* 28 (2000), p. 281. E. Hornung, *op. cit.*, p. 39 translates: "So war es, daß Sachmet enstand, das Gebräu der Nacht, um in ihrem Blute zu waten."
[91] S. Quirke, *Ancient Egyptian Religion* (London, 1992), p. 164 dates it to the time of King Tut. See also A. Spalinger, *op. cit.*, p. 259, who observes: "We are forced to date this literary narrative to Dynasty XVIII *at the earliest*."

pyramid we read that the flame from Horus's Eye produced a prodigious storm (*nšn*) shaking the very foundations of heaven:

"I [Horus] will put flame in my eye, and it will encompass you and set storm among the doers of (evil) deeds, and its fiery outburst among these primeval ones. I will smite away the arms of Shu which support the sky."[92]

So, too, the Coffin Texts are replete with cryptic allusions to the apocalyptic disaster associated with the Eye of Horus. Spell 316 emphasizes the terrifying power of the raging goddess:

"I am the fiery Eye of Horus, which went forth terrible, Lady of slaughter, greatly awesome, who came into being in the flame of the sunshine, to whom Rēʿ granted appearings in glory…What Rēʿ said about her: Mighty is the fear of you, great is the awe of you, mighty is your striking-power…all men have been in the sleep of death because of you and through your power."[93]

The Eye of Horus is here likened to a heaven-spanning "flame" (*ns*). Indeed, the catastrophic context of the warring Eye-goddess is everywhere apparent: "Its flame is to the sky."[94] In Spell 946, as elsewhere, the Eye is associated with fire falling from the sky: "I am a fire in sky and earth, and all my foes are under my flame."[95] Other hymns confirm that the Eye's rampage was incendiary in nature: "The fire will go up, the flame will go up…the fiery one will be against them as the Eye of Rēʿ."[96]

At one time or another, every major Egyptian goddess is identified with the Eye of Horus: Hathor, Isis, Wadjet, Mut, Wepset, etc. The traditions attached to Sakhmet aptly illustrate the fundamental nature of the warring Eye-goddess. In the Bremner-Rhind papyrus, it is Sakhmet who protects the king and wards off his enemies as the raging Eye:

---

[92] *PT* 298-299.
[93] *CT* IV: 98-100.
[94] *CT* III:343.
[95] *CT* VII:162.
[96] *CT* V: 264.

"Thou art (condemned) to this fire of the Eye of Rē'; it sends forth (?) its fiery blast against thee in this its name of Wadjet; it consumes thee in this its name of 'Devouring Flame'; it has power over thee in this its name of Sakhmet; it is fiery against thee in this its name of 'Glorious Serpent'."[97]

The image of Sakhmet as a raging serpentine goddess is abundantly attested in the religious inscriptions discovered at Philae. Here, as elsewhere, Sakhmet is identified as the "Eye of Horus":

"Sakhmet, the strong one (*wsrt*), is in Bigeh in her form as the Eye of Horus, the living [eye…] while [spreading fire (?)] with the flame when she goes round, while scorching the rebels with the heat of her mouth. She is the primeval snake (*ḳrḥt*)."[98]

In the temple texts from Edfu, Sakhmet is once again compared to a flame-spewing serpent and celebrated for her protective powers. Witness the following passage:

"O Sekhmet, Eye of Rē', great of flame, Lady of protection who envelops her creator…O Sekhmet who fills the ways with blood, Who slaughters to the limits of all she sees, Come towards the living image, the living Hawk, Protect him, and preserve him from all evil."[99]

The terrifying goddess who "fills the ways with blood" and slaughters to the limits is here urged to approach Horus—the living Hawk and star-god—and serve as his protector. Indeed, Horus's protection by the fire-spitting uraeus-serpent is a prominent thematic pattern in Egyptian religion.[100]

According to various traditions preserved in the Pyramid and Coffin Texts, the raging Eye-goddess was eventually pacified or otherwise

---

[97] R. Faulkner, "The Bremner-Rhind Papyrus— IV," *Journal of Egyptian Archaeology* 24 (1938), p. 45.
[98] 81,15-16 as translated in J. F. Borghouts, "The Evil Eye of Apophis," *Journal of Egyptian Archaeology* 59 (1973), p. 136.
[99] Quoted from A. Roberts, *Hathor Rising* (Devon, 1995), p. 13.
[100] Thus a royal hymn assures King Thutmose III: "The glowing diadem [*ȝḫt*] protects you." See M. Lichtheim, *Ancient Egyptian Literature, Vol. II* (Berkeley, 1976), p. 36.

dissuaded from her terrifying campaign of destruction. The following account from the Coffin Texts alludes to this motif: "The storm of Her who is mighty of dread, Mistress of the land, is quelled(?)."[101] Another Coffin Text summarizes this turn of events as follows: "So the fighting has ended, the tumult is stopped, the fire which went forth is quenched, the anger in the presence of the Tribunal of the Gods is calmed…"[102] Here it is the "fire" (sḏt) and "anger" (dšrw) of the raging Eye that is extinguished or calmed.

The "pacification" of the raging Eye, in turn, is typically attributed to the heroic interventions of either Shu or Onuris (the two gods were commonly identified). In Spell 325 from the Coffin Texts, for example, Shu is described as follows: "He subdued the Eye when it was angry and fiery, that he might lead the Great Ones and have power over the gods…."[103] The same idea is alluded to in Spell 75, wherein Shu is made to announce:

"I have extinguished the fire, I have calmed the soul of her who burns, I have quietened her who is in the midst of her rage…(even she) the fiery one who severed the tresses of the gods."[104]

The phrase translated by Faulkner here as "extinguished the fire"—ꜥhm sḏ.t—seems to have served as a *terminus technicus* for the calming of the raging Eye.

Numerous texts from the Ptolemaic period likewise allude to the pacification of the raging Eye by Shu or Onuris, often aided and abetted by Thoth. Thanks in large part to the painstaking detective work and incisive scholarship of Herman Junker, these widely scattered fragmentary texts were pieced together and have since come to be known

---

[101] *CT* VII:36.
[102] *CT* I:21-22.
[103] *CT* IV:154.
[104] *CT* I:378.

by the generic name of the *Wandering Goddess* theme.[105] Although they were inscribed nearly two thousand years later than the Pyramid and Coffin Texts, such texts frequently preserve archaic motifs and are thus well worthy of careful study—this despite the fact that they also betray rather clumsy attempts to humanize and localize the myth of the raging Eye goddess, originally celestial in nature.

The basic plot of the *Wandering Goddess* tale finds the Eye goddess (variously identified as Hathor, Tefnut, Wadjet, Mut, etc.) going into exile and abandoning Egypt for some distant land—typically Nubia or Libya—whereupon she goes on a destructive rampage in the form of a raging eye or lion. It is only through the magical interventions of Shu, Onuris, or Thoth that the warrior-goddess is eventually pacified and induced to return to Egypt.[106]

The Wandering Goddess as raging Eye formed a recurring theme in various New Year's rituals celebrated throughout Egypt during the Ptolemaic period, the latter being characterized by boisterous music, bouts of drinking, the brandishing of torches, and ecstatic dancing.[107] A measure of the ritual's ideological importance can be seen from the fact that Egyptian monuments from this period depict the pharaoh emulating (or reenacting) the role of Shu/Onuris by performing a series of gyrating dances and other magical acts, such as the vigorous rattling of sistrums.[108] Such ritual reenactments were evidently conducted in the belief that they

---

[105] H. Junker, *Der Auszug der Hathor-Tefnut aus Nubien* (Berlin, 1911). See also the valuable discussion in B. Richter, *The Theology of Hathor of Dendera* (Atlanta, 2016), pp. 1-6.

[106] R. Krauss, "Stellar Power and Solar Components in Ancient Egyptian Mythology and Royal Ideology," in M. Rappenglück et al eds., *Astronomy and Power* (Oxford, 2016), p. 138 would explain this myth by reference to the regular interactions of the Moon and Venus: "The loss of the eye corresponds astronomically to the two-month invisibility of Venus before the planet reappears as the evening star. The role of the moon god who finds the lost eye, brings it back, and heals it (PT 82; CT 249), can be seen as reflecting the frequent encounter of the waxing moon and the evening star."

[107] B. Richter, "On the Heels of the Wandering Goddess," in M. Dolinska &. H. Beinlich eds., *Ägyptologische Tempeltagung* (Wiesbaden, 2010), p. 155 writes: "one of the most important festivals celebrated during the Ptolemaic Era."

[108] H. Junker, *op. cit.*, pp. 9, 72, 85. See also B. Richter, *op. cit.*, p. 161.

would help stave off or calm (*sḥtp*) the Eye's raging (*nšn*) and thereby maintain or restore order to the world.[109]

Although the precise manner of the pacification of the Eye of Horus is never spelled out as explicitly as we might wish, it seems clear that, upon being calmed, the Eye was returned or otherwise restored to the god Horus.[110] Indeed, a wealth of evidence suggests that the Eye-goddess eventually came to adorn the Horus-star as his royal headband or crown. An exemplary text in this regard is Utterance 220/221 from the Pyramid Texts, wherein the Eye-goddess is addressed by a series of epithets identifying her as the Red Crown (*Nt*):

"He has come to you, O *Nt*-crown; he has come to you, O Fiery Serpent; he has come to you, O Great One; he has come to you, O Great of Magic, being pure for you and fearing you…How kindly is your face, for you are content, renewed, and rejuvenated, even as the father of the gods fashioned you. He has come to you, O Great of Magic, for he is Horus encircled with the protection of his Eye, O Great of Magic…Ho, Crown great of magic! Ho Fiery Serpent! Grant that the dread of me be like the dread of you; Grant that the fear of me be like the fear of you…If Ikhet the Great has borne you, Ikhet the Serpent has adorned you; If Ikhet the Serpent has borne you, Ikhet the Great has adorned you, Because you are Horus encircled with the protection of his Eye."[111]

As stated here in no uncertain terms, it is the "encircling" (*šn*) of Horus by the fire-spewing uraeus-goddess—addressed as Ikhet the Serpent, "Great of Magic," and other archaic epithets—which endows the star-god with his "Eye" and thereby provides him with a magical rampart of

---

[109] According to John Darnell, "Hathor Returns to Medamud," *JEA* 22 (1995), pp. 92-93: "Their noisy revelry [of the celebrants] appeasing the ever more calm goddess, and the cacophony driving away baleful influences."

[110] J. Darnell, "The Apotropaic Goddess in the Eye," *Studien zur altägyptischen Kultur* 24 (1997), p. 47 cites a Ptolemaic text from Elkab in which Ra announces: "Welcome! Come back upon the head of him whom you have protected, that head from which you went forth!" See also the wealth of evidence provided by B. Richter, *The Theology of Hathor of Dendera* (Atlanta, 2016), pp. 165-172.

[111] *PT* 194-198.

protection (*s3*).¹¹² Essential to understanding the symbolism involved is the report that the raging Eye is "calmed" (*shtp*) upon returning to and encircling the Horus-star as a crown—hence the Eye's description as "content" (*htp*) in *PT* 195c.

The same basic idea recurs throughout Egyptian history. In the coronation hymn of Haremhab (circa 1319 BCE), we read that the uraeus-serpent—explicitly addressed as "Great of Magic"—was deemed responsible for the "crowning" of the Egyptian pharaoh: "[her arms] in welcoming attitude, and she embraced his beauty and established herself on his forehead, and the Divine Ennead…were in exultation at his glorious rising."¹¹³

The return of the raging Eye/uraeus to its rightful place atop the brow of the Horus-star, in addition to providing the royal crown, endows the latter with awe-inspiring glory and power and forms a prominent episode in the Egyptian account of creation. Indeed, it is no exaggeration to say that the Eye-Goddess "invests" the Horus-star as the King of the Gods through this act of encirclement or "conjunction."¹¹⁴ Susan Johnson summarized the primeval mythological events in question as follows:

"The god of creation appeased the eye, which had become a cobra, by placing it on his forehead as the uraeus, *i'rt* [Iaret], 'the Risen One', who guards the crown. The pacification of the cobra thus marked the establishment of monarchy, and the uraeus became the protective symbol of legitimate kingship and unity."¹¹⁵

---

¹¹² See L. Zabkar, *Hymns to Isis in Her Temple at Philae* (Hanover, 1988), p. 133: "As the uraeus-diadem of the sun-god, 'the Coiled One on his head,' or as an anthropomorphic deity, the goddess travels with Re in his barque and protects him from his enemies."
¹¹³ A. Gardiner, "The Coronation of King Ḥaremḥab," *JEA* 39 (1953), p. 29.
¹¹⁴ With specific reference to Haremhab's coronation, K. Bosse-Griffiths, "The Great Enchantress in the Little Golden Shrine of Tutʿankhamun," in J. Gwyn Griffiths ed., *Amarna Studies and Other Selected Papers* (Fribourg, 2001), p. 118 observed: "By fixing the uraeus on the forehead of Ḥaremḥab, his right to be king is established."
¹¹⁵ S. Johnson, *The Cobra Goddess of Ancient Egypt* (London, 1990), p. 6.

Johnson's conclusion is right on the money and bears underscoring: It is the joining together or *reunion of the Eye/uraeus with the Horus-star* which marks the establishment of kingship.[116] The pacification of the raging Eye, moreover, signals the restoration of world order after the terrifying cosmic upheaval attending its destructive rampage.[117]

Even from this brief survey it is evident that the Eye of Horus plays a central role in Egyptian cosmogonic myth and ideas about kingship and divinity. How, then, are we to explain the peculiar traditions attached to the raging Eye-goddess? James Allen, together with the vast majority of Egyptologists, would identify the Eye of Horus with the Sun:

"The uraeus-goddess is essentially the destructive power of the sun. She is a goddess because the sun is viewed in this case as the eye of the sun-god (Horus or Re), which is feminine (*jrt*). She is normally represented as a cobra (*wadjet*, also feminine) because of the notion of a power that can strike and kill: the hieroglyphic representation of this is N6 (sun-disk with cobra) [☉]. The same power is viewed as inherent in the king's headgear, which is why it also has a uraeus. The primary thing to keep in mind, however, is the notion of the eye. In myth she represents both the sun as an eye and its destructive power. Her common epithet 'Great of Magic' (*weret-hekau*) derives from the idea of the eye as conveyor of intent—same notion as the 'evil eye' (which also existed in ancient Egypt). Through syncretism, she is associated with other major goddesses, such as Isis and Hathor."[118]

---

[116] R. T. Clark, *Myth and Symbol in Ancient Egypt* (London, 1959), p. 94 wrote: "The return of the Eye marks the assumption of kingship by the High God and the end of the age of inchoate chaos." K. Goebs, *Crowns in Egyptian Funerary Literature* (Oxford, 2008), p. 143 has recently offered a similar assessment: "The return of the Eye(s) corresponds with the investiture of the new Horus-king, and—on a cosmic level—to the daily rising of the sun."

[117] B. Richter, *op. cit.*, p. 156, wrote: "With her pacification, the order of the cosmos is also restored."

[118] Personal correspondence, 8-29-2010.

Yet if the Eye of Horus is to be identified with the Sun, how are we to understand its departure from Horus (or Re in the *The Destruction of Mankind*)? For if Horus himself is to be identified with the Sun, as Allen assures us, one is left with the seemingly paradoxical situation wherein the Eye/Sun departs and, after threatening the world with destruction, returns to encircle or "crown" *itself*![119]

It must also be asked why Egyptian skywatchers would conceptualize one and the same celestial body as simultaneously both male (Horus) and female (the Eye as Hathor or Sakhmet). Insofar as the Horus-star represented the celestial prototype of the masculine war-god, while the Eye represented the archetypal mother goddess, this interpretation of the Egyptian myth would appear to be at odds with the facts and more than a little strained.

Equally problematic is the fact that the explicit catastrophic imagery attending the raging of the fire-spewing Eye is difficult to explain by the solar hypothesis. In what sense is the Sun displaced while presenting a terrifying fire-spewing serpentine form? Under what circumstances does the Sun threaten to destroy mankind? What is there about the Sun's familiar appearance that would lead it to be conceptualized as a serpentine-goddess "protecting" the Horus-star by encircling it as a luminous crown or headband?

Far from being a reference to one and the same star, Horus's relationship to the Eye is best understood as reflecting a close interaction or conjunction between two entirely different celestial bodies. On this

---

[119] J. Quack, "A Goddess Rising 10,000 Cubits into the Air," in J. Steele & A. Imhausen eds., *Under One Sky* (Münster, 2002), p. 287 offered a similar opinion: "As the goddess is always designated as the daughter of the sun-god to whom she returns, any interpretation identifying the goddess herself with the sun runs into serious trouble: one sun would have to play two roles at once." So, too, R. Krauss, "The Eye of Horus and the Planet Venus: Astronomical and Mythological References," in J. Steele & A. Imhausen eds., *Under One Sky* (Münster, 2002), p. 194: "If this myth reflects reality or nature, then the eye which leaves the sun god and afterwards returns to him cannot be identical with the sun disk itself."

matter the preponderance of evidence is clear: The Eye of Horus is to be identified with the mother goddess and, as such, it represents an entirely different star from that associated with the masculine Horus (Mars).[120] In ancient Egypt, as around the globe, only one star fits the bill as the celestial prototype for the mother goddess—namely, Venus.[121] In this conclusion we find ourselves in complete agreement with Rolf Krauss who, in a number of publications investigating Egyptian astral religion, has argued that the Eye of Horus is to be identified with the planet Venus.[122]

Granted the possibility that Venus is the subject of the Egyptian traditions regarding the Eye of Horus, how are we to understand the cataclysmic imagery attending its destructive rampage? Whence derives the Eye's pronounced capacity for raining fire and destruction on mankind? Why would the planet Venus be conceptualized as a raging serpent at one moment and as "pacified" or calmed on another? On these all-important questions Krauss had nothing substantive to offer, noting simply: "It remains unclear how the observer understood raging and peacefulness."[123]

As strange and improbable as the Egyptian traditions attached to the Eye appear, striking parallels exist in Mesopotamia and elsewhere that describe the planet Venus in analogous terms—i.e., as a terrifying agent of sky-borne disaster, one prone to assuming the form of a fire-spewing serpent.[124] It was in the latter guise, according to the archaic traditions

---

[120] R. T. Clark, *Myth and Symbol in Ancient Egypt* (London, 1959), p. 220: "Hence we get the fundamental symbol equation of Egyptian religion: Eye=Flame=Destructive Goddess=Cobra=Crown."

[121] E. Cochrane, *The Many Faces of Venus* (Ames, 2001), pp. 7-13; 159-165.

[122] R. Krauss, *Astronomische Konzepte und Jenseitsvorstellungen in den Pyramidentexten* (Wiesbaden, 1997), pp. 193-208. It will be noted that Talbott and I offered this identification well over a decade before Krauss.

[123] *Ibid.*, p. 201.

[124] See here the discussion in E. Cochrane, *Fossil Gods and Forgotten Worlds* (Ames, 2010), pp. 77-123.

preserved in the Sumerian text known as *The Exaltation of Inanna,* that the war-mongering planet-goddess rained fire from heaven:

"Like a dragon you have deposited venom on the land, When you roar at the earth like Thunder, no vegetation can stand up to you. A flood descending from its mountain, Oh foremost one, you are the Inanna of heaven and earth! Raining the fanned fire down upon the nation…When mankind comes before you In fear and trembling at your tempestuous radiance."[125]

Virtually identical imagery is to be found in early literary accounts of the Semitic goddess Ishtar who, like the Sumerian Inanna, was explicitly identified with the planet Venus. The following passage is representative:

"I rain battle down like flames in the fighting, I make heaven and earth shake (?) with my cries…I constantly traverse heaven, then (?) I trample the earth. I destroy what remains of the inhabited world."[126]

Here, as in the Sumerian hymns describing Inanna, *it is the planet Venus* that is raining fire and destruction from the sky. The celestial context of the imagery in question could hardly be more patently obvious or unequivocal.

In ancient Mesopotamia, as in Egypt, the raging planet-goddess brings an apocalyptic storm in her wake. The testimony of a Sumerian text known as BM 23820 is instructive:

"Inanna, who pours down rain over all the lands, over all the people, loud-thundering storm. Hierodule, who makes heavens tremble, who makes the earth quake, Who can soothe your heart? You who pour down firebrands over the earthly orb, who flash like lightning over the highland…Whose cry reaches heaven and earth, whose roar is all-destructive…Your angry heart is a terrifying flood-wave."[127]

In this hymn, as in various other early Sumerian texts, Inanna/Venus rains down fire and flood from the skies much as was reported of the

---

[125] W. Hallo & J. van Dijk, *The Exaltation of Inanna* (New Haven, 1968), pp. 15-17.
[126] B. Foster, *Before the Muses* (Bethesda, 1993), p. 74.
[127] S. Kramer, *From the Poetry of Sumer* (Berkeley, 1979), p. 89.

raging Eye in Egyptian texts dating from the same general period (circa 2000 BCE). The cataclysmic nature of the goddess's rampage is evident: "Wherever she spits venom there is a storm and strife makes the ground groan (?)."[128]

The similarities between Inanna/Venus and the Egyptian Eye goddess extend to the finest details. Remembering that the return of the Eye marked the establishment of kingship in Egyptian tradition, it is significant to find that similar reports surround Inanna/Venus in Sumerian lore. This archaic symbolism is most clearly expressed in the third-millennium text *Enmerkar and the Lord of Aratta*, called "probably the finest piece of poetic storytelling ever produced by Old Babylonian authors."[129] There we learn of the early king Enmerkar who, as the beloved of Inanna, engages in a sacred marriage with the planet-goddess, although much of the language and imagery is allusive and cryptic in nature.[130] In the final lines of the epic Enmerkar credits the planet-goddess with investing him with kingship: "The ever-sparkling lady gives me my kingship."[131]

The word translated as "ever-sparkling" here is mul-mul-e, "to shine, or radiate," a verb formed from the Sumerian word for star (mul) and hence referring to the luminous splendor of Venus itself. The clear import of this passage, beyond any shadow of a doubt, is that kingship was a gift of the planet Venus.[132] Far from being figurative in nature, the language of *Enmerkar and the lord of Aratta* is best understood in literal fashion: It

---

[128] Line 28 from Inana C as translated by M. Cohen, *An Annotated Sumerian Dictionary* (London, 2023), p. 1392.

[129] H. Vanstiphout, *Epics of Sumerian Kings* (Leiden, 2004), p. 49.

[130] C. Woods, "Sons of the Sun: The Mythological Foundations of the First Dynasty of Uruk," *JANER* 12 (2012), p. 33 notes: "Enmerkar, of course, represents Dumuzi in the sacred marriage ritual."

[131] Line 632 from "Enmerkar and the lord of Aratta," *ETCSL*.

[132] E. Cochrane, *On Fossil Gods and Forgotten Worlds* (Ames, 2021), pp. 162-176. See also the discussion in J. Westenholz, "King by Love of Inanna," *NIN* 1 (2000), pp. 75-82.

is the planet Venus who "makes" the king by enveloping him with a starry mantle or crown of "glory."

Even from this cursory survey the striking parallels between the mythological traditions describing Inanna/Venus and those attached to the Eye of Horus are readily apparent. Yet in the dozens of monographs devoted to the Egyptian Eye goddess—not to mention the hundreds of articles that have addressed the peculiar symbolism surrounding the raging Eye of Horus—I am unaware of a single scholar who has even commented on the manifold correspondences between the Eye and Inanna/Venus, much less offered a systematic cross-cultural analysis of the traditions. Suffice it to say that expertise in comparative mythology is not prevalent in Egyptological circles. As a result, modern Egyptology remains mired in the same outdated solar interpretations that dominated scholarship at the turn of the 20th century, wholly oblivious to the fact that the ancient Egyptian descriptions of the raging Eye of Horus share a virtual one-to-one correspondence with Sumerian accounts of the raging Inanna/Venus.[133]

To return to the Egyptian testimony, it will be remembered that the raging Eye produced an all-encompassing storm. In the following account from Unis's pyramid, quoted earlier, the flame from Horus's Eye is likened to a raging storm:

"I [Horus] will put flame in my eye, and it will encompass you and set storm among the doers of (evil) deeds, and its (fiery) outburst among these primeval ones. I will smite away the arms of Shu which support the sky."[134]

As for how we are to understand the "storm" (*nšn*) in question, it is evident that it is a meteorological disturbance of cosmic proportions—in the Coffin Texts the same word is repeatedly used to denote an

---

[133] E. Cochrane, *Fossil Gods and Forgotten Worlds* (Ames, 2010), pp. 77-123.
[134] *PT* 298-299.

apocalyptic disturbance.[135] Yet in Spell 335 from the Coffin Texts the same word is employed to describe the "wrath" of the raging Eye-goddess: "I raised the hair from the Sacred Eye at its time of wrath."[136] The seemingly incongruous reference to "hair" (*šn*) in conjunction with a stellar Eye is addressed—if not fully clarified—by a gloss appended to the spell in question:

*"What is the Sacred Eye at its time of wrath? Who raised the hair from it? It is the right Eye of Re when it was wroth with him after he had sent it on an errand. It was Thoth who raised the hair from it."*[137]

Here the disaster-bringing "wrath" (*nšn*) of the raging Eye is explicitly linked to its "hair" (*šn*). Taking these two traditions together, it seems evident that the "wrath" or "storm" associated with the Eye of Horus was somehow connected to its extraterrestrial "hair."

The same conclusion is supported by the apparent etymological relationship between the Egyptian words *šnj*, "hair," and *šnjt*, "storm," the latter term being employed to denote the catastrophic storm that accompanied the deceased king's ascent to heaven (as in *PT* 1150b, quoted earlier).[138] So, too, this very term is elsewhere substituted for *nšn*: Witness the following passage—"N will dispel the storm."[139] (It will be noted that the word translated as "dispel" here is *ts*, an apparent cognate of the word *ts* translated by Faulkner as "raised" in the passage above

---

[135] *CT* IV:40, IV:396, VI:306, and VII:376. R. Caminos, *The Chronicle of Prince Osorkon* (Rome, 1958), p. 90 observes that *nšn* denotes "the rage of heaven" or a "convulsion of the sky." See also S. Quirke, *Going out in Daylight* (London, 2013), p. 214: "The storm is a recurrent term to refer to, without mentioning directly, the attack on Osiris."
[136] *CT* IV: 238.
[137] *CT* IV: 239-240.
[138] On the former word see R. Hannig, *Ägyptisches Wörterbuch I* (Mainz, 2003), p. 1309, entry 33121. On the latter word see *Ibid.*, entry 33154.
[139] *CT* VII:110. See *PT* 2366 and *CT* V:150, VI:330. See also the discussion in R. Faulkner, *The Ancient Egyptian Coffin Texts* (Oxford, 1973), p. 8.

describing Thoth's raising of the hair from the Sacred Eye). Also relevant here is the word *šnṯ*, denoting the Eye-goddess's "wrath."[140]

Here, then, is the probable answer to the question which so baffled Krauss regarding the Egyptian traditions describing the Eye of Horus as the planet Venus—namely, how to explain its peculiar propensity for "raging": The Eye/Venus was conceptualized as raging because it displayed disheveled "hair" while wandering about the sky—this while raising a "storm" and spewing forth immense volumes of fiery material.[141] Thus it is that, in some accounts of the Eye-goddess's return, she shakes her disheveled hair.[142] The adjective employed here is *tḥtḥ*, denoting disheveled.[143] Yet the same word also describes a rebellion of the gods *in illo tempore*.[144]

If this much is fairly obvious and straightforward, it remains to be shown how or why the planet Venus could ever be conceptualized as suddenly displaying disheveled or "storm"-laden hair. The answer to this question, it must be said, will not sit well with the Central Dogma of modern astronomy, which holds that the visible planets have not changed their appearance or orbits in any fundamental manner for many millions of years. Yet it is necessary to follow the evidence wherever it happens to lead. As Sherlock Holmes was wont to say, "When you have eliminated the impossible, whatever remains, however improbable, must be the truth."[145] As improbable as it must appear at first sight, the testimony of ancient skywatchers with regards to Venus's recent history tells a very

---

[140] *CT* VI:46h. R. van der Molen, *A Hieroglyphic Dictionary of Egyptian Coffin Texts* (Leiden, 2000), p. 626.
[141] See the discussion in E. Cochrane, *The Many Faces of Venus* (Ames, 2022), pp. 73-82 wherein analogous traditions surrounding the Indic goddess Kali are discussed.
[142] J. Darnell, "A Midsummer Night's Succubus…," in S. Melville & A. Slotsky eds., *Opening the Tablet B*ox (Leiden, 2010), p. 114.
[143] R. Faulkner, *The Ancient Egyptian Pyramid Texts* (Oxford, 1969), p. 251.
[144] *PT* 392d. See R. Hannig, *op. cit.*, p. 1435, entry 46534.
[145] *The Sign of the Four*.

consistent story—namely, that of a planet run amok while displaying comet-like hair.[146]

In order to clarify the nature of Venus's "hair" from the standpoint of natural science, it is instructive to revisit the Egyptian traditions recounting how the Eye-goddess came to encircle the Horus-star with a royal headband. Utterance 510 from the Pyramid Texts is especially informative. There the Eye is addressed as Ikhet the Great: "I am this head-band of red colour which went forth from Ikhet the Great; I am this Eye of Horus which is stronger than men and mightier than the gods."[147] Here the all-powerful Eye of Horus is specifically identified with a headband emanating from the Ikhet-Serpent. The headband associated with the Eye is also alluded to in another equally enigmatic passage from Utterance 519: "So that I may ferry across in it together with that headband of green and of red cloth which has been woven from the Eye of Horus in order to bandage therewith that finger of Osiris that has become diseased."[148]

The word translated as "head-band" in both of these Utterance is *sšd*, determined with the following glyph: ⌒ɣ. If the Eye of Horus is to be identified with a celestial body, as all Egyptologists agree, how are we to explain this choice of determinative?[149] This question is directly related to another: Why would a "headband" be likened to—or identified with—a terrifying serpentine form which rains fire and "is stronger than men and mightier than the gods"?[150]

---

[146] D. Talbott, "The Great Comet Venus," *Aeon* 3:5 (1994), pp. 5-51. See also E. Cochrane, *The Many Faces of Venus* (Ames, 2022), pp. 78-88.
[147] *PT* 1147.
[148] *PT* 1202-1203.
[149] C. Manassa, *The Late Egyptian Underworld* (Wiesbaden, 2007), p. 26 suggests that the reference is to the Milky Way: "The *sšd*-fillet in this Pyramid Text passage [Spell 519] may also allude to the Milky Way, providing further evidence for the Egyptian association of the eye of Horus with astral bodies other than the sun and moon."
[150] It will be noted that the *sšd*-headband is also identified with the Eye of Horus in *PT* 96c.

A decisive clue is provided by the fact that, in addition to denoting "headband," the word *sšd* also signifies a comet-like object or flame-scattering star.[151] Indeed, there are a number of Egyptian texts which describe a *sšd*-star streaking across the sky and scattering fire. In the so-called Poetical Stela found at Karnak, for example, the warring Thutmose III is likened to an *sšd*-star "strewing its fire in flame and yielding its downpour."[152] As Gerald Wainwright pointed out in his discussion of the royal inscription in question, the terrifying specter of the *sšd*-star is a decided point of emphasis in the Egyptian texts: "Its dangerous nature is certified by the desire of the Pharaoh to seem to his enemies in battle to be like the *sšd*."[153]

Hitherto overlooked, however, is the fact that the *sšd*-star's propensity for strewing flames of fire and inspiring dread is mirrored in Egyptian reports of the raging Eye of Horus. Recall again the passage from Unis's pyramid, quoted earlier, wherein the flame from Horus's Eye is likened to a raging storm: "I [Horus] will put flame in my eye, and it will encompass you and set storm among the doers of (evil) deeds, and its fiery outburst among these primeval ones."[154]

The Eye of Horus is here said to unleash a fiery "outburst" (*ḥfḥft*) or swell of efflux on the primeval ones.[155] This tradition recalls the fact that

---

[151] R. Hannig, *Ägyptisches Wörterbuch I* (Mainz, 2003), p. 1244, entry 30768. J. Zandee, *Der Amunhymnus des Papyrus Leiden I 344, Verso, Vol. 1* (Leiden, 1992), p. 356 translates *sšd* as "Komet."

[152] Line 15 of the king's Poetical Stela as translated in R. Faulkner, "'The Pregnancy of Isis': A Rejoinder," *JEA* 59 (1973), p. 219, citing Urk. IV, 615, 13-15. K. Goebs, *Crowns in Egyptian Funerary Literature* (Oxford, 2008), p. 373 translates the passage as "a shooting star that scatters its flame of fire."

[153] G. Wainwright, "Letopolis," *JEA* 18 (1932), p. 162. R. Faulkner, "'The Pregnancy of Isis': A Rejoinder," *JEA* 59 (1973), p. 219 translated *sšd* as "lightning-flash," arguing "such a description is not applicable to a star, but is most appropriate to a thunderstorm." The fact that *sšd* is determined with a star in Thutmose's stela undermines Faulkner's strained interpretation.

[154] *PT* 298-299.

[155] R. Faulkner, *op. cit.*, p. 190 translates the word as "flood." The very same word is used to describe a flood unleashed by the Eye of Horus in the *Coffin Texts* (VII:235h).

a "downpour" of fiery efflux (*jdt*) was associated with the *sšd*-star on Thutmose's Poetical Stela.[156] How, then, are we to explain the Eye's peculiar association with a flood of fire?

That there was a celestial basis for such imagery is strongly suggested by the fact that an extraterrestrial "flooding" and raining of fire is precisely the disaster dispensed by Inanna/Venus, as evinced not only by the Sumerian story quoted above (BM 23280) but by the following hymn as well:

"Like a dragon you have deposited venom on the land…A flood descending from its mountain, Oh foremost one, you are the Inanna of heaven and earth! Raining the fanned fire down upon the nation."[157]

The fiery "flood" (*ḥfḥft*) associated with the raging Eye of Horus, in turn, finds a close structural analogue in the wrath-like "flood" associated with the incendiary rampage of Inanna/Venus.[158] Witness the following passage: "Her wrath (is)…a devastating flood which no one can withstand."[159]

In light of the detailed parallels between the Egyptian traditions describing the Eye of Horus and Sumerian hymns celebrating Inanna/Venus, it is necessary to ask whether the respective traditions are describing the same celestial body? On this point the evidence is unambiguous: The Eye of Horus, like Inanna, is to be identified with the planet Venus. It was the Queen of Heaven that was conceptualized as a raging warrior-goddess throughout the ancient Near East (Inanna, Ishtar, Astarte, al-'Uzza, etc.), thereby paralleling the behavior accorded the Eye-goddess in Egyptian texts.[160] So, too, it was the planet Venus that formerly

---

[156] *Jdt* elsewhere denotes the "wrath" of the Eye of Horus. See *CT* IV:108.
[157] W. Hallo & J. van Dijk, *The Exaltation of Inanna* (New Haven, 1968), pp. 15-17.
[158] See lines 204-205 of "The death of Ur-Nammu (Ur-Namma A)," *ETCSL*. See also the discussion in E. Cochrane, *On Fossil Gods and Forgotten Worlds* (Ames, 2010), pp. 77-113.
[159] Line 29 from "A hymn to Inana (Inana C), *ETCSL*.
[160] It will be noted that the Egyptian *Astarte Papyrus* describes the planet-goddess Astarte as *qndt nšny*, "furious/raging storm." See here the discussion in N. Ayali-

presented a comet-like form while spewing fire across the sky, an event mythologized as a fire-scattering "comet" (*sšd*) or as a fire-spewing serpent (the Inanna-dragon or uraeus-goddess).[161]

To summarize our findings in this chapter: A wealth of evidence confirms that the Eye of Horus is to be identified with the planet Venus. This finding, in turn, has profound and wide-ranging ramifications for the proper understanding of ancient Egyptian religion insofar as the Eye's history is catastrophic from start to finish, being explicitly associated with an apocalyptic cosmic disaster *in illo tempore*. After an indefinite period of time during which it was conceptualized as waging war against mankind amidst darkness and chaos, the raging Eye was eventually pacified or "calmed," whereupon order was restored to the cosmos. According to the archaic account preserved in Utterances 220-221 from the Pyramid Texts, the Eye came to encircle the star-god Horus as a serpentine goddess (Ikhet the Serpent), thereby providing him with an aegis-like headband or crown. The Eye-goddess's "encircling" of the Horus-star, in our view, has direct reference to extraordinary astronomical events in which the planet Venus appeared to conjoin with Mars (Horus) and encircle it with a comet-like band (*sšd*)—hence the reason why this one word denotes at once Ikhet's head-band as well as a flame-scattering star ("comet or meteor"). Indeed, the mere fact that the word *sšd* is elsewhere determined by the N6 glyph— ☉ —confirms its intimate relationship with the uraeus-serpent that came to form the encircling crown of Horus.[162]

---

Darshan, "The Other Version of the Story of the Storm-god's Combat with the Sea...," *JANER* 15 (2015), p. 33.

[161] E. Cochrane, *The Many Faces of Venus* (Ames, 2001), pp. 113-151.

[162] W. Barta, "Zur Bedeutung des Stirnbands-Diadems *sšd*," *Göttinger Miszellen* 72 (1984), p. 8. The archaic symbolism attached to the seshed-band is still preserved in a temple hymn from Dendera: "Wearing the (royal) crown. Words to say: Take for yourself the seshed band, It has encircled your forehead. The uraeus is united (*ḥnm*) with your head." Translation in B. Richter, *The Theology of Hathor of Dendera* (Atlanta, 2016), p. 95.

It is telling that strikingly similar traditions are attached to Inanna/Venus in Sumerian religion. The name Inanna was written with an archaic pictograph known as the MUŠ₃-sign (see figure one). Peter Huber, a noted authority on ancient Near Eastern astronomical traditions, acknowledged that the pictograph in question resembled a cometary object: "The Inanna symbol sometimes looks like a comet."[163] Yet the MUŠ₃-sign was also employed to determine the king's headband, much like the Egyptian *sšd*-band. Witness the statement of Piotr Steinkeller:

"As for its specific meaning, we undoubtedly find here a type of band. Since suh is compared to 'crown' (men) and 'tiara' (aga), and since it may have been decorated with lapis lazuli, it certainly was an object of considerable importance and value, which was worn over the head. A translation 'diadem' would thus not be inappropriate…It would seem, therefore, that the archaic symbol of Inanna depicts a scarf or headband."[164]

Figure 1

Sumerian tradition emphasizes the fact that the investiture of the king with a MUŠ₃-headband was central to the coronation ritual. A Sumerian temple hymn from the third millennium BCE describes the mother goddess as tying a MUŠ₃-headband around the king:

---

[163] Quoted in L. Rose, "Just Plainly Wrong: A Critique of Peter Huber," in L. Greenberg & W. Sizemore, eds., *Velikovsky and Establishment Science* (Glassboro, 1977), p. 109.
[164] P. Steinkeller, "Inanna's Archaic Symbol," in J. Braun et al eds., *Written on Clay and Stone* (Warsaw, 1998), p. 95.

"The (new)born king, she binds the mùš (around his head), The (new)born lord, she sets the crown (on his head), he is (secure) in her hand."¹⁶⁵

It is notable that Egyptian tradition preserves a similar story about the goddess Isis. According to the Pyramid Texts, Isis tied a headband or fillet on Horus: "Great Isis—she who tied the headband on her son Horus as a young boy."¹⁶⁶ In the passage in question the word for "headband" is *mdḥ*. The fact that this very word is employed to describe the king's headband or crown in the Coffin Texts suggests that it originally signified the crown of sovereignty. Witness the following passage:

"Come, that you may see me adorned with a fillet [*mdḥ*] and wearing the royal head-cloth. Joy is given to me by means of it."¹⁶⁷

Figure 2

The most common ideogram or determinative for *mdḥ* is depicted in figure two.¹⁶⁸ The resemblance between this ideogram and the Sumerian MUŠ₃-sign employed to denote Inanna/Venus is evident at once. The fact that both ideograms were used to describe the king's headband or crown confirms their fundamental affinity and suggests that their spiraling volute-like form traces to a common celestial prototype.¹⁶⁹

---

¹⁶⁵ Lines 501-503 from "The temple hymns," *ETCSL*.
¹⁶⁶ PT 1214b as translated in J. Allen, *The Ancient Egyptian Pyramid Texts* (Atlanta, 2005), p. 161.
¹⁶⁷ *CT* V:158.
¹⁶⁸ M. Betrò, *Hieroglyphics* (New York, 1996), p. 186.
¹⁶⁹ The same hieroglyph was employed to write the Egyptian word *sšd*. See W. Barta, "Zur Bedeutung des Stirnbands-Diadems," *Göttinger Miszellen* 72 (1984), p. 8. See also the perceptive remarks of B. Gunn, "Note," *JEA* 25 (1939), pp. 218-219. It will be noted that the Egyptian headband typically displays two dangling "tails," not unlike certain variants of the Sumerian MUŠ₃-sign. E. Kern-Lileso, "Stirnband und Diademe,"

To paraphrase a famous taunt from inner city playgrounds: The pictographs don't lie. And in the final analysis, it is the detailed parallels between the Sumerian planet-goddess Inanna and the Egyptian Eye-goddess that make the case for planetary catastrophism and signal the need for a wholescale revolution in our understanding of ancient Egyptian cosmogonic myth and religion.

---

*Lexikon der Ägyptologie* 1 (Wiesbaden, 1975), col. 46 calls these dangling threads "streamers," a most apt description of a comet-like tail. Doubtless it is no coincidence that similar streamers distinguish the royal headband in early Minoan and Aztec iconography.

## Horus: Lord of Appearances

> "In the [Egyptian] texts the concepts of creation, sunrise, and kingly rule are continually merged; the verb $ḫ\'i$ (which marks the appearance of Pharaoh on the throne) denotes sunrise and is written with the hieroglyph ⌒ that depicts the sun rising over the Primeval Hill."[170]

> "In the Old Kingdom determinatives usually had been mere pictograms, representations of the signified objects."[171]

Creation, according to the earliest Egyptian texts, was a decidedly tumultuous affair. Horus's role in these singular events is regularly alluded to but is never clearly spelled out in any early narrative account. What we find instead are scattered and all-too-brief allusions to the god's conception, birth, danger-laden infancy, and triumphant accession to the throne as the Lord of All.

One of the most important texts in this regard is Utterance 257 from the Pyramid Texts. There it is recounted how Horus first ascended to the throne during the epochal events recalled as the forcible separation of heaven and earth (in ancient Egypt, as around the globe, the separation of these two primordial entities constituted a pivotal phase in Creation[172]):

"There is tumult in the sky; 'We see something new', say the primeval gods. O you Ennead, Horus is in the sunlight, the possessors of forms make salutation to him, all the Two Enneads serve him, for he sits on the throne of the Lord of All. The King takes possession of the sky, he cleaves

---

[170] H. Frankfort, *Kingship and the Gods* (Chicago, 1978), p. 151.
[171] A. Bolshakov, *Man and his Double in Egyptian ideology of the Old Kingdom* (Wiesbaden, 1997), p. 155.
[172] E. Hornung, "Ancient Egyptian Religious Iconography," in J. Sasson ed., *Civilizations of the Ancient Near East, Vol. 3/4* (Farmington Hills, 1995), p. 1717 observed: "The most important event of the creation: the separation of heaven and earth." The earliest Sumerian traditions repeat the same claim. See J. Westenholz, "Heaven and Earth," in *Gazing on the Deep* (Bethesda, 2010), p. 304: "Creation began with the separation of heaven and earth."

its iron…The King shines anew in the East, and he who settled the dispute will come to him bowing. Make salutation, you gods, to the King, who is older than the Great One, to whom belongs power on his throne…Rejoice at the King, for he has taken possession of the horizon."[173]

If we are to judge by this particular account, Horus first became manifest as a "new" or "reborn" star during the turbulent natural events attending Creation and the concomitant separation of heaven and earth (The cleaving of the celestial iron amidst "tumult in the sky" is a patent reference to the forcible separation of heaven and earth).[174] And it was in the immediate aftermath of that profoundly awe-inspiring and mind-altering occasion—*the prototypical Hierophany*, as it were—that the Horus-star took possession of the "horizon" (*akhet*) and assumed the celestial throne as the "King of the Gods."

Here, *in nuce*, is the Egyptian myth of creation. And insofar as cosmogonic myth serves as the historical reference point for virtually every aspect of Egyptian civilization—see the discussion in chapter twenty-five—it is essential that we seek to decipher and reconstruct the specific events described in this text.

Additional insight into the singular celestial events in question is provided by Utterance 519 from the Pyramid Texts, wherein Horus—expressly identified as the "Morning Star"—is said to have appeared ($ḥꜥ$) at the time that heaven and earth were first separated. This all-important passage reads as follows:

"O Morning Star, Horus of the Netherworld, divine Falcon, $wꜣḏꜣḏ$-bird whom the sky bore…give me these your two fingers which you gave

---

[173] *PT* 304-307.
[174] Our interpretation is confirmed by the fact that the parallel passage in the *Coffin Texts* reads $pšn(w)=j\ bjꜣ$: "I have divided the firmament." See here *CT* IV:161a. In ancient Egypt, as in other ancient cultures, the firmament was thought to be composed of meteoritic stone or "iron." On the meteoritic nature of the Egyptian sky, see L. Lesko, "Ancient Egyptian Cosmogonies and Cosmology," in B. Shafer ed., *Religion in Ancient Egypt* (Ithaca, 1991), p. 117. See also M. Almansa-Villatoro, "The Cultural Indexicality of the N41 Sign for *bjꜣ*: The Metal of the Sky and the Sky of Metal," *Journal of Egyptian Archaeology* 105 (2020), pp. 73-81.

to the Beautiful, the daughter of the great god, when the sky was separated from the earth, when the gods ascended to the sky, you having a soul and appearing in front of your boat of 770 cubits which the gods of Pe bound together for you, which the eastern gods built for you."[175]

The verb translated here as "appearing"—ḥʿ—is the very term regularly employed to describe the deceased king's glorious epiphany in heaven as an Imperishable Star.[176] This convergence of formulaic terminology suggests that the Egyptian pharaoh's much-anticipated post-mortem apotheosis as a star was expressly patterned after the prehistoric—i.e., prototypical and *exemplary*—appearance of the Horus-star during the momentous natural events remembered as Creation. Indeed, the appearance (ḥʿ) of the transfigured king is compared to that of the Horus-star elsewhere in the Pyramid Texts: "O King…you having appeared to them as a jackal, as Horus at the head of the living."[177] Horus's canine epithet here must remind us of *PT* 1719, quoted earlier, wherein the Morning Star, as Horus, was likened to a jackal:

"Rēʿ summons you into the zenith(?) of the sky as the Jackal, the Governor of the Two Enneads, and as Horus *Ḥnty-mnit-f*; may he set you as the Morning Star in the midst of the Field of Rushes."[178]

A similar scenario is recounted in the so-called "Cannibal Hymn." In that archaic text the deceased king—clearly conceptualized as a star—ascends to heaven and assumes the *akhet*-throne in the midst of cosmic upheaval:

"The sky is overcast, the stars are darkened, the celestial expanses quiver, the bones of the earth-gods tremble, the planets (?) are stilled, for they have seen the King appearing in power…The glory of the King is in

---

[175] *PT* 1207-1210.
[176] C. Eyre, *The Cannibal Hymn* (Liverpool, 2002), p. 78 observes that "The juxtaposition of *ḥʿj* and *bꜣ* is formulaic for the divine manifestation of the king appearing in the sky."
[177] *PT* 2103.
[178] *PT* 1719.

the sky, his power is in the horizon…The King has appeared again in the sky, he is crowned as Lord of the horizon."[179]

The word translated herein as "appear"—as in the phrases "appearing in power" (*PT* 394) and "appeared again in the sky" (*PT* 409)—is the aforementioned ḫʿ, written with the following ideogram: ⊖. As one of the most important icons describing the deceased king's manifestation as a transfigured star—evidently as the Morning Star—it is imperative that we gain a better understanding of the original celestial referent of the hieroglyph in question.

Egyptologists, understandably, have sought to interpret the ḫʿ-glyph by reference to the familiar solar system.[180] For John Wilson the sign encodes the prototypical sunrise:

"The Egyptian hieroglyph which means the primeval 'hillock of appearance' means also 'to appear in glory.' It shows a rounded mound with the rays of the sun streaming upward from it (⊖), graphically portraying this miracle of the first appearance of the creator-god."[181]

Yet this interpretation is problematic for a host of reasons. Granted that this glyph depicts the rising of the present sun, how are we to conceptualize the hill-like structure over which the rays of the sun allegedly appeared? Are we to believe that a prehistoric Egyptian skywatcher suddenly woke up one morning and invented wholecloth the myth of the rising sun as a god appearing in glory from an invisible primeval hill—this while accompanied by an otherwise invisible uraeus-serpent? Such an interpretation flies in the face of everything we know about the Egyptian mindset and the genesis of ancient religious beliefs.

In an effort to determine the original meaning and semantic range of this term, Donald Redford conducted a comprehensive review of the

---

[179] *PT* 393-409 as quoted in R. Faulkner, *op. cit.*, pp. 80-82.
[180] J. Allen, *Middle Egyptian* (Cambridge, 2014), p. 161. See also H. R. Hall, "Review of *De Egyptische Voorstellingen betreffende den Oerheuvel*," *JEA* 10 (1924), p. 186.
[181] J. Wilson, "Egypt," in H. Frankfort et al eds., *Before Philosophy* (Baltimore, 1946), p. 60.

relevant Egyptian texts. He offered the following summary of the imagery in question:

"The verb ḫʿy means basically 'to shine forth in dazzling splendour, to appear in glory, to arise,' and was used primarily of the sun. It could also be used of any celestial body, e.g. a star, that made a spectacular appearance in the sky. In the Pyramid Texts the king is spoken of as appearing 'as a star,' or 'as a great god,' and the literal meaning of ḫʿy here is graphically illustrated by the use in parallel texts of qꜣ, 'be high,' and bꜣ, 'appear in the sky as a *bai*.' By a slight semantic extension, a cult image that put in an appearance at a festival could be said to have 'arisen in glory'; and this rather frequent use gave rise to the noun 'festival'."[182]

Insofar as it was Horus who represented the mythical "first king" and divine model for Egyptian kingship, it stands to reason that it was the epochal "appearance" of that god's stellar doppelgänger that formed the natural-historical prototype for these archaic conceptions surrounding the ḫʿ-glyph (it will be noted that Horus is the only god celebrated as the "King of the Gods" in the Pyramid Texts).[183] It is certain that the ancient Egyptians recognized an inherent connection between the Horus-star and "appearances" of a celestial nature. An inscription from King Userkaf's mortuary temple dating from around 2500 BCE invokes Horus as the "Lord of Appearances": "He of Behdet, the Great God, the colorfully feathered one, who has come forth from the horizon, the perfect god, the lord of appearances."[184] It is this very phrase—*nb ḫʿ*, "Lord of Appearances"—that would come to serve as an epithet of kings in the Pyramid Texts and throughout Egyptian history, presumably because they were thought to incarnate the divine prototype, the Horus-star.[185]

---

[182] D. Redford, "Ḫʿy and Its Derivatives," in D. Redford, *History and Chronology of the Eighteenth Dynasty of Egypt* (Toronto, 1967), pp. 4-5.
[183] *PT* 1458e.
[184] N. Strudwick, *Texts From the Pyramid Age* (Atlanta, 2005), p. 83.
[185] *PT* 7 and 8, for example. See also J. Allen, *Middle Egyptian* (Cambridge, 2010), p. 64.

One of the earliest attested examples of the *ḫʿ*-glyph—an Early Dynastic domain name from the reign of Hetepsekhemwy (ca. 2890 BCE) depicted in figure one—finds it being employed as an epithet of the Horus-star (Toby Wilkinson translated the phrase *Ḥr-ḫʿ-sbȝ* as "Horus rising as a star").[186] Such evidence, considered alongside the fact that Utterance 519 from the Pyramid Texts describes Horus as "appearing" (*ḫʿ*) as the "Morning Star" in conjunction with the separation of heaven and earth at the Time of Beginning (*zp tpj*), suggests that it was the Horus-star—and not the present Sun—that embodied the prototypical "god of appearances." If so, this finding has profound ramifications for the scientific study of the natural-historical (astronomical) foundations of ancient Egyptian religion.

Figure 1

Equally telling is an archaic tradition reporting that the *ḫʿ*-mound was the cosmic site upon which the falcon-god Horus alighted *in illo tempore*.[187] A pivotal moment in cosmogonic history, Horus's appearance atop the Primeval Hill came to serve as the mythological charter for numerous Egyptian temples:

"The place where creation began was given various names— 'primeval hill,' 'sacred mound,' 'place of coming forth,'—and its

---

[186] T. Wilkinson, *Early Dynastic Egypt* (London, 1999), pp. 119-121.

[187] K. Goebs, *Crowns in Egyptian Funerary Literature* (Oxford, 2008), p. 24 points out: "The earliest attestation of the verb *ḫʿj* and the related noun, as well as the symbolism of the hieroglyph ◠ (Gardiner sign-list N28), relate to the arising of the solar creator from the primeval mound." See also T. Wilkinson, *op. cit.*, p. 309.

symbolism was potent and ubiquitous in Egyptian writing as well as in artistic representation. Every temple was supposedly erected upon a primeval hill, and to that end an artificial lake was often included in the precinct to replicate the primeval waters (this is what Herodotus saw in Chemmis)…The birthplace of Horus, the first king of Egypt and the prototype for the pharaoh, was also imagined as a primeval hill, hence Horus too was a type of creator, and his birth the 'first time.' This event could be conveyed by the image of Horus as a child or again by the Horus-falcon within a papyrus swamp."[188]

The prototypical appearance of the Horus-star, as noted earlier, occurred in the general context of "tumult in the sky," the latter marked by shaking, thunder, darkness and chaos. And if we are to judge by the testimony of the Egyptian texts, it was the Horus-star's inaugural appearance or "dawning" that brought light to a cosmos previously enshrouded in darkness—hence the familiar theme of Horus as the prototypical "light-bringer."[189] The latter idea formed a recurring theme in the texts at the god's temple in Edfu, as evidenced by the following passage:

"Words to speak by! Horus Behedeti, the great god, the lord of heaven, the colorfully feathered one, who arises from the *akhet*…who originated at the beginning, who began the lighting."[190]

The Egyptologist Barbara Watterson elaborated on these epochal events as follows:

---

[188] S. Stephens, *Seeing Double: Intercultural Poetics in Ptolemaic Alexandria* (Berkeley, 2003), pp. 58-59. See also T. Wilkinson, *The Rise and Fall of Ancient Egypt* (New York, 2010), pp. 17-18: "Throughout the long course of pharaonic history, every temple in Egypt sought to emulate this moment of creation [Horus's lighting on a mound], siting its sanctuary on a replica of the primeval mound in order to re-create the universe anew."

[189] J. Assmann, *Egyptian Solar Religion in the New Kingdom* (London, 1995), p. 106, citing Theban Tombs 179: "Great hawk with colourful feathers who makes light for mankind."

[190] 86, 10-12 as translated in D. Kurth, *Edfou VII: Übersetzungen* (Wiesbaden, 2004), p. 147: "Worte zu sprechen von Horus Behedeti, dem großen Gott, dem Herrn des Himmels, dem Buntgefiederten, der aus dem Horizont hervorkommt…der am Anfang enstand, der das Leuchten begann." Author's translation.

"All was in darkness, and the waters of Nun covered the earth…A falcon [Horus] emerged from the surrounding darkness and alighted on the stick. Immediately, light broke over Chaos, and the falcon sitting on his perch transformed the island into a holy place. The antiquity of this tradition is attested by the fact that, in the Archaic Period, the hieroglyphic sign for 'god' consisted of a falcon sitting on a perch."[191]

As the falcon perched atop a pole-like standard, Horus is to be understood as the god *par excellence* of archaic Egypt.[192]

How, then, are we to understand the Horus-star's appearance atop the Primeval Hill from the standpoint of natural science? Egyptologists, as we have seen, interpret this archetypal cosmogonic myth as a reference to the peaceful rising of the Sun over an invisible mound along the eastern horizon. It is evident, however, that there was much more to the imagery in question than an elaborate fantasy based upon the familiar sunrise. Far from being a product of creative imagination or allegory, the Primeval Hill was a key concept in the Egyptian creation account and must needs have reference to an objective celestial structure.

A decisive clue is provided by the fact that the word $ḥˁ$ also denotes the "crowning" of the Egyptian pharaoh.[193] Thus it is that the king himself was "Lord of Crowns" ($ḥˁw$), while the ritual affixing of the pharaoh's royal crown was known as *smnt ḥˁ*, literally a making firm of the crown.[194] This terminology, in our opinion, suggests that the prototypical

---

[191] B. Watterson, *The Gods of Ancient Egypt* (London, 1984), pp. 105-106.
[192] O. Goldwasser, *Prophets, Lovers and Giraffes* (Wiesbaden, 2002), p. 114 points out that Horus on the standard is the "only classifier" for Divine in the Pyramid Texts. See also J. Baines, "On the symbolic context of the principal hieroglyph for 'God'," in U. Verhoeven & E. Graefe eds., *Religion und Philosophie im alten Ägypten* (Leuven, 1991), p. 32.
[193] K. Goebs, *Crowns in Egyptian Funerary Literature* (Oxford, 2008), pp. 24-25: "Already in the Old Kingdom—for example, on the Palermo Stone—the term is used to designate the assumption of crowns by the terrestrial ruler."
[194] A. Gardiner, "The Coronation of King Haremhab," *JEA* 39 (1953), p. 24. See also K. Bosse-Griffiths, "The Great Enchantress in the Little Golden Shrine of Tut'Ankhamun," in J. Gwyn Griffiths ed., *Amarna Studies and Other Selected Papers* (Fribourg, 2001), p. 119.

"appearance" of the Horus-star necessarily involved its "crowning"—a deduction that is abundantly confirmed in early Egyptian texts. A telling text is recorded on the so-called Turin statue, wherein we read that the uraeus-serpent was responsible for "crowning" the Egyptian pharaoh: "[her arms] in welcoming attitude, and she embraced his beauty and established herself on his forehead, and the Divine Ennead…were in exultation at his glorious rising."[195]

It will be noted that the pharaoh's "crowning" at the hands of the uraeus-serpent is concomitant with his glorious rising—$ḫʿ$.[196] (The reference to the exulting Divine Ennead, in turn, recalls the circumstances prevailing in the creation account in Utterance 257, quoted earlier, wherein the Horus-star is greeted by the Divine Ennead upon making his inaugural appearance in the sky.[197]) The Pyramid Texts offer complementary testimony: There it is reported that the primordial sun-god appeared in unison with the uraeus-serpent: "Rēʿ arises, his uraeus upon him."[198] Such traditions suggest that there was an inherent relationship between the star-god's glorious "appearance" *in illo tempore* and his "crowning" at the hands of the uraeus-goddess. Yet it is difficult to see why this should be the case given the conventional understanding of the $ḫʿ$-glyph, which views it as a representation of the uneventful sunrise. Where in the modern sky is a fire-spewing uraeus-serpent that appears to "crown" the sun?[199]

Equally problematic for the conventional explanation of the $ḫʿ$-glyph as a pictograph describing the familiar sunrise is the abundant testimony to the effect that the star which "appeared" at the time of Creation

---

[195] *Ibid.*, p. 29.
[196] A. Roberts, *Hathor Rising* (Devon, 1995), p. 42 observed: "Only after the palace snake had coiled herself around Haremhab's brow does he make his 'glorious rising.'"
[197] So, too, in Spell 326 from the Coffin Texts celebrating Horus's prototypical appearance it is reported that "the Enneads of Re serve him."
[198] *PT* 442.
[199] J. Assmann, *Egyptian Solar Religion in the New Kingdom* (London, 1995), p. 52 would explain the uraeus as follows: "This icon represents the experience of the aggressive heat of summer."

presented a greenish form and effected a spectacular "greening" of the celestial landscape.[200] Thus it is that the *Book of the Dead* describes the Horus-star as radiating a turquoise (*mfkꜣt*) color upon appearing (*ḫʿt*) in the *akhet*:

"[Harmachis] When thou appearest in the horizon of heaven, hymns to thee are in the mouths of everyone, thou being beautiful and youthful in the sun-disk within the arms of thy mother Hathor. How thou shinest in every place, thy heart rejoicing forever…How thou shinest in the horizon of heaven. Thou hast strewn the Two Lands with turquoise."[201]

The Horus-star is expressly linked to a greening of the cosmos in other texts as well. Witness the following hymn from the reign of Haremhab (circa 1300 BCE): "How you have appeared in the *akhet* of heaven. You have strewn both lands with turquoise."[202]

The same idea recurs in Horus's temple at Edfu, a temple known to preserve archaic traditions. Witness the following passage: "The sky was cleared for him by the north wind, and the Two Lands were strewn with Upper Egyptian emeralds [*stj tꜣwj m wꜣḏ šmʿj*], because Horus has built his war-galley in order to go therein to the fen to overthrow the enemies of his father."[203]

The cult of the sun reached its greatest heights during the New Kingdom (1500-1200 BCE). Yet even in these later texts the sun-god is expressly associated with a greening of the cosmos: "Hail to you who rises

---

[200] For a general discussion of such references, see J. Zandee, *Der Amunhymnus des Papyrus Leiden I 344, Verso, Vol. 1* (Leiden, 1992), pp. 349-364. See also E. Cochrane, *The Case of the Turquoise Sun* (Ames, 2023), pp. 28-34.
[201] H. Stewart, "Traditional Egyptian Sun Hymns of the New Kingdom," *Bull. Inst. Arch.* 6 (1967), p. 52.
[202] Lines 11-12 from *Urkunden* IV 2095 as cited in J. Zandee, *Der Amunshymnus des Papyrus Leiden I 344 verso, Vol. 1* (Leiden, 1992), p. 362: "Wie bist du erschienen im Lichtland des Himmels (*ḫʿ wj tw m ꜣḫt nt pt*), du hast die Beiden Länder bestreut mit Türkis (*stj.n.k tꜣwj <m> mfkꜣt*)." Translation by author.
[203] A. Blackman & H. Fairman, "The Myth of Horus at Edfu—III," *JEA* 29 (1943), p. 13.

in Turquoise" (*jnd ḥr.k wbnw m mfkt*).²⁰⁴ Such imagery is so commonplace that Egyptologists readily concede the point even though it stands in direct contradiction to astronomical reality. Witness the following observation of Joris Borghouts: "In certain hymns the sun is said to strew the sky with turquoise."²⁰⁵ Jan Zandee, likewise, offered the following commentary: "In many passages turquoise is specifically associated with the rising sun." ²⁰⁶

To bring the argument full circle: The intrinsic connection between the prototypical appearance of the Horus-star and a greening of the celestial landscape is evidently encoded in the earliest hieroglyphic signs. As Margit Schunck documented in her authoritative analysis of the imagery attached to the Egyptian *ḫʿ*-glyph ⌒, the logogram's corona was typically accorded a brilliant greenish-blue color:

"Für die Farbgebung der Sonnenkorona über dem Hügel der Hieroglyphe wurde in der Mehrzahl ein kräftiges Grün, Blaugrün oder…wechselnd blaue und grüne Strahlen gewählt."²⁰⁷

Yet why should this be the case if the logogram's point of reference was the familiar sunrise as per the conventional view? Who among us has witnessed an explosion of turquoise-green radiation associated with the current Sun's appearance over the eastern horizon?

The brilliant colors reflected in the *ḫʿ*-sign will also serve to clarify the archaic Egyptian traditions referencing the multi-colored or "mottled" plumage traditionally accorded the Horus-star. Recall again the inscription from King Userkaf's mortuary temple dating from the mid-third millennium BCE: "He of Behdet, the Great God, the colorfully

---

²⁰⁴ TT 53 as translated in J. Assmann, *Egyptian Solar Religion in the New Kingdom* (London, 1995), p. 15.
²⁰⁵ J. Borghouts, *Book of the Dead [39]: From Shouting To Structure* (Wiesbaden, 2007), p. 52, citing Budge *Book of the Dead* 11.10.
²⁰⁶ J. Zandee, *Der Amunshymnus des Papyrus Leiden I 344 verso, Vol. 1* (Leiden, 1992), p. 364: "In vielen Belegstellen hängt 'Türkis' besonders mit der aufgehenden Sonne zusammen." Translation by author.
²⁰⁷ M. Schunck, *Untersuchungen zum Wortstamm ḫʿ* (Bonn, 1985), pp. 8-9.

feathered one, who has come forth from the horizon, the perfect god, the lord of appearances."[208] Here the Horus-star, in his guise of "Lord of appearances"—*nb ḫʿ*—is expressly identified as "the colorfully feathered one" (*sȝb šwt*).[209] Analogous epithets would reverberate for millennia, although their original celestial context had long since been forgotten. The following text from Horus's temple at Edfu, inscribed well over two thousand years later, offers a case in point and serves to underscore the extraordinary conservativeness of the Egyptian traditions recounting Creation:

"Falcon-of-the-mottled plumage, Horus-of-Behdet…For you are the divine god who came into being on the first occasion…"[210]

This imagery has long puzzled Egyptologists.[211] For what could it mean that a particular star has iridescent plumage or is plentiful of colors (Horus is elsewhere described as *ʿȝ iwn.w*, "plentiful of colors")?[212]

The fact that the present Sun does not display glorious plumage or a wide range of colors in the blue-green spectrum prompts us to look elsewhere for the origin of these archaic epithets. The key to deciphering the imagery in question is to view the phrase "the colorfully feathered one" as complementary to, or in apposition with, the phrase "lord of

---

[208] N. Strudwick, *Texts From the Pyramid Age* (Atlanta, 2005), p. 83.
[209] K. Goebs, "Receive the Henu—that You May Shine Forth in it like Akhty," in F. Coppens, J. Janák & H. Vymazalová eds., *Royal versus Divine Authority* (Wiesbaden, 2015), p. 172 translates the epithet *sȝb šwt* as "iridescent."
[210] Edfu VI, 181, 9-10 as translated in R. Finnestad, *Image of the World and Symbol of the Creator* (Wiesbaden, 1985), p. 25.
[211] H. Frankfort, *Kingship and the Gods* (Chicago, 1978), p. 40, confesses his befuddlement: "It seems difficult, at first sight, to bring the elusive and somewhat uncanny 'Horus feathered in many hues' within the family group of the Osiris cycle."
[212] The Lord of Appearances is alternately described as *sȝb šwt*, "the colorfully feathered one" and as *ʿȝ iwn.w*, "plentiful of colors." Theban Tombs 33 offers a case in point: "Lord of glorious appearances in the early morning [*nb ḫʿ(.w) m nhp*], plentiful of colors, [*ʿȝ iwn.w*], at the sight of whom—within his protective serpent—the gods rejoice [*ḥʿʿ nṯr.w m mȝn=f m-ḫnw n Mḥn.t=f*]." See also J. Zandee, *Der Amunhymnus des Papyrus Leiden I 344, Verso, Vol. 1* (Leiden, 1992), p. 109: "Das Epitheton 'Farbenreicher' wird oft mit dem Falkengott verbunden und bezieht sich wie *ṯhn jrw* und *sȝb šwt* auf die Flügel."

appearances": It is the Horus-star's glorious "appearance" (ḫꜥ) that is being likened to a bird with multi-colored feathers.²¹³ Early examples of the ḫꜥ-glyph, in fact, depict a feather-like corona, with the "feathers" in question painted in rich turquoise-green and blue colors (see figure two).²¹⁴

Figure 2

To summarize our findings in the present chapter: Far from being an imaginative interpretation of the familiar sunrise, as per the unanimous opinion of several generations of Egyptologists, a wealth of evidence suggests that the myth of the Horus-star's glorious appearance at the Time of Beginning encodes *singular* and inherently *catastrophic* events. It was on that memorable occasion—presumably in the late fifth or early fourth millennium BCE—that the Horus-star burst forth in nova-like splendor and flooded the sky with turquoise radiation, a series of events remembered as the prototypical "sunrise." And it was this decidedly extraordinary event—not the familiar sunrise—that the deceased king hoped to emulate and reexperience in his post-mortem ascent to heaven.

Absolutely essential for understanding the multivalent symbolism in question is the fact that there was an inherent relationship between the star-god's glorious "appearance" and his "crowning" at the hands of the Eye-goddess, identified here with the planet Venus. To be more specific:

---

²¹³ See here especially K. Goebs, *op. cit.*, pp. 158-159: "Such examples [of the ḫꜥ-glyph] lend a particular meaning to the solar epithet sꜣb šwt, 'colourful of plumage', of gods such as (Horus) Behedeti, whose representations usually display the same colour scheme."

²¹⁴ *Ibid.*, p. 155: "It is noteworthy that the older writings (First and Second Dynasty) of the hieroglyph mostly display distinct rays emanating from the corona of the rising sun or primeval mound."

It is our opinion that the ḥʿ-glyph depicts Horus's prototypical appearance as the "Morning Star" atop the Primeval Hill, at which time the heaven-spanning "rays/feathers" emanating from Venus appeared to encircle and "crown" the smaller red orb (Mars is located in front of Venus in this reconstruction, as depicted in figure three).[215] It is in this wholly concrete sense, then, that the planet Venus invested the Horus-star with its crown—its corona or "glory," as it were—at the time of the falcon-god's coronation *in illo tempore*. The Egyptian skywatchers who witnessed this spectacular conjunction of planetary powers interpreted it as signifying that the Horus-star had been "crowned in glory" (ḥʿ) and enthroned as Universal King—the celestial prototype for all pharaohs.

If this deduction is well-founded, it stands to reason that the "crowning" of the Horus-star (Mars) necessarily involved a close conjunction between the red planet and the planet Venus. This insight, in turn, leads us to conclude that the Egyptian hieroglyph of the Primeval Hill—⌒—actually encodes an *extraordinary* conjunction of planets moving in remarkably close proximity to the Earth.

Figure 3

---

[215] Special thanks to Rick Smith for permission to use this image generated by him.

## The Greening of the Cosmos

> "In mythology, as in any other scholarly or scientific activity, it is important to recall that the datum itself is more important than any theory that may be applied to it."[216]

The greening of the cosmos associated with the Horus-star's explosive appearance at the Time of Beginning forms a recurring theme in the Egyptian funerary hymns describing the king's glorious transfiguration in the celestial Hereafter. This idea is evident in the following Utterance recounting the king's post-mortem ascent as Sobek, an archaic crocodile god identified with Horus:

"Unis is Sobek, green of plumage, with alert face and raised fore, the splashing one who came from the thigh and tail of the great goddess in the sunlight. Unis has come to his canals in the flood-shore in the Great Immersion, to the place of rest with green marshes in the Akhet, that Unis might make green the vegetation on the Akhet's shores, that Unis might get the faience of the great eye in the marsh's midst, that Unis might receive his seat that is in the Akhet."[217]

As clearly stated in this text, the *akhet* was "greened" in the wake of the deceased king's ascent to heaven and transfiguration, presumably because the latter myth was purposefully modeled upon the extraordinary natural events attending the Horus-star's appearance *in illo tempore*. Yet how are we to make sense of such imagery from the standpoint of modern Egyptology, which views the *akhet* as an invisible region located beneath the horizon?

One of the most important texts describing the central events of Creation is Utterance 519 from the Pyramid Texts, referenced earlier. There the Horus-star was likened to a brilliant green bird at the time of his

---

[216] J. Puhvel, *Comparative Mythology* (Baltimore, 1987), p. 19.
[217] *PT* 507-510 as translated in J. Allen, *The Ancient Egyptian Pyramid Texts* (Atlanta, 2006), p. 60. On the god's identification with Horus, see M. Lichtheim, *Ancient Egyptian Literature, Vol. 1* (Berkeley, 1975), p. 201.

glorious "appearance" in heaven, much as Sobek was singled out for his green plumage:

"O Morning Star, Horus of the Netherworld, divine Falcon, *wȝdȝd*-bird whom the sky bore…give me these your two fingers which you gave to the Beautiful, the daughter of the great god, when the sky was separated from the earth, when the gods ascended to the sky."[218]

The epithet *wȝdȝd* constitutes a reduplication of the root *wȝd*, "green," presumably in order to provide emphasis. In light of this testimony, it is evident that the Egyptian scribes were keen to accentuate the fact that a brilliant "greening" of the celestial landscape distinguished the glorious appearance of the transfigured Horus-star.

Elsewhere in the same hymn it is reported that the celestial landscape became "greened" at the time of the Morning Star's prototypical appearance. Witness the following passage: "These are they whom Nut bore, who have gone down upon you with their garlands on their heads…who make green the Nt-crowns of the canals of the Field of Offerings for Isis the Great, who tied on the fillet in Chemmis."[219]

Such passages have typically been met with bemusement and disbelief on the part of Egyptologists. Samuel Mercer, in his commentary on this particular Utterance, spoke of "a collection of incoherent figures of speech and allusions":

"The children of Nut cause the crowns…of the canals (or, watercourses) of the Marsh of Offerings to flourish. The reduplicated verb *ȝhȝh* in the causative means 'to cause to be green,' or 'to cause to flourish.'…As the imagery with which we are dealing is a mixture of celestial and terrestrial, 'the crowns of the canals of the Marsh of Offerings,' if it is not a collection of incoherent figures of speech and allusions, may mean that these celestial ones, the children of Nut enhance (i.e., 'cause to flourish') the authority of Lower Egypt (i.e. the red crowns

---

[218] *PT* 1207-1210.
[219] *PT* 1213-1214.

of the ruler of Lower Egypt, whether now among the deceased or still ruling) in the watercourse."[220]

Far from being a collection of incoherent figures of speech, it is patently obvious that the greening of the celestial landscape formed a memorable phase in the Egyptian creation account. Certainly it can be no accident that the very word used to describe the "greening" or "flourishing" of the cosmos at the time of the Horus-star's inaugural appearance—*sꜣḫꜣḫ*, "to become green, blossom"—is simply a causative of *ḫꜣḫ*, a word employed in the Horus-texts at Edfu and elsewhere to describe the verdant greenery associated with the falcon-god's prototypical appearance at Creation.[221] Witness the following passage, wherein "bloom" is *ḫꜣḫ*:

"Words to speak to Horus Behedeti, the great god…the multi-colored feathered one, who comes forth from the *akhet*…who illuminates the darkness, through whose glance all flowers bloom, at whose appearance the plants sprout forth."[222]

Analogous imagery is evident in the creation account preserved in the *Book of the Heavenly Cow*. Although the passage in question is damaged, the context clearly implies that a greening of the celestial landscape accompanied the sun's appearance at the Time of Beginning. Alicia Maravelia translated the passage as follows:

"'I shall provide it [the sky] with everything! And the *ḫꜣḫw*-stars came into being!'"[223]

---

[220] S. Mercer, *op. cit.*, pp. 602-603.
[221] R. Finnestad, *Image of the World and Symbol of the Creator* (Wiesbaden, 1985), pp. 38-40.
[222] 83, 8-9 as translated in D. Kurth, *Edfou VII: Übersetzungen* (Wiesbaden, 2004), p. 142. Author's translation: "Worte zu sprechen von Horus Behedeti, dem großen Gott…dem Buntgefiederten, der aus dem 'Horizont' hervorkommt…das die Dunkelheit erhellt, durch dessen Blick jede Blume erblüht, bei dessen Aufgehen die Pflanzen aufspreißen."
[223] A. Maravelia, "The function and importance of some special categories of stars in the Ancient Egyptian funerary texts, 1," in G. Rosati & M. Guidotti eds., *International Congress of Egyptologists XI* (Oxford, 2017), p. 372.

Laslow Kákosy, in his commentary on this passage, acknowledged that a greening of the cosmos was involved: "It must be noted that the verb ꜣḫꜣḫ (jḫjḫ) seems to carry the connotation 'twinkle or sparkle in green light'."[224] Wilhelm Müller, similarly, translated the term as "verdant stars."[225] Already in the Pyramid and Coffin Texts the same word is employed to describe the stars present at Horus's epiphany: "I am Horus on the day of his accession…who navigates in front of the stars of the sky."[226] In short, given the evidence adduced here there can be no denying the fact that a "greening" (sꜣḫꜣḫ) of the sky formed a central theme in the Egyptian myth of creation.[227]

It is the greening of the Horus-star and celestial landscape during the momentous natural events attending Creation, presumably, that explains why Egyptian pharaohs aspired to become "green" (wꜣḏ) upon ascending to heaven and conjoining with the mother goddess. A prayer from Teti's pyramid captures this symbolism precisely: "Teti is green as the papyrus-head of your eye in which heat is, and Teti will be green with you."[228] Complementary testimony comes from Utterance 352 inscribed on Pepi II's pyramid: "Your papyrus-plant is the green of the turquoise of the stars, your papyrus-plant is the green of the King, (even as) living rush is green, and the King is green with you."[229]

---

[224] L. Kákosy, "Astral Mythology in Egypt," *Acta Antiqua* 40 (2000), pp. 213-214.
[225] Wilhelm Müller, "Egyptian Mythology," in L. Gray ed., *The Mythology of All Races, Vol.* 12 (Boston, 1918), p. 61. E. Hornung, *Der ägyptische Mythos von der Himmelskuh* (Freiburg, 1982), p. 42 translated the term as "immerleuchtenden Sterne."
[226] *CT* III:263. See also *PT* 1143, wherein the deceased king announces: "I take possession of the sky, its pillars and its stars."
[227] In her discussion of this passage, Nadine Guilhou, *La Vieillesse de Dieux* (Montpellier, 1989), p. 125 offered the following summary: "d'autre part le nom de ces étioles: jḫjḫ, 'les Verdoyantes', or 'les Brillantes': le vert, lumineux, est la couleur de la vegetation qui pousse." Translation by Birgit Liesching: "On the other hand, the name of these stars, jḫjḫ, the 'green ones' or 'shiny ones': the shiny green is the color of growing vegetation."
[228] *PT* 702 as translated in J. Allen, *The Ancient Egyptian Pyramid Texts* (Atlanta, 2006), p. 92.
[229] *PT* 569.

It will be noted that the king's coloration is specifically likened to the green (w3ḏ) of the "turquoise of the stars."

But there is more. In light of the fact that the eternal resting place of the deceased king was distinguished by a verdant greening (3ḫ3ḫ)—not to mention a singular collection of stars bearing a cognate name (3ḫ3ḫw)—it is worth considering whether the very idea of *akhification* describing the deceased king's transfigured state was itself connected to the concept of greening. As Faulkner pointed out many years ago, the root 3ḫ is evidently reduplicated in the aforementioned word for verdant greenery and/or "stars": "3ḫ, otherwise unrecorded, is clearly the simplex which is reduplicated in 3ḫ3ḫ 'grow green', 'flourish'."[230] Alicia Maravelia made much the same point: "From the etymology of the word 3ḫ3ḫ (=*bright stars, grow green, twilight*, etc.) it is evident that the stem 3ḫ-, hints clearly to *brightness, transfigured sanctity* (3ḫ), light (i3ḫw), etc."[231]

It is our opinion, in fact, that the Egyptian myth of the deceased king's "akhification" within the celestial *akhet* was directly inspired by the *greening* of the Horus-star within a greenish celestial enclosure. Recall again the *Book of the Dead*'s account of the Horus-star's appearance at Creation:

"[Harakhti] When thou appearest in the horizon of heaven, hymns to thee are in the mouths of everyone, thou being beautiful and youthful in the sun-disk within the arms of thy mother Hathor. How thou shinest in every place, thy heart rejoicing forever…How thou shinest in the horizon of heaven. Thou hast strewn the Two Lands with turquoise."[232]

Here the Horus-star is described as beautiful (nfr), youthful (ḥwn), and rejuvenated (rnp) upon his epiphany—i.e., the very terms employed to

---

[230] R. Faulkner, *The Ancient Egyptian Coffin Texts* (Oxford, 1973), p. 143.
[231] A. Maravelia, "The function and importance of some special categories of stars in the Ancient Egyptian funerary texts, 1," *International Congress of Egyptologists XI* (Oxford, 2017), p. 370.
[232] H. Stewart, "Traditional Egyptian Sun Hymns of the New Kingdom," *Bull. Inst. Arch.* 6 (1967), p. 52.

describe the deceased king upon his hoped-for akhification.[233] This can scarcely be a coincidence. The clear implication of this passage and others is that the Horus-star assumed a radically new and sublimely beautiful appearance upon ascending to heaven and being transfigured within the akhet. Hitherto overlooked by all Egyptologists is the fact that the greening of the Horus-star is essential to its status as a new, rejuvenated, and beautiful god.

If our reconstruction of these prehistoric natural events is well-founded, it stands to reason that the "greening" of the Horus-star *in illo tempore* will provide us with the most likely explanation for why the Egyptian scribes chose the crested ibis as the avian form best suited to denote the concept *akh*—i.e., the term employed to describe the transfigured state of the deceased king as an Imperishable Star.[234] The bird in question, it will be noted, is distinguished by its iridescent turquoise-blue plumage and peculiar crest (the latter quite possibly believed to resemble the star-god's feathery *coma*-like corona or multi-colored "feathers" as illustrated in figure two in the previous chapter).[235] Insofar as the Horus-star was expressly identified with an exotic "green bird" in the classic account in the Pyramid Texts (519) describing that god's prototypical appearance and glorious transfiguration—the aforementioned *wꜣḏꜣḏ* (-bird)—it is only natural that the Egyptian scribes would choose a green bird to represent the transfigured star-god.

Truth be told, the archaic traditions describing the greening of the cosmos at the time of the Horus-star's glorious appearance (*ḥꜥ*) hold the

---

[233] Of *nfr*, Allan Lloyd, "Expeditions to the Wadi Hammamat," in J. Hill et al eds., *Experiencing Power, Generating Authority* (Philadelphia, 2013), p. 370 observed: "*Nfr* (and its affiliates) is another word that is impossible to translate but whose core of meaning lies in the area of 'youthful vigour and creative force' (James 1953:12; Donohue 1978: 143ff.)."

[234] B. Kemp, *100 Hieroglyphs* (London, 2005), p. 122: "It is not clear if the hieroglyph for spirit—a crested ibis (*Ibis comata*)—was conceptually associated with a bird, or whether it was chosen on account of its phonetic similarity with the bird's name."

[235] See the discussion in J. Hancock et al, *Storks, Ibises and Spoonbills of the World* (London, 1992), pp. 231-236. There the authors note: "The base plumage of the adult is a dark metallic green, which is tinged with a purple iridescence."

key to a proper understanding of Egyptian ideas of creation and, it follows, an elucidation of the king's post-mortem peregrinations in the earliest funerary hymns (the latter, after all, were purposefully patterned after the glorious transfiguration of the Horus-star).[236] Yet from the vantage point of modern Egyptology, the greening of the celestial landscape in *zp tpj* is routinely dismissed as imaginative hyperbole together with the detailed traditions describing the cosmic tumult attending the prototypical sunrise and the disaster associated with the Eye of Horus—an interpretation that makes the Egyptian skywatchers out to be inveterate fantasists and liars. This default position, in turn, begs the following question: If the Egyptian scribes can't be trusted to accurately describe the prototypical sunrise at the time of creation—the alleged *fons et origo* and multi-millenial fixation of their funerary religion according to the conventional view—how can their testimony be trusted on any score?

---

[236] See here S. Wiebach-Koepke, "The Growth of Plants in the Light of the Sun-God," in A. Maravelia ed., *In Quest of Light* (Montpellier, 2009), pp. 51-70.

## The Return of the Eye of Horus

"The myth of the return of the goddess has a distinct astronomical background. It is a description in mythological terms of natural phenomena associated with the heliacal rising of Sirius. Such a result shows quite clearly that research on Egyptian astronomy cannot afford to concentrate on 'pure' scientific texts while neglecting the religious background. Rather, it is typical for the Egyptians that astronomical background is presupposed in religious texts."[237]

"Elsewhere, I have suggested that this episode [the bloodbath associated with the Eye's rampage *in illo tempore*] may be related to the daily reddening of the sky at dawn, which, in Egyptian terms, coincides with the slaying of the solar enemies. The return of the goddess would then represent the rising of the sun, which coincides with the redness in the sky. The periods during which the goddess is absent would, accordingly, correspond to the nighttime."[238]

A systematic examination of the ancient Egyptian texts will confirm that the mother goddess played a pivotal role in the greening of the celestial landscape during the time of creation. As a case in point, consider the tradition reported in Utterance 350 from the Pyramid Texts, wherein a female star is invoked as follows:

"O you who stride out greatly, strewing green-stone, malachite, turquoise of (?) the stars, if you are green, then the King will be green, (even as) living rush is green."[239]

A literal reading of this text reveals that the goddess in question—likely Wadjet or Nut—scattered greenish-colored stellar material as she moved about the sky. Mercer's commentary on this passage is right on the

---

[237] J. Quack, "A Goddess Rising 10,000 Cubits into the Air," in J. Steele & A. Imhausen, *Under One Sky* (Münster, 2002), p. 291.
[238] K. Goebs, "A Functional Approach to Egyptian Myth and Mythemes," *Journal of Ancient Near Eastern Religions* 2 (2002), p. 55.
[239] *PT* 567.

money even though he avoids offering any astronomical explanation for the imagery in question:

"The feminine sower may be Nut (cf. 568b and 569b). However, she may be *W3di.t*, the serpent-goddess of Buto…The thought in this line seems to be that stars had their origin in the sowing of precious stones, and especially those of a green colour…The greenness of the goddess is the result of the green stones which she sows…The deceased king as a star belongs to the green stones, and the greenness, therefore, has the meaning of 'fresh,' 'well.'…This brief utterance presents a vision of beauty and power—the goddess of heaven, striding widely across the sky, strews far and wide across the heavens green, luminous pebbles of emerald, malachite and turquoise, which are our stars and planets (cf. 1203a)."[240]

As the uraeus-goddess, Wadjet was conceptualized as the "green one" and celebrated as she who "makes green the two Lands and guides the gods in this her name of Wadjet."[241] An echo of the "greening" effect associated with the goddess can be discerned in the following passage from the *Book of the Dead*, wherein she is identified with the Eye of Re:

"Every god is afraid because so great and mighty is my protection of the god from him who would vilify him. Malachite glitters for me, I live according to my will, for I am Wadjet, Lady of the Devouring Flame, and few approach me…As for Wadjet, Lady of the Devouring Flame, she is the Eye of Re."[242]

Wadjet is elsewhere said to provide Horus or the deceased king with his headband. It is this act which "rejuvenates" the god, an act that is inseparable from the "greening" of the cosmos associated with the Eye-

---

[240] S. Mercer, *The Pyramid Texts in Translation and Commentary, Vol. 2* (New York, 1952), pp. 276-277. This passage finds a possible parallel in lines 495-496 of *Lugalbanda in the Wilderness*: "The matriarch made (them) rise. (In) a clear sky the numerous stars rose." The translator, H. Vanstiphout, *Epics of Sumerian Kings* (Leiden, 2004), p. 163 observed of this passage: "Here [Inanna] seems to cause the stars and constellations to rise."
[241] R. Faulkner, "The Bremner-Rhind Papyrus—II," *JEA* 23 (1937), p. 13.
[242] R. Faulkner, *The Ancient Egyptian Book of the Dead* (Austin, 1972), p. 50.

goddess. This idea is evident in the following text from Osiris's chapel in the temple of Seti I at Abydos:

"*Spell for donning the green/Wadjit-cloth.* May Wadjit, the mistress of flame/*Nbyt*, arise...may it/she refresh (him) through what is in her freshness/greenness, (so that) he will be young through it."[243]

Here it will be noted that the word translated as "refresh" by Goebs is *swꜣḏ*, literally "to make green" (the latter word is cognate with the name of the Eye Goddess Wadjet). As Goebs points out, the entire spell is full of word-plays:

"The ritual episode employs wordplays that involve, on the one hand, terms for greenness/freshness (*wꜣḏ*), rejuvenation (*swꜣḏ*), and haleness (*swḏꜣ*), and—on the other—the fiery solar disc and uraeus Wadjit, who is said to 'arise' or 'shine forth' (*ḫꜥj*). This latter statement moreover points to the luminous associations of the term *wꜣḏ* and the goddess associated with it."[244]

Similar traditions surround Hathor, who, like Wadjet, was described as an Eye-goddess who came to encircle the Horus-star. According to the Coffin Texts, she too was associated with a greening of the celestial landscape:

"The mountain is broken, the stone is split, the caverns of Hathor are broken open; she ascends in turquoise and is covered with her royal wig-cover."[245]

The word translated as "turquoise" here is *mfkꜣt*, elsewhere translated as "malachite" as in Utterance 350 above. A turquoise-colored gemstone, malachite came to serve as a special symbol of the Egyptian Eye-goddess

---

[243] The New Kingdom Daily Cultic Ritual as translated in K. Goebs, "King as God and God as King," in R. Gundlach & K. Spence eds., *Palace and Temple* (Wiesbaden, 2011), pp. 66-67.
[244] *Ibid.*, p. 67.
[245] *CT* VI:631-64c.

(Hathor herself was commonly invoked as the "Mistress of Malachite").[246]

A wealth of evidence confirms that the greening of the celestial landscape constitutes a memorable phase in the extraordinary natural events alluded to in the Egyptian myth of the Eye-Goddess's return and pacification. Although the extant Egyptian texts typically reference these dramatic events by means of brief allusions couched in exceedingly obscure language, a comparative approach allows us to discern the underlying patterns and reconstruct their general cosmogonic context and temporal order.

As documented in chapter four, the Eye of Horus is said to have experienced a period of wandering or exile during the cataclysmic events attending the death of Osiris—or, according to an alternative tradition recounted in the *Destruction of Mankind*, during the rebellion of mankind—whereupon it departed from its customary celestial station alongside the Horus-star and went on a rampage, seemingly hellbent on destroying mankind. While wandering abroad the Eye was represented as "raging," a phenomenon typically described with the Egyptian term *dšrw* "wrath," or *dšr jb*, "red of heart."[247] The clear implication is that, during its period of wrath and wandering, the Eye of Horus (Venus) presented a ruddy red form.[248] Indeed, the Eye's marked propensity for strewing "fire" and "blood" during a veritable *bloodbath* associated with its primeval rampage is incomprehensible apart from a catastrophic scattering of red celestial efflux by Venus.

We know this to be the case because Inanna/Venus is described in strikingly similar terms in Sumerian lore. Thus, if one text makes Inanna

---

[246] P. Nicholson & I. Shaw, *Ancient Egyptian Materials and Technology* (Cambridge, 2000), p. 43.
[247] *CT* I:21-22. See the discussion in A. Joseph, "Divine Wrath in Ancient Egypt," *Études et Travaux* 31 (2018), p. 38.
[248] Witness K. Goebs, *Crowns in Egyptian Funerary Literature* (Oxford, 2008), p. 54: "that it may redden the raging one [*nšnt*]."

announce that "An has made me terrifying throughout heaven,"[249] another reports that the planet-goddess flooded the landscape with blood: "She filled the wells of the Land with blood."[250] In text after text Inanna is described as covered in blood as she threatened to destroy mankind:

"Inana…drenched in blood, rushing around in great battles…covered in storm and flood…In heaven and on earth you roar like a lion and devastate the people."[251]

To return to Egyptian cosmogonic myth: If the period associated with the Eye's raging was remembered as one of cosmic upheaval marked by "storm," darkness, and the raining of ruddy-colored extraterrestrial debris, the subsequent period associated with its "pacification" and return to the immediate vicinity of the Horus-star was distinguished by an equally spectacular scattering of green stellar efflux. Egyptian texts describe this remarkable turn of events as the Eye Goddess's raining blood suddenly becoming turquoise in color. The *Brooklyn Papyrus* (ca. 450 BCE), for example, recounts the remarkable transformation as follows: "The blood came forth from her and it transformed into turquoise."[252] Analogous testimony is attested from the sacred texts adorning the temple at Esna dating from the Graeco-Roman period: "A monograph in the temple of Esna has Tefnut returning in rage and transforming herself into turquoise when Shu pacifies her."[253]

The material scattered by the Eye-goddess after her return from exile is likened to *ṯhn*, a word commonly translated as "faience" but clearly referencing a shiny, green-colored substance.[254] In a survey of the

---

[249] Line 66 of "Inana and Ebiḫ," *ETCSL*.
[250] Line 131 of "Inana and Šukaletuda," *ETCSL*.
[251] Lines 2-7 from "Inana and Ebiḫ," *ETCSL*. See here the discussion in E. Cochrane, *The Many Faces of Venus* (Ames, 2001), pp. 18-20.
[252] J. Jorgensen, "Myths, Menarche and the *Return of the Goddess*," in R. Nyord & K. Ryholt eds., *Lotus and Laurel* (Copenhagen, 2015), p. 135, citing *Papyrus Brooklyn* 47.218.84.
[253] *Ibid.*, p. 136, citing *Esna* 58, 4.
[254] S. Wiebach-Koepke, "The Growth of Plants in the Light of the Sun-God," in A. Maravelia ed., *In Quest of Light* (Montpellier, 2009), pp. 57-60. See also F. Friedman ed., *Gifts of the Nile: Ancient Egyptian Faience* (Leuven, 1992).

Wandering Goddess theme, Jens Jorgensen points out that a Delta manual traces the origin of faience to the Eye of Horus:

"In the Heliopolis section of the Delta manual we find a related aetiology for faience, which comes into being when the anger or flames (*bst*) of the bright eye is extinguished. The underlying premise in both cases is the transformation of the dangerous red of blood and fire into the greenish or blue minerals."[255]

The greening of the celestial landscape associated with the Eye of Horus, in turn, is inextricably linked to the catastrophic events described in a previous chapter during which the Eye returns from exile and comes to encircle the Horus-star with a green headband (*sšd*), thereby signaling the latter's transfiguration and coronation. The following passage from the Pyramid Texts alludes to this archaic conception: "Here is Horus's green eye, which he put on as a headband."[256] The same idea is apparent in the following passage from Unis's pyramid: "Osiris Unis, accept Horus's green eye: prevent him from putting it on as a headband."[257]

As is evident from these archaic hymns, the so-called Green Eye (*wɜḏt*) describes the Eye *after* its pacification and reunion with the Horus-star, whereupon it comes to form the god's royal headband (*sšd*). If the period marked by the wandering of the raging Eye was remembered as a time of cosmic crisis and apocalyptic disorder, the return of the Eye and encircling of the Horus-star with the green headband signaled a restoration of world order.[258] Alternatively, if the Eye was conceptualized as "bewailing" or "injured" during its period of wandering, its return signaled the onset of health, well-being, and joy. It is by reference to this

---

[255] J. Jorgensen, *op. cit.*, pp. 141-142.
[256] *PT* 108c as translated in J. Allen, *The Ancient Egyptian Pyramid Texts* (Atlanta, 2005), p. 257.
[257] *PT* 96c as translated by *Ibid.*, p. 27. The fact that the *sšd*-headband is determined with the uraeus-serpent here rather than the linen sign encodes the inherent relationship between the *sšd*, uraeus-serpent, and green eye.
[258] B. Richter, "On the Heels of the Wandering Goddess," in M. Dolinska & H. Beinlich eds., *Ägyptologische Tempeltagung* (Wiesbaden, 2010), p. 156: "With her pacification, the order of the cosmos is also restored."

singular planetary history, then, that we would understand the Green Eye's epithet *wḏꜣt*, denoting the "sound" or perhaps "restored" one.[259]

And insofar as the Green Eye was associated with a return of health—not to mention the beautification or "rejuvenation" of the Horus-star—it came to serve as a magical talisman guaranteeing health, fertility, and resurrection. Indeed, the Green Eye's beneficial properties are the subject of countless spells and proverbs in the ancient Egyptian texts. Witness the following passage from the Pyramid Texts: "Pepi Neferkare, Horus's sound [eye has been tied on for you]."[260] The same idea is evident in the following passage: "Osiris Pepi Neferkare, here is Horus's green eye, which he acquired."[261]

It is noteworthy that the word denoting the "sound eye," *wḏꜣt*, is commonly employed by the Egyptian scribes in various plays on the word for "green," *wꜣḏ*.[262] In the Pyramid Texts, for example, the presentation of green eye-paint to the deceased king is introduced as follows: "O Osiris the King, I paint an uninjured Eye of Horus [*wḏꜣt*] on your face for you—green [*wꜣḏ*] eye-paint."[263] In the *Papyrus Ebers*, the origin of the green paint is traced to the Eye of Horus:

"The green eye-paint comes, the green eye-paint comes, the green one comes, the liquid from the eye of Horus comes…Recitation over green eye-paint mixed with fermented honey, Cyperus is added to it, and (it) is put on the eye."[264]

---

[259] C. Andrews, *Amulets of Ancient Egypt* (London, 1994), p. 6. See also D. Meeks & C. Favard-Meeks, *Daily Life of Egyptian Gods* (Ithaca, 1998), p. 33.
[260] *PT* 634c as translated in J. Allen, *The Ancient Egyptian Pyramid Texts* (Atlanta, 2005), p. 261.
[261] *PT* 107 as translated in *Ibid.*, p. 257.
[262] *PT* 704, for example, features a play upon the two words *wꜣḏ* and *wḏꜣ*, wherein the Eye of Horus is said to rejuvenate the deceased king. See also the discussion in N. Billing, *Performative Structure* (Copenhagen, 2018), pp. 527-528.
[263] *PT* 54 as translated in R. Faulkner, *The Ancient Egyptian Pyramid Texts* (Oxford, 1969).
[264] R. Nyord, *Breathing Flesh: Conceptions of the Body in the Ancient Egyptian Coffin Texts* (Copenhagen, 2009), pp. 118-119.

In a ritual in which ointment was applied to the god's head, the offering was identified as the Eye of Horus. Here, too, the raging Eye of Horus, as Wadjet-Sakhmet, is described as greening Horus:

"The heart of Horus rejoices at meeting his bodily Eye. May it refresh you, may it adorn you in this its name of Wadjit."[265]

Here it will be noted that the word translated as "refresh" by Goebs is *swȝd*, literally "to make green."[266]

The green paint favored by the Old Kingdom makeup artists was commonly derived from malachite, a form of copper carbonate which regularly produces a shiny green color. Thus it is that Egyptian texts make reference to *wadj ḥmty*, "copper green" or "coppery green" as a name for the pigment used as eye makeup by women.[267] (Doubtless it is no coincidence that copper is the very metal—and green the color—commonly associated with the planet Venus by ancient writers as well as alchemists of the Medieval period.[268])

It bears repeating that the Pyramid Texts themselves expressly point out that the turquoise in question was "of the stars" (*mfkȝt sbȝw*) and that it had been scattered by the Eye Goddess herself during catastrophic events *in illo tempore*. Recall again the passage addressing the Eye quoted earlier:

"O you who stride out greatly, strewing green-stone, malachite, turquoise of (?) the stars, if you are green, then the King will be green, (even as) a living rush is green."[269]

---

[265] Daily Cultic Ritual as translated by K. Goebs, "A Functional Approach to Egyptian Myth and Mythemes," *JANER* 2 (2002), p. 44.
[266] It is this word that is used to describe the pacification of Sakhmet.
[267] G. Majno, *The Healing Hand* (Cambridge, 1975), p. 112. See also T. Sherkova, "Solar Notions, Rituals and Images in Pre-Dynastic Egypt," in A. Maravelia ed., *In Quest of Light* (Montpellier, 2009), p. 136: "The mythological reconstruction of the sound Eye of Horus was reproduced in the ritualistic lining of the eyes with *malachite green*, thus symbolizing the regeneration of life."
[268] G. Irby-Massie & P. Keyser, *Greek Science of the Hellenistic Era* (London, 2002), p. 226. See also E. Krupp, *Beyond the Blue Horizon* (Oxford, 1991), p. 183.
[269] *PT* 567.

The scattering of green stars described here and elsewhere in the Pyramid and Coffin Texts has reference to the strewing of green stellar material by the Eye of Horus (Venus) upon its return to and conjunction with the Horus-star. How interesting, then, to find that Egyptian rituals celebrating the Eye-goddess's return featured a scattering of a greenish-colored material. Barbara Richter, in a recent study of Hathor's cult at Dendera during the Graeco-Roman period, noted that the ritual in question featured a procession of the Eye-goddess:

"Green powder, made sparkling by the addition of gold, was sprinkled on the ground in front of Hathor's statue, which went out in procession. The whole earth 'sparkled with her radiance' (*thn t3 dr=f <m> ꜥhw=t*)."[270]

So, too, in texts from Esna, the Eye-Goddess is said to have strewn (*wpš*) the greenish-colored material throughout the land: "When she opened the sky with a sparkle of light [*thn.t*] and strewed the ground with sparkling green powder [*thn.t*]."[271] The passage in question is illustrated in figure one, wherein *thn* is determined by the mound-like object and *wpš* is determined by the sun-like body surrounded by tiny dots (N55).[272] This imagery recalls that attested in the much older text from the Pyramid Texts (567b), quoted above, wherein the word "strew" (*st*) is determined with a sign 𓀃 elsewhere determining *wpš*. The greenish material of the stars, in turn, is determined by the 𓈔 sign, otherwise associated with *thn*, "faience" (the same sign serves as the ideogram for malachite). Clearly the two traditions are homologous in nature and point unequivocally to an

---

[270] B. Richter, *op. cit.*, p. 265.
[271] J.-C. Goyon, "Répandre l'or et éparpiller la verdure...," in J. van Dijk, *Essays on Ancient Egypt in Honour of Herman te Velde* (Groningen, 1997), p. 96, as translated in B. Richter, *op. cit.*, p. 185.
[272] *Esna* 236 as adapted from J.-C. Goyon, *op. cit.*, p. 96.

explosive astronomical event in which the Eye-goddess scattered greenish material throughout the visible celestial landscape.²⁷³

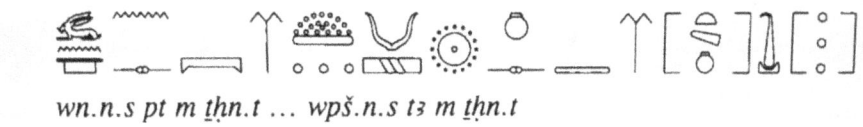

wn.n.s pt m ṯhn.t ... wpš.n.s t3 m ṯhn.t

Figure 1

To recap our discussion in the present chapter: A survey of a wide variety of Egyptian texts from different historical periods has revealed that the Eye of Horus underwent a dramatic metamorphosis in appearance over time, assuming a ruddy red color during its period of destructive "raging" and later transforming into a sparkling "turquoise green" once it returned to the Horus-star and settled down as if "pacified." Indeed, it is precisely because the raging red Eye of Horus transformed into a tranquil greenish form upon being pacified that we can understand the various references in ancient Egyptian texts for the desire to "put turquoise in place of carnelian."²⁷⁴ The following Egyptian proverb is representative of this archaic belief-system: "Ich vertrieb das Leid (ḥrst), ich brachte Freude (mfk3t)."²⁷⁵ It will be noted that the word translated as "Leid" here is ḥrst, derived from the Egyptian word for carnelian. The word translated as "Freude" is derived from the Egyptian word for turquoise (mfk3t).²⁷⁶

---

²⁷³ B. Richter, *op. cit.*, p. 325 observes: "The idea of 'scattering light' alludes to the ritual of 'répandre l'or,' during which sparkling green powder was strewn on the fields during the month of Epiphi in order to guarantee the agricultural cycle."
²⁷⁴ See the insightful discussion in A. Roberts, *Hathor Rising* (Devon, 1995), p. 10: "The need to transform violent, uncontrolled female rage into a radiant beneficient force—or as Graeco-Roman texts express it, 'to put turquoise in place of carnelian'—lies at the core of myths about the serpent Sun Eye."
²⁷⁵ *Denderah* II 53b as quoted from M. Schunk, *Untersuchungen zum Wortstamm ḥr* (Bonn, 1985), p. 7.
²⁷⁶ E. Brunner-Traut, "Farben," *Lexikon der Ägyptologie 2* (Wiesbaden, 1977), col. 125: "Alle grünfarbenen Dinge haben in magischen Sinne die Sympathiewirkung der grünen Farben als des jungen, frischen Wachsens und gesunden Gedeihens. Grüne Materialien konnten Metapher sein fur 'Friede' und 'Freude', so dass man zur Besanftigung 'Türkis anstelle von Karneol setzte'. Das gesunde Horusauge war

Such, in essence, is the metamorphosis undergone by the Eye of Horus upon its return to the Horus-star.

The evidence adduced above is consistent with the hypothesis that the Eye of Horus presented the appearance of a ruddy, comet-like form during its destructive rampage in the pre-Creation period. The Egyptian traditions surrounding the so-called Green Eye, on the other hand, describe Venus *after* it had returned to the Horus-star and encircled (*šn*) it as a green headband (*sšd*).

In addition to the dramatic metamorphosis in color from red to green, the Eye-goddess's pacification was also marked by a notable reordering of her hair, thereby giving rise to the mythological interpretation that it had been "lifted up," "tied up," or otherwise brought under control. Witness the otherwise obscure language from Spell 335 in the Coffin Texts: "I have tied together her hair as the *wḏɜt*-eye."[277] With the tying together of the disheveled hair and the greening of the Eye, raging (*nšn*) and disorder (*jzft*) were replaced by pacification (*ḥtp*) and cosmic order (*mɜꜥ*).[278]

While Egyptologists find themselves at a loss to explain a single one of the major mythological motifs associated with the Eye of Horus—its role as an agent of apocalyptic disaster, its storm-laden "hair," its function as a powerful warrior-goddess and protector of the Pharaoh, its return to Horus, its function as an enclosure of the Horus-star, its intimate association with the royal headband/crown, its identification with various items of offering, its function as a talisman guaranteeing prosperity, etc.—

---

grün...." For a detailed discussion of green sun imagery see M. van der Sluijs, *On the Origin of Myths, Vol. One* (Vancouver, 2019), pp. 129-131.

[277] *CT* IV: 238 as translated in R. Nyord, *Breathing Flesh: Conceptions of the Body in the Ancient Egyptian Coffin Texts* (Copenhagen, 2009), p. 229: "Ik heb het haar samengebonden als wedzjatoog." Translation courtesy of Marinus van der Sluijs. See also the comparable passage in the *Book of the Dead*: "Hair is bound on the wedjat-eye in its time of rage." See S. Quirke, *Going out in Daylight* (London, 2013), p. 58, citing EA 9900.

[278] It will be noted that *mɜꜥ* likewise denotes an ordering of the hair. See R. van der Molen, *op. cit.*, p. 153.

the historical reconstruction advanced here offers a perfectly straightforward and coherent explanation for each and every aspect of the Eye's multifaceted mythology. The Eye of Horus was conceptualized as an agent of terrifying celestial disaster precisely because, during one particular phase in its history, it presented the appearance of a fire-spewing comet-like body (*sšd*) that played a prominent role in a number of extraordinary cataclysms during the prehistoric period. Indeed, it was because the Eye of Horus had formerly assumed a prodigious comet-like form while waging "war" against mankind that it came to be viewed as an awe-inspiring weapon or aegis-like source of protection for the Horus-star once it came to encircle the latter as a headband-like crown (*sšd*) (Egyptologists, being completely unaware of Venus's incendiary history, are left grasping at straws trying to explain why it is that an "eye" could ever be thought of as an angry or terrifying agent of heaven-sent disaster).

The Eye was deemed the archetypal offering, finally, because its return and reunion with the Horus-star effected the latter's transfiguration into an Imperishable Star, whereupon it appeared as if renewed and empowered.[279] It is in this very concrete sense, then, that the Eye of Horus, as the planet Venus, was the decisive agent of transfiguration with respect to the Horus-star (Mars)—the celestial prototype for the Egyptian pharaoh—for it was the conjunction of the Eye with Horus that endowed the latter with the headband-like crown (*sšd*) and thereby invested it as the King of the Gods (Universal Sovereign). And as the principal divine agent responsible for the Horus-star's transfiguration, rejuvenation, and "healing," the Green Eye was memorialized as a powerful talisman guaranteeing health, prosperity, and magical protection.

---

[279] R. Wilkinson, *Reading Egyptian Art* (London, 1992), p. 43: "The restored eye which was presented by Horus to his father became an archetype of the act of offering and an offering itself."

## Horus in the *Akhet*

> "Hieroglyphic texts reflect the ancient Egyptian view of the world. Understanding these texts is not just a matter of translation: it also requires an appreciation of ancient Egyptian geography."[280]

> "Unlike the modern concept of 'horizon,' the Egyptian *akhet* was conceived originally as a specific and concrete locale in the sky, as opposed to an imaginary line where earth and sky appear to meet (Assmann 1980, 3)... The importance of the *akhet* as a feature of cosmic geography cannot be overstated...."[281]

> "The word normally translated 'horizon' means, really, 'Land of Light' or 'Mountain of Light.' It is the place of sunrise, originally conceived quite concretely as mountains to the east of the Nile Valley."[282]

The *locus classicus* of the Horus-star, according to the Pyramid Texts, was the *akhet*—hence the god's epithet *Harakhte*, repeated *ad infinitum* throughout three thousand years of Egyptian history.[283] Indeed, it is fair to say that the concept of the *akhet* stands at the very heart of ancient Egyptian ideas of celestial geography and funerary symbolism, for it was there—within the *akhet*—that Horus experienced its transfiguration into an Imperishable *akh* or star, the central theme of Egyptian funerary religion. PT 928 is representative in this regard:

> "I go up on this eastern side of the sky where the gods are born, and I am born as Horus, as Him of the horizon."[284]

---

[280] J. Allen, *Middle Egyptian* (Cambridge, 2014), p. 25.
[281] J. Roberson, "The Iconicity of the Vertical: Hieroglyphic Encoding and the *Akhet* in Royal Burial Chambers of Egypt's New Kingdom," in I. Zsolnay ed., *Seen Not Heard* (Chicago, 2023), p. 41.
[282] H. Frankfort, *Kingship and the Gods* (Chicago, 1948), p. 354.
[283] J. Allen, "The Celestial Realm," in D. Silverman ed., *Ancient Egypt* (Oxford, 1997), p. 119.
[284] *PT* 928.

Yet if scholars are agreed as to the *akhet's* paramount importance in Egyptian cosmography and religion, there is little consensus as to what it originally represented or how it is to be understood from the standpoint of human experience or natural science. Now here is a truly remarkable situation: How is it possible that Egyptologists are unable to point to an obvious celestial prototype or tangible structure for what is arguably the single most important cosmological concept in all of Egyptian religion?[285] And if this is indeed the case, what does this say about the theoretical foundation of modern Egyptology in general?

In order to introduce this difficult subject—but also to summarize conventional opinion—a number of leading authorities will be quoted at some length. Jan Assmann, the author of the standard entry on the *akhet* in the *Lexikon der Ägyptologie*, explored this subject in great detail in a number of seminal works on Egyptian religion:

"They [pyramids] are not iconic signs; they are not an image of anything…The pyramid does not *stand* for anything visible, it *makes* something visible. Its elevation makes it a pointer to the heavens…The central concept here is the *akhet*, a word which we traditionally translate as 'horizon' but that in Egyptian refers to a region of the heavens where the sky nears the earth and the sun god ascends from the underworld in the morning and returns in the evening. In Egyptian the pyramid of Cheops (whose Egyptian name was Khufu) is called *akhet* of Khufu. *Akhet* is the threshold region between the sky, the earth, and the underworld; in particular, *akhet* is the place where the sun rises. The etymological root of the word has the meaning of 'blaze, be radiant'; likewise, the hieroglyph for *akhet* has nothing in common with the pyramid, but is a pictogram of the sun rising or setting between two

---

[285] K. Jansen-Winkeln, "'Horizont und Verklärtheit': Zur Bedeutung der Wurzel *ȝḫ*," *Studien zur altägyptischen Kultur* 23 (1996), p. 215 deems the *akhet* to be the key term in Egyptian religion: "fur viele der Schlüsselbegriffe der ägyptischen Religion zutrefft."

mountains [◯]. The pyramid does not represent such an *akhet*, but symbolizes it in an aniconic way. The term of comparison between *akhet* and pyramid is the idea of 'ascent to heaven.' As the sun god ascends from the underworld to the *akhet* and appears in the sky, so the king interred in the pyramid ascends to heaven by way of his *akhet*, his threshold of light."[286]

What is true of the pyramid is also true of the temple complex and palace—indeed, of all sacred monumental structures in ancient Egypt: Such structures derived their intrinsic symbolic value from the fact that they were thought to represent or somehow embody the celestial *akhet*—the locus of the Horus-star's transfiguration. Thus it is that each and every local Egyptian temple was celebrated as *the akhet* and deemed to be a terrestrial replica of the celestial prototype.[287]

Asked to provide a celestial referent for the *akhet*, Egyptologists typically point to the "horizon" or to some nondescript mountain range to the east of Cairo.[288] For Mark Lehner, the *akhet* was an invisible region *below* the horizon:

"*Akhet* is usually translated as 'horizon', where land and skies touch, but it meant much more in the Egyptian world concept. Written with the same root as the word *akh*, the *Akhet* was where the dead were transformed into effective inhabitants of the world beyond death. As part of the sky, it was also the place into which the sun, and therefore the king, was reborn from within the *Duat*. It is not hard to imagine the early Egyptians being inspired by the pre-dawn glow in the eastern horizon, and by the sunset flaming in the west, to see the area just below the horizon as

---

[286] J. Assmann, *The Mind of Egypt* (Cambridge, 2002), pp. 57-58.
[287] J. Assmann, *The Search for God in Ancient Egypt* (Ithaca, 2001), pp. 36-37 notes that "From the New Kingdom on, innumerable texts emphasize that the temple is 'like the *akhet* of the sky' or an 'image of the celestial *akhet*.'"
[288] Z. Hawass, *Mountains of the Pharaoh* (Cairo, 2006), p. 116, would identify the *akhet* with the horizon. J. Assmann, *The Mind of Egypt* (Cambridge, 2002), p. 58 identifies it with the "sun rising or setting between two mountains."

the place of glorification…As the place where the deceased becomes an *akh*, a suggested translation is 'Spirit' or 'Light Land'."[289]

Remarkably, Lehner is arguing that the ancient Egyptian skywatchers were so impressed by the "pre-dawn glow in the eastern horizon" that they would make an invisible region *below the horizon* the focal point of their mystery religion involving the transfiguration of the deceased king. James Allen has offered a similar opinion:

"Between the day and night skies was a region known as the Akhet (Egyptian *3ḥt*), into which the sun set before descending into the Duat, and into which he rose before appearing in the morning sky. The concept of the Akhet was a practical explanation of why light fades gradually after sunset and appears gradually before sunrise, instead of disappearing and reappearing with the sun all at once."[290]

To reiterate: Jansen-Winkeln, Lehner, and Allen would have us believe that the supreme mystery of Egyptian religion—the akhification of the Horus-star within the *akhet*—takes place somewhere beneath the horizon and thus out of view of the Egyptian skywatchers. According to this understanding, it follows that the manifold Egyptian traditions telling of Horus's glorious transfiguration within the *akhet* at the hands of the great mother goddess must needs be largely imaginative or fictional in nature. So, too, it follows that the pyramids and other monumental structures designed to model the *akhet* were inspired by an imaginary or speculative concept (recall Assmann's claim that the pyramid "does not stand for anything visible"). We would challenge this entire line of thought: For if the study of Egyptian religion and language teaches us anything it is that the ancient Egyptians had a decided preference for concrete imagery and thus it seems most unlikely that they would construct a complex and remarkably coherent myth of a post-mortem

---

[289] M. Lehner, *The Complete Pyramids* (London, 1997), p. 29.
[290] J. Allen, *Middle Egyptian* (Cambridge, 2014), p. 26.

journey to the celestial Hereafter around an abstract concept like the astronomical "horizon" or the invisible "area just below the horizon."

In order to gain a better understanding of what the Egyptians had in mind when invoking the *akhet*, it is instructive to briefly review the orthography and semantic range of the term in question. In the Pyramid Texts the word *ꜣḫt* is written with the following hieroglyphs: . The bird depicted in the first hieroglyph—a biliteral known to have the phonetic value *ꜣḫ*, the root of the word *akhet*—is commonly identified with the *Ibis comata*, the latter being renowned for its iridescent greenish plumage and singular crest.[291] The second sign, a complement to the first, is associated with the sound *ḫ* and is of unknown origin.[292] The third sign is thought to depict a loaf of bread and is associated with the *t*-sound; employed as a suffix, it marks the word as being feminine in nature.[293] The final oval sign—the determinative for the word in question—is thought to depict an island[294] or, according to Allen, a "place" or "womb."[295]

A few related words are of interest here. The word *ꜣḫt*—determined with the uraeus-sign —denotes the fire-spewing serpent associated with the royal crown.[296] This archaic concept is evident in Utterance 256, wherein the uraeus-serpent is expressly identified with the mother goddess, there invoked by the name Ernutet: "The flaming blast of my uraeus is that of Ernutet who is upon me."[297] Elsewhere in the Pyramid

---

[291] F. Friedman, "The Root Meaning of *ꜣḫ*: Effectiveness or Luminosity," *Serapis* 8 (1984/5), p. 145.
[292] J. Allen, *Middle Egyptian* (Oxford, 2014), p. 505.
[293] M. Betrò, *op. cit.*, p. 185.
[294] *Ibid.*, p. 157.
[295] Personal communication: "The original determinative, the elongated oval, reflects the nature of the Akhet both as a place and as the womb (like Nut)."
[296] R. Hannig, *Ägyptisches Wörterbuch I* (Mainz, 2003), p. 15, entry 392.
[297] *PT* 302.

Texts it is said that the sun-god makes his glorious appearance in unison with the *ȝḫt*-serpent: "Rēʿ arises, his uraeus upon him."²⁹⁸

The word *ȝḫt*, spelled like the previous word but with the following determinative 👁, denotes the Eye of Horus.²⁹⁹ The Eye of Horus, in turn, shares a fundamental affinity with the uraeus-serpent as evinced by the following passage from the Coffin Texts, wherein the falcon-god is made to announce:

"I am Horus, son of Osiris, born of the divine Isis. I am king in Chemmis, my face is formed as that of a divine falcon; I created my Eye in flame, I am alert, and my Sacred Eye is united with his Sacred Eye. I made my Eye, a living serpent."³⁰⁰

As is evident from the passages quoted above, the Eye of Horus was commonly conceptualized as being serpentine in appearance and flame-like in nature. This imagery, in turn, dovetails perfectly with the evidence presented in the previous chapter, wherein it was documented that the Eye was described as a fire-spewing celestial body—one that presented a serpentine form and eventually came to encircle the Horus-star as a headband or crown. Inasmuch as *akhet* was one of the many names for this Eye-like enclosure, it would appear that we are close to identifying the celestial prototype for the ever-elusive *akhet*.

Certainly, it is significant that each of the aforementioned *ȝḫt*-words is employed to describe the Egyptian mother goddess—"uraeus-serpent" and "Eye," respectively. This convergence of sacred terminology confirms the fundamental affinity of the two *ȝḫt*-terms in question and suggests the possibility that the *akhet* itself originally shared an inherent relationship with the mother goddess. This, in fact, is precisely our claim: the original celestial prototype for the *akhet* was simply a fiery enclosure circumscribed around the Horus-star by the uraeus-goddess (Wadjet,

---

[298] *PT* 442.
[299] R. van der Molen, *op. cit.*, p. 7.
[300] *CT* IV:91e-k.

Ikhet, Hathor, Isis, Ernutet, etc). In this sense the *akhet* is functionally and structurally identical with the Eye-enclosure formed when the Ikhet-serpent encircled the Horus-star as recounted in Utterances 220-221 (Ikhet is simply another spelling of *akhet*).[301] Recall again the passage in question, wherein the mother goddess is addressed by a series of epithets identifying her as a fiery serpent, Red Crown, and Eye, respectively:

"He has come to you, O *Nt*-crown; he has come to you, O Fiery Serpent; he has come to you, O Great One; he has come to you, O Great of Magic, being pure for you and fearing you…He has come to you, O Great of Magic, for he is Horus encircled with the protection of his Eye, O Great of Magic…Ho, Crown great of magic! Ho Fiery Serpent! Grant that the dread of me be like the dread of you; Grant that the fear of me be like the fear of you…If Ikhet the Great has borne you, Ikhet the Serpent has adorned you; If Ikhet the Serpent has borne you, Ikhet the Great has adorned you, Because you are Horus encircled with the protection of his Eye."[302]

The archaic mythological motif identifying the mother goddess as an Eye-like enclosure housing the Horus-star—hitherto virtually unexplored[303]—represents a decisive key to the proper understanding of Egyptian religion. The same basic conception is encoded in the name of Hathor—*Hwt Hrw*—which denotes "enclosure of Horus."[304] Hathor herself, moreover, was specifically identified with the fire-spewing Eye as well as with the uraeus-serpent.

References to a Mansion of Horus in the sky evidently allude to the very same enclosure. In the Pyramid Texts the Mansion in question was represented as the ultimate goal and intended destination of the deceased

---

[301] S. Johnson, *The Cobra Goddess of Ancient Egypt* (London, 1990), p. 10: "'Ikhet' and 'Akhet' represent different vocalizations of the same word."
[302] *PT* 194-198.
[303] David Talbott's *The Saturn Myth* (New York, 1980) and assorted writings represent a notable and groundbreaking exception in this regard. See also E. Cochrane, *The Many Faces of Venus* (Ames, 2001), pp. 175-179.
[304] J. Allen, *Middle Egyptian* (Cambridge, 2010), p. 32.

king, thereby mirroring the role otherwise ascribed to the *akhet*.[305] Witness the following spell: "He shall ascend to the Mansion of Horus which is in the sky."[306] Yet the Mansion of Horus—*Ḥwt-ḥr*—as Faulkner observed in his commentary on an analogous passage in the Coffin Texts, "has to be taken here as the name of the goddess."[307]

As noted above, the Egyptian pyramids derived their numinous power precisely because they modeled or materialized the celestial *akhet* housing the Horus-star. Yet the pyramid itself, according to the Pyramid Texts, was conceptualized as the Mansion of Horus: "As for anyone who shall lay a finger on this pyramid and this temple which belong to me and my double, he will have laid his finger on the Mansion of Horus in the firmament."[308] Such explicit testimony underscores the essential identity between the Mansion of Horus and the *akhet*.

To summarize our argument in this chapter: A review of the evidence confirms that there is zero justification for the conventional view that ancient Egyptian traditions of the *akhet* point to an invisible region "just below the horizon." On the contrary, the rich and exquisitely detailed imagery associated with the *akhet* can only be properly understood by reference to a perfectly visible celestial prototype—namely, a fiery serpentine-shaped enclosure housing the Horus-star. The akhification of the Horus-star within the *akhet*, in turn, was something that happened in plain view while it was in conjunction with the mother goddess—i.e., the planet Venus. Hence, we would understand the otherwise baffling Egyptian texts which describe the god's akhification as occurring within

---

[305] R. Anthes, "The Original Meaning of *mꜣꜥ ḫrw*," *JNES* 13 (1954), p. 49 observes: "This 'house of Horus' therefore is the goal of the gods and, at the same time, of the deceased." See also S. Mercer, *op. cit.*, p. 629: "The pyramid enclosure here seems to be paralleled to the house of Horus in heaven."

[306] *PT* 1025-1026. The same idea is evident in *PT* 1327.

[307] R. Faulkner, *The Ancient Egyptian Coffin Texts, Vol. II* (Warminster, 1977), p. 300. R. Anthes, "Das Sonnenauge in den Pyramidentexten," *ZÄS* 86 (1961), p. 13 made the same point many years ago: "machen die Pyramidentexte keinen Unterschied zwischen dem 'Haus des Horus' und der Göttin Hathor; diese beiden Begriffe sind das gleiche."

[308] *PT* 1278.

a giant serpent.[309] Early illustrations which depict Horus within a serpent, the latter clearly analogized to the *akhet* (as witnessed by the god's *akhet*-shaped seat), doubtless encode the same basic idea (see figure one).[310]

Figure 1

---

[309] J. Zandee, *Der Amunhymnus des Papyrus Leiden I 344, Verso, Vol. 1* (Leiden, 1992), p. 403: "Der Prozess der Weidergeburt der Sonne ereignet sich im Innern einer riesigen Schlange." See also S. Quirke, *Going out in Daylight* (London, 2013), p. 566: "Lord of the sky, horizon-god, Horus of the East…Praise to you! As you rise in the Coiled goddess," wherein Coiled goddess is *mḥnt*.

[310] Adapted from *The Papyrus of Herytwebkhet* (Twenty-first Dynasty).

## Return to the Motherland

> "Nut personified the Elysian realm the deceased hoped to enter."[311]

> "An additional factor that has to be considered is the conception of a celestial, and in most cases, stellar, afterlife that the early texts describe."[312]

The singular and seemingly obsessive goal of the Egyptian pharaoh's postmortem journey was to ascend to the celestial Hereafter, wherein he hoped to be reunited with the mother goddess and experience akhification. Often the goal is explicitly identified as the *akhet*. Indeed, a common expression for the funerary procession was "to let the god ascend to his horizon [*akhet*]."[313]

Given the fact that there is a fundamental identity between the *akhet* and the uraeus-serpent, as documented in the previous chapter, it is hardly surprising to find Egyptian texts proclaiming that the deceased king longed to (re)unite with the uraeus-goddess. The following passage from the Pyramid Texts reflects this archaic belief:

"I have laid down for myself this sunshine of yours [i.e., of Re's] as a stairway under my feet on which I will ascend to that mother of mine, the living uraeus which should be upon me."[314]

Here, as so often in the early Egyptian texts, the deceased king's mother is identified with the uraeus-goddess (Wadjet). It is Wadjet who will suckle him and, as a result, render him as one reborn: "She will have compassion on me and will give me her breast that I may suck it."[315]

---

[311] J. Assmann, *Death and Salvation in Ancient Egypt* (Ithaca, 2005), p. 279.
[312] K. Goebs, "A Functional Approach to Egyptian Myth and Mythemes," *JANER* 2 (2002), p. 41.
[313] J. Assmann, "Death and Initiation in the Funerary Religion of Ancient Egypt," in W. Simpson ed., *Religion and Philosophy in Ancient Egypt* (New Haven, 1989), p. 137.
[314] *PT* 1108.
[315] *PT* 1115.

It scarcely needs to be pointed out that the idea of the pharaoh suckling from the teats of a serpent has no foundation in biological reality. Biology notwithstanding, the uraeus-goddess as suckler of the Pharaoh is a recurring theme in Egyptian religion and, as such, represents merely one of countless anomalies that the researcher will encounter in the earliest Egyptian texts and iconography.[316] In order to properly understand the imagery in question, it is essential to recognize that the serpentine goddess is inseparable from the Great Mother and based upon a celestial prototype—one that has long since disappeared.

The uraeus-goddess, in turn, is expressly identified with the Eye of Horus/Re. Thus it is to be expected that the Egyptian scribes would make the goal of the king's post-mortem ascent to be conjunction with the Eye itself. The following hymn is representative:

"Rise up to the Eye of Rēʿ for this name of yours which the gods made for Horus of the Netherworld, for Horus *Sksn*, for Horus […]. Raise yourself and sit on this iron throne of yours…"[317]

Although the names and symbolic forms of the goddess are many and varied, the ultimate goal of the pharaoh's post-mortem journey is always the same—to ascend to and reunite with the celestial mother goddess. As is well known, a number of the most informative passages in this regard identify the mother goddess with Nut. In the following ascension hymn from the Pyramid Texts the deceased king is identified as the "Great Star":

"(O Nut), set your hand on me with life and dominion, that you may assemble my bones and collect my members…May I ascend and lift myself up to the sky as the great star in the midst of the East."[318]

Analogous statements are to be found throughout the Pyramid and Coffin Texts. Another ascension text identifies the deceased king as "the sole star" within Nut:

---

[316] See the discussion in S. Budin, *Images of Woman and Child from the Bronze Age* (Cambridge, 2011), pp. 38-44. See also N. Billing, *Performative Structure* (Leiden, 2018), pp. 324-325.
[317] *PT* 1734.
[318] *PT* 1036-1038.

"Ho, Pepi!...You will wear the headband as the sole star in Nut's midst."[319]

The deceased king is elsewhere identified as an Imperishable Star set within Nut's body:

"O Great One [Nut], who came into being in the sky, you have achieved power, you have achieved strength, and have filled every place with your beauty...And you have set this King as an Imperishable Star who is in you."[320]

A recurring thematic pattern finds the ascending king longing to enter into Nut's embrace, wherein he will find everlasting life and *akhdom*. The following hymn is representative:

"Equip yourself as Horus, being young...Go up, open your way by means of the bones of Shu, the embrace of your mother Nut will enfold you."[321]

In an insightful analysis of Nut's role in the Pyramid Texts, Nils Billing observes that the goddess is commonly invoked as the "Great Embracer"—*ḥnmt wr*. With reference to her role in the ascension hymns quoted above, he observed: "All these passages establish Nut as the goal of the king's trajectory."[322]

As is evident from this brief sampling of passages, the express goal of the pharaoh's post-mortem ascent to heaven is to conjoin with the mother goddess. To be more specific: the deceased king longs to spend eternity *within* the body of Nut, where he will be akhified, rejuvenated (*ḥwntj*), and shine forth as a headbanded star.[323] How, apart from some witnessed

---

[319] *PT* 1048 as translated in J. Allen, *op. cit.*, p. 134. See also the Papyrus of Nebseny, circa 1375, as translated in S. Quirke, *Going out in Daylight* (London, 2013), p. 441: "He has opened his place in the midst of the stars that are at this sky. You are indeed the sole star of Nut."
[320] *PT* 782.
[321] *PT* 206-208.
[322] "Text and Tomb: Some spatial properties of Nut in the Pyramid Texts," in Z. Hawass et al eds., *Egyptology at the Dawn of the Twenty-first Century, Vol. 2* (Cairo, 2003), pp. 131-132.
[323] H. Frankfort, *Kingship and the Gods* (Chicago, 1948), p. 365 made the same point many years ago: "The king desired to enter the body of the goddess Nut in order to be

*celestial* precedent—in our view, a conjunction of planets—is it possible to understand the origin of these richly detailed and remarkably coherent traditions?[324]

Questions of origin aside, the archaic Egyptian traditions describing the celestial peregrinations of the Horus-star *in illo tempore* eventually became incorporated into funerary rituals. And so it was that the coffin—as the pharaoh's final resting place—became assimilated to Nut herself. It is Jan Assmann, perhaps, who has done more than anyone to emphasize that the goal of the pharaoh's ascent to heaven necessarily involved a reunion with the mother goddess:

"In accordance with the principle of 'transfiguration,' as the correlation of this world's symbolic objects and actions with yonder world of values and realities, the coffin becomes the body of the sky-and mother-goddess, thus enabling the 'placing of the body in the coffin' to be transfigured into the ascent of the deceased to the heavens and the return to the mother-goddess (*regressus ad uterum*). In Egypt, the sky is conceived as a female entity…The sky-goddess is the Egyptian manifestation of the Great Mother…The texts underline the indissolubility of this bond, or more precisely of the embrace into which the deceased, when laid in his coffin, enters with the sky—the mother-goddess, the goddess of the dead. The concept of rebirth, however, still plays an important role: 'I shall bear thee anew, rejuvenated,' exclaims the sky-goddess to the deceased in one of many such texts inscribed on or in nearly every coffin and tomb. 'I have spread myself over thee, I have

---

reborne by her, and there are indications (Sethe, *Komm.* 3, 11-12 and Erman IV, 566, 14) that these texts may possibly convey that the king entered the body of the mother-goddess by means of sympathetic magic, using an object which had come forth from her."

[324] The fact that the name Nut is thought to denote "oval" or ball is certainly suggestive of a planetary orb. See here J. Allen, "The Cosmology of the Pyramid Texts," in W. Simpson ed., *Religion and Philosophy in Ancient Egypt* (New Haven, 1989), pp. 16-17: "Nut's name may be identical with the word *nwt*, meaning 'ball' or 'oval,' which appears in later funerary texts. An oval, in fact, is used in place of the sky sign to determine her name in two instances in the Pyramid Texts, and in others a round sign is used in place of the *nw*-jar."

born thee again as a god.' Through this rebirth, the deceased becomes a star-god, a member of the AKH-sphere, a new entity. This rebirth, however, does not imply a delivery, a separation, but takes place inside the mother's womb, inside the coffin and the sky. The constellative relationship of the deceased and mother-goddess, as shown in the pictorial representations and texts, is interpreted and activated in the sense of affiliation and rebirth. It does not represent a transitional state, but the eternal, unalterable basis for a new and higher form of existence."[325]

Although Assmann does not attempt to explain the natural-historical origins of Nut's role as the final resting place and rejuvenator of the deceased king, it is interesting to find him referring to the "constellative relationship of the deceased and mother-goddess" for that is *exactly* what the Egyptian skywatchers were endeavoring to describe. The explicit message of the ascension hymns in the Pyramid Texts is that the deceased king (as Horus) will only find everlasting life as an Imperishable Star by returning to and conjoining with the *celestial* mother goddess. Whether known by the name of Nut, Hathor, Wadjet, or Isis, it is solely by means of the mother goddess's embrace that the deceased king will be transfigured into an *akh*. The following hymn invoking Nut is exemplary: "May you akhify this Pepi inside you, and he will not die ."[326] Here, as elsewhere, the akhification of the deceased king takes place *within* the body of Nut. (Several late illustrations, in fact, actually depict the Horus-child as residing within the mother goddess's belly, as in figure two).[327]

---

[325] J. Assmann, "Death and Initiation in the Funerary Religion of Ancient Egypt," in W. Simpson ed., *Religion and Philosophy in Ancient Egypt* (New Haven, 1989), pp. 139-140.
[326] *PT* 781 as translated in J. Allen, *The Ancient Egyptian Pyramid Texts* (Atlanta, 2005), p. 103.
[327] See the discussion in W. Waitkus, "Die Geburt des Harsomtus aus der Blüte," *Studien zur altägyptischen Kultur* 30 (2002), pp. 376ff. See also figures two and four in M. Rashed, "The Significance of the Hieroglyph [deleted] 'The Egg with the Young Bird Inside', in G. Miniaci eds., *The World of Middle Kingdom Egypt (2000-1500 BC)* (London, 2015), p. 315.

Figure 2

In short, the *mysterium conjunctionis* that stands at the very core of the Egyptian funerary traditions describing the pharaoh's post-mortem ascent to heaven is a conjunction of stars—specifically, a conjunction between a star conceptualized as masculine, alternately identified as Horus or as the "Great Star," and an even larger star conceptualized as female, alternately identified as Nut, Hathor, Isis, the uraeus-goddess, or the Eye. The male star, as we have argued, is to be identified with the planet Mars. The female star— the intended *goal* of the post-mortem journey—is to be identified with the planet Venus. To state the obvious: Egyptian funerary religion will forever remain enigmatic and inexplicable so long as Egyptologists continue to ignore the formative role of these two planets in the genesis of ancient mythological traditions.

## Horus *spd*

"[Sothis:*spdt*] The morning star, Sirius, seen by the Egyptians as a goddess. In Egypt the star disappears below the horizon once a year for a period of some seventy days; its reappearance in midsummer marked the beginning of the annual inundation and the Egyptian year. The star's rising was also seen as a harbinger of the sunrise and therefore associated with Horus in his solar aspect, occasionally specified as Horus in Sothis *(ḥrw jmj spdt)*, Sothic Horus *(ḥrw spdtj)*, or Sharp Horus *(ḥrw spd)*."[328]

"Our knowledge of ancient Egyptian astronomy relies on a variety of sources, including religious texts, funerary decorations, and building records. Matching the ancient data to the sky itself, however, is not easy…Achievements and problems in the study of ancient Egyptian astronomy may be summarized as follows: our understanding of mechanisms and notation has certainly improved over the years, but the identification of the majority of the stars mentioned in the ancient sources remains an unsolved problem. The introduction of computer-generated models that help to reconstruct the ancient sky has had a significant impact but has not produced results that have met with the general consensus. In general, it is interesting to note that a better comprehension of the ancient sources has weakened, rather than reinforced, some earlier undisputed assumptions, thus opening the way for further research."[329]

In a number of passages from the Pyramid Texts the Horus-star is equipped with the epithet *spd*. The identity of this particular star has long puzzled scholars. For Kurt Sethe and other Egyptologists, Horus *spd* is to be understood as the Sun. According to Otto Neugebauer and Richard Parker, the star in question is to be identified with Sirius. Indeed, they go so far as to claim that the matter is not open to question: "That *spd* and

---

[328] J. Allen, *The Ancient Egyptian Pyramid Texts* (Atlanta, 2005), p. 441.
[329] C. Rossi, "Science and Technology: Pharaonic," in A. Lloyd ed., *A Companion to Ancient Egyptian, Vol. 1* (Oxford, 2010), p. 394.

*spd.t* 'Sothis' are both identified with Sirius is one of the rare certainties in Egyptian astronomy."[330] Rolf Krauss and other scholars have since endorsed this opinion.[331]

The word *spd* denotes "sharp" or "to be pointed" and it is this meaning that would seem to be reflected in its determinative, which features a pointed triangular object—△.[332] The same conception is evident in the following Pyramid Text, wherein the deceased king ascends to heaven as Sopdu: "You should go forth toward them, ba as one fully born, sharp as one fully born, in your identity of Sopdu."[333]

A decisive key to understanding the original nature of Horus *spd* is his identification as the "seed" of Osiris. This motif is evident in a mythological fragment found in Utterance 366, wherein Osiris is addressed as follows:

"Your sister Isis has come to you, around [for] love of you. You have put her on your phallus so that your seed might emerge into her, sharp as Sothis, and sharp Horus has emerged from you as Horus in Sothis. You have become akh in him in his identity of the Akh in the Djenderu-Bark."[334]

As the seed of Osiris, Horus *spd* is explicitly conceptualized as masculine in nature and clearly distinguished from Sothis. Sothis/*spdt*, whose feminized name is formed from the same root *spd*, is identified as Osiris's consort. Whether identified as *spdt* or as Isis, the stellar goddess in question represents the female receptacle of Osiris's seed—i.e., Horus *spd* himself. It is our opinion that it is impossible to make sense of this

---

[330] *Egyptian Astronomical Texts I* (London, 1960), p. 25.
[331] N. Billing, *The Performative Structure* (Leiden, 2018), p. 323: "Sothis (*Spdt*) was identified with Osiris's sister Isis, whereas their son Horus could be projected on Sirius (*Spd*)."
[332] R. Hannig, *Ägyptisches Wörterbuch I* (Mainz, 2003), p. 1111 entry 27525. See also the discussion in A. Gardiner, *Egyptian Grammar* (Oxford, 1957), p. 484. According to Faulkner, the same word also came to mean "effective" or "pre-eminent."
[333] *PT* 1534 as translated in J. Allen, *The Ancient Egyptian Pyramid Texts* (Atlanta, 2005), p. 184.
[334] *PT* 632-633 as translated in J. Allen, *op. cit.*, pp. 81-82.

passage or of the numerous other references to Horus *spd* in the Pyramid Texts without first recognizing the fact that the names *spd* and *spdt* denote two entirely different stars, one conceptualized as masculine and the other as feminine in nature. We thus arrive at the following equations:

*spd*=Horus=masculine seed of Osiris.

*spdt*=Isis=female receptacle of Osiris's seed=enclosure of Horus *spd*.

The crux presented by *PT* 632 has generated a good deal of discussion and speculation. Rudolf Anthes's analysis of this particular spell is particularly confused: He would identify "Horus who is in Sothis" as the star Sirius because of the reference to *spdt*, which he would understand as Sothis/Sirius. *Spd*, in turn, he would understand as an epithet of Horus but one devoid of any reference to a star apart from its relationship to Sothis/Sirius. Of Horus Sopd, Anthes writes: "We understand it with Sethe as 'the top Horus,' whatever the significance of *spd* as an adjective may be."[335]

Anthes's hypothesis, amazingly, ignores the clear distinction between Horus *spd* and Isis *spdt*. The latter celestial body, as noted above, is always female in nature and embodies the womb or receptacle within which Horus *spd* is implanted. The deceased king, on the other hand, is consistently identified with Horus *spd*—not *spdt*—and therefore the myth of his ascent to heaven implies that Horus *spd* represents an independent star prior to its interaction or conjunction with Isis/*spdt*. By ignoring the possibility that Horus *spd* had a stellar dimension apart from his relationship to *spdt*, Anthes drew the erroneous conclusion that he, too, was to be identified with Sirius.

In order to clarify the manifold issues involved here it is instructive to examine the various attestations of *spd* in the earliest Egyptian texts. This exercise, in turn, will require that we review the mythological traditions surrounding Horus.

---

[335] R. Anthes, "Horus als Sirius in den Pyramidentexten," *ZÄS* 102 (1975), p. 4.

Horus's identification with the divine seed is a recurring theme in Egyptian religious tradition. This conception is alluded to in the following passage from the Pyramid Texts, wherein the deceased king is identified as Horus:

"Pepi your seed, Osiris, which is sharp in your identity, (O seed), of Horus in the Great Green, Horus at the fore of the akhs."[336]

As the "seed" of Osiris, Horus appears in the very role ascribed to Horus *spd* in *PT* 632=1636. Indeed, the word translated as "sharp" here is *spd.t(y)*, a patent reference to *spd* as the (sharp) seed of Osiris. Most important, however, is the fact that the spell in question leaves no doubt about Horus's stellar nature in his role as the divine seed:

"Pepi is your seed, Sun, which is sharp in your identity, (O seed), of Horus at the fore of the akhs, the star which crosses the Great Green."[337]

In addition to identifying the deceased king as the divine seed—here Re has been substituted for Osiris—this passage unequivocally identifies the seed in question as Horus and as a star to boot. This testimony supports our deduction, stated above, that the divine seed—as Horus *spd*—is to be distinguished from *spdt*.[338]

The express purpose of the Pyramid Texts, it will be remembered, was to aid the deceased king in making his way to the celestial Hereafter. Upon reaching heaven, the Egyptian pharaoh hoped to become transfigured into an *akh* and join the Imperishable Stars. In the following hymn the deceased king is identified as an *akh*—translated here as "spirit":

"Raise yourself, King…being a spirit at the head of the spirits…that you may have a soul thereby, that you may be effective thereby, that you may be powerful thereby…O King, you are a spirit and your survivor is a spirit."[339]

---

[336] *PT* 1505 as translated in J. Allen, *The Ancient Egyptian Pyramid Texts* (Atlanta, 2005), p. 182.
[337] *PT* 1508-1509 as translated in *Ibid.*, p. 182.
[338] See also R. Krauss, *Astronomische Konzepte und Jenseitsvorstellungen in den Pyramidentexten* (Wiesbaden, 1997), p. 161, who offers a similar interpretation.
[339] *PT* 859.

The pharaoh here receives the epithet "at the head of the spirits," an epithet otherwise associated with Horus (in *PT* 1505 and 1508 above and elsewhere). This epithet implies that the deceased king was identified with Horus. Equally noteworthy is the fact that the king is described as *spd*, sharp or "effective," a likely reference to the stellar form Horus *spd*.

Allusions to the same mythological theme are evident elsewhere in the Pyramid Texts as well. In the following passage the deceased king—as Horus—is identified with a star:

"Unis is a great one: Unis has emerged from the Ennead's thighs. Unis has been conceived by Sekhmet, and Shezmetet is the one who gave birth to Unis, a star with sharp front and extreme goings, who fetches what the above has for the Sun every day."[340]

The phrase as "sharp front" by Allen and "brilliant" by Faulkner is *spd ḥȝt*—unequivocal evidence that a star characterized as *spd* was deemed to be the celestial prototype or counterpart of the deceased king.[341] The clear import of this passage, in our opinion, is that the deceased king was identified with the star otherwise denoted as Horus *spd*.

---

[340] *PT* 262-263 as translated in J. Allen, *op. cit.*, p. 42.
[341] So S. Mercer, *op. cit.*, p. 121: "The deceased king is born anew from between the thighs of the Ennead…The star with the piercing front (*spd ḥȝ.t*) may be compared with the star in 537a, with uplifted brow, and with the crocodile-god with vigilant countenance in 507b, all referring to the deceased king, newborn."

## Spd Wr

A number of spells describe the pharaoh's post-mortem journey and ensuing transfiguration as an occasion of great tumult and danger, distinguished by a disturbance of the stars and the shaking of heaven and earth (see chapter three). One of the most important texts in this regard would compare (or identify) the ascending king with a stellar form denoted as *Spd-wr:*

"Geb will laugh, Nut will chuckle, before him as Pepi goes up to the sky. The sky will shout for him, the earth will shake for him…He will become sharp as the great sharp one and go forward to the fore of the Dual Shrines."[342]

In the guise of *Spd-wr*—literally "the great sharp one"[343]—the deceased pharaoh assumes rule at the front or head (*ḫnt*) of the Two Conclaves, thereby recalling the enthroning of the king in the passage above (*PT* 262-3). The fact that the king in *PT* 262 was expressly compared to an *spd*-Star can scarcely be a coincidence.

In his notes with regards to this passage, Faulkner does not even mention *Spd-wr*, much less seek to explain its significance therein. Nor did *Spd-wr* receive any mention in Faulkner's comprehensive survey of Egyptian star-religion.[344]

Anthes's discussion of this passage is equally indifferent. Indeed, the renowned Egyptologist goes so far as to deny that *Spd-wr* has any reference to a star at all:

"The fact that *spd wr* seems to have survived in the Edfu-temple probably does not help us any further. I can only understand *spd wr* as 'the great top,' whatever that may mean, and see no indication that it is a star."[345]

---

[342] *PT* 1149-1159 as translated in J. Allen, *op. cit*, pp. 153-154.
[343] So translated by James Allen, *op. cit.*, p. 154.
[344] R. Faulkner, "The King and the Star Religion in the Pyramid Texts," *JNES* 25 (1966), pp. 153-161.
[345] R. Anthes, *op. cit.*, p. 3.

Contrary to Anthes's opinion, the testimony of the Edfu texts is decisive here. Witness the following passage: "Words to speak to Sopdu, the great Sopdu in the house of the Sycamore, Behedeti, the great god, the multicolored-feathered one...whose rays illuminate both lands."[346] Here *Spd-wr* is identified as Sopdu and as Horus Behedeti, both of whom were clearly conceptualized as stars.

Much more helpful and in harmony with the evidence is the analysis offered by Samuel Mercer; he would understand *Spd-wr* as a reference to the archaic war-god Sopdu:

"The word s*pd* is 'to be sharp'; ...The 'great *spd*' is most likely the god Sopdu, a warlike god, Asiatic in type, and worshipped as 'smiter of the Asiatics.'...There is a play on words between *spd*, 'sharp' and *spdw*, 'Sopdu'."[347]

Understanding *Spd-wr* here as a pseudonym for Sopdu makes perfect sense given the deceased king's fundamental affinity with Horus *spd*.[348] The passage in question, after all, has to do with the pharaoh's post-mortem ascent to heaven, an event known to involve him in a stellar capacity (often as Horus). Indeed, in the analogous passage in Utterance 248, quoted above, the deceased king is explicitly identified as the *spd*-star. Anthes rejected Mercer's obvious solution, claiming that there was no evidence for Sopdu's cult as early as the building of the pyramids, but this claim is demonstrably false (A funerary text from the mortuary temple of Unis at Saqqara states: "Soped wishes that Unas may live").[349] Indeed,

---

[346] 162, 2-3 as translated in D. Kurth, *Edfou VII: Übersetzungen* (Wiesbaden, 2004), p. 292: Worte zu sprechen von Sopdu, dem Soped-ur im Haus-der-Sycamore, Behedeti, dem groSen Gott, dem Buntegefiederten...dessen Strahlen die Beiden Länder erleuchtet." Translation by the author.
[347] S. Mercer, *The Pyramid Texts in Translation and Commentary, Vol. 3* (New York, 1952), p. 571.
[348] Inke Schumacher offers a similar opinion in *Der Gott Sopdu der Herr der Fremdländer* (Göttingen, 1988), pp. 48, 317.
[349] Quoted from R. Giveon, "Soped in Sinai," *Festschrift für Westendorf, Vol. 2* (Göttingen, 1984), p. 782.

the god's cult is attested already during the First Dynasty reign of Semerkhet.[350]

By now a recurring thematic pattern should be evident: The deceased king, as a star, journeys to heaven in order to claim his rightful throne. In multiple passages that star is explicitly identified as *spd* or Horus *spd*. The star in question, moreover, is clearly and consistently distinguished from Sothis.

Other passages also point to a clear distinction between *spd* and Sothis in the earliest sources. Especially relevant here is the following ascension text from the Pyramid Texts (Utterance 302):

"The sky has been bled, the Sharp Star lives, for I am the living one, Sothis's son. The Dual Ennead have become clean for me as Striker, an imperishable star."[351]

As the "living one, Sothis's son," we would recognize a reference to the star *spd*. Faulkner acknowledges that this epithet has reference to a star, although he does not mention *spd* by name nor comment on the difficulties in translating this passage.[352] Anthes, meanwhile, observes that Unis's Pyramid (W) contains a variant text wherein the living one is identified as *spd*: "W on the other hand clearly shows that NN is the *spd*-Star as the living one, the son of Sothis, who has become visible in the morning sky."[353]

The variant text preserved in Unis's pyramid is instructive insofar as it serves to bolster the hypothesis that the *spd*-star, as Horus *spd*, was conceptualized as the stellar avatar of the deceased king. And as Sothis's son the masculine *spd*-star is explicitly distinguished from Sothis.

---

[350] T. Wilkinson, *Early Dynastic Egypt* (London, 1999), p. 296. See also I. Schumacher, *op. cit.*, pp. 4-52; R. Giveon, "Sopdu," *Lexikon der Ägyptologie* 5 (Wiesbaden, 1984), cols. 1107-1110.

[351] *PT* 458-459 as translated in J. Allen, *Grammar of the Ancient Egyptian Pyramid Texts, Volume 1: Unis* (Winona Lake, 2017), p. 351.

[352] R. Faulkner, *Ancient Egyptian Pyramid Texts* (Oxford, 1969), p. 92 footnote 3.

[353] R. Anthes, *op. cit.*, p. 1.

Granted that the pharaoh ascends to heaven as Horus *spd*, how are we to reconcile this testimony with other passages that identify the deceased king with the Morning Star (*Nṯr-dwꜣj*)? The conventional view is that such seemingly contradictory traditions reflect a conflation of originally distinct conceptions about the precise stellar identification of the deceased king. Such is the view expressed by Anthes, for example, who sought to identify Horus *spd* with Sirius: "Still, the star is apparently not in all cases the same heavenly body, but very often it is identified with the Morning Star..."[354]

It is our opinion that there is a more logical and economical solution to the matter. Indeed, we would interpret *Nṯr-dwꜣj* "Morning Star" and *spd* as simply different epithets for the same celestial body—namely, the planet Mars. Thus, we would understand the respective traditions surrounding *spd* and "Morning Star" as analogous and complementary in nature and reject the thesis that there was a "conflation" of originally independent and contradictory views with respect to the identity of Horus's star.

There are several different lines of circumstantial evidence that support this deduction.[355] Certainly it is significant to find that the Egyptian scribes substituted Horus *spd* for Horus Duat within the Pyramid Texts. In *PT* 331a, for example, the name Horus *spd* replaces Horus Duat. If nothing else, this substitution hints at a fundamental affinity between Horus *spd* and Horus Duat. Thomas Allen entertained the same possibility many years ago:

"*Ḥr spd* and *ymy Dwꜣ.t* in vocative have interchanged places in W and T texts of 330 and 331. Are they identified?"[356]

If Horus *spd* and Horus Duat were simply different names for the same stellar body the apparent discrepancy between these two variant passages disappears. Yet once admit this possibility and it becomes extremely

---

[354] *Ibid.*, p. 10.
[355] R. Krauss, *op. cit.*, pp. 93 and 288 raised the same possibility.
[356] T. Allen, *Horus in the Pyramid Texts* (Chicago, 1916), p. 30.

difficult to avoid the conclusion that Horus *spd* is to be identified with the Morning Star in light of the fact that Horus Duat is identified with *Neter Dwɜ* in *PT* 1207.

The same conclusion is supported by the fact that both star-gods are placed in close proximity to a celestial ship. Thus, *PT* 1637 describes Horus *spd* as follows: "Ḥar-Sopd has issued from you in his name of 'Horus who is in Sothis'; you have power through him in his name of 'Spirit who is in the *Dndrw*-bark'."[357] Of Horus Duat, similarly, we read that he was identified as the Morning Star and positioned in front of a giant celestial boat:

"O Morning Star, Horus of the Netherworld, divine Falcon, *wɜdɜd*-bird whom the sky bore…give me these your two fingers which you gave to the Beautiful, the daughter of the great god, when the sky was separated from the earth, when the gods ascended to the sky, you having a soul and appearing in front of your boat of 770 cubits which the gods of Pe bound together for you, which the eastern gods built for you."[358]

The fact that *spd* is expressly identified with the obscure ocular god *Dwɜw* in *PT* 480 and *PT* 994b is also relevant here.[359] In the former passage the deceased king is invoked as follows: "The Fields of Rushes worship you in this your name of *Dwɜw* as Sopd who is under his *ksbt*-trees." Here *Sopdu-Dwɜw* is seemingly localized either within or in close proximity to the Fields of Rushes. Yet the Field of Rushes is identified as the dwelling-place of the Morning Star in *PT* 1719:

"Rēꜥ summons you into the zenith(?) of the sky as the Jackal, the Governor of the Two Enneads, and as Horus *Ḫnty-mnit-f*; may he set you as the Morning Star in the midst of the Field of Rushes."[360]

---

[357] *PT* 1637. See also *PT* 633, where the same statement is repeated.
[358] *PT* 1207-1210.
[359] See the discussion in S. Mercer, *op. cit.*, p. 214.
[360] *PT* 1719.

The name *Dwꜣw*, like *Nṯr Dwꜣ*, means "of the morning"[361]—both names being written with a star-determinative. The fact that these two gods were identified with the deceased king (as Horus) and clearly conceptualized as a star in the "morning sky" would appear to argue for their fundamental affinity and probable identity.[362]

The star-god *ḥd-tꜣ*, mentioned in several obscure spells in the Coffin Texts, is also of interest here. Although precious little is known regarding this particular god, it is significant to find him described as the "son of Sothis" in Spell 760. The passage in question reads as follows:

"My mother is Sothis, and she prepares my path, she sets up a stairway to this very great plain of Nenmut for my ascent from the Valley of the Mountain of the *Seḥseḥ*-bird on the north within my river-banks, at the place whence Orion issues."[363]

The name of the god, according to Faulkner and Krauss, denotes "He of the Dawn."[364] Krauss, together with Goebs, would identify *ḥd-tꜣ* with the morning star.[365] That this is the correct interpretation is bolstered by the fact that *ḥd-tꜣ* elsewhere appears at the bow of Re's boat—i.e., in the very position assumed by Horus Duat as the Morning Star.[366] Granted that this particular "son of Sothis" can be identified with the Morning Star—and we concur with Krauss and Goebs on this matter—it is difficult to deny the deduction that Horus *spd*—expressly identified as the "son of Sothis" in PT 458—is likewise to be identified with the Egyptian Morning Star.

To summarize our findings in this chapter: A wealth of evidence suggests that by Horus *spd* the ancient Egyptians were describing the star

---

[361] E. Otto, "Dua," and "Duai," in W. Helck ed., *Lexikon der Ägyptologie I* (Wiesbaden, 1975), cols. 1147-1148.
[362] I offered much the same argument in "Sothis and the Morning Star," *Aeon* 3:5 (1994), pp. 77-94.
[363] *CT* V:389.
[364] R. van der Molen, *op. cit.*, p. 369 translates the name as "dawn-god."
[365] R. Krauss, *op. cit.*, p. 288.
[366] See here *CT* VI:349, wherein one reads: "*ḥd-tꜣ…jmj ḥꜣt wjꜣ Rꜥw.*"

known elsewhere as Horus Duat. The star-god Horus Duat, in turn, was explicitly identified with the Morning Star by the authors of the Pyramid Texts. Insofar as Horus Duat—as the prototypical "Morning Star"—is to be identified with the planet Mars, it follows that Horus *spd* likewise had reference to the red planet. This identification will prove to have profound and far-reaching ramifications when we turn to consider the celestial identification of Sothis in the next chapter.

# Sothis, Sirius, and the Astronomical Foundations of Egyptian Chronology

> "Isis owes her cosmic aspect to her early identification with Sothis (=Sirius), the star announcing the annual inundation."[367]

> "The surviving records of observations of the heliacal rising of the dog-star Sirius serve both as the linchpin of the reconstruction of the Egyptian calendar and its essential link with the chronology as a whole."[368]

> "Whether we like it or not, the chronology of the second millennium B.C.E. found in every handbook is Sothic."[369]

There is a general consensus among Egyptologists that the ancient Egyptians were preoccupied with the observation and veneration of the star Sirius already at the dawn of history. According to Richard Parker, author of the vastly influential study *The Calendars of Ancient Egypt*, a sophisticated calendar organized around careful observations of Sirius was already in place by 3100 BCE.[370] Inasmuch as Parker's thesis has dominated Egyptology for the past 60 years and launched hundreds of studies in the meantime, a lengthy quote will be offered to give the reader some idea of the nature of his views:

> "The earliest calendar of which we have any record in Egypt was one based on the moon and the star Sirius, the brightest star in the sky, called by the Egyptians Sothis. In the ages before this historical calendar…we suppose with great probability that primitive man in Egypt, as elsewhere,

---

[367] J. Assmann, "Isis," in K. van der Toorn et al, *Dictionary of Deities and Demons in the Bible* (Leiden, 1995), col. 856.

[368] I. Shaw, "Introduction: Chronologies and Cultural Change in Egypt," in I. Shaw ed., *The Oxford History of Ancient Egypt* (Oxford, 2000), p. 10.

[369] L. Depuydt, "Sothic Chronology and Old Kingdom," *Journal of the American Research Center in Egypt* 37 (2000), p. 171.

[370] J. Belmonte and J. Lull, *Astronomy of Ancient Egypt* (Cham, 2023), p. 308 observe that "Richard Parker's *Calendars* has reigned supreme in the view of a majority of scholars as the last word on Egyptian calendrical matters."

had counted time in days and lunar months and had become aware of the rhythm of the seasons with the inundation of the river valley through the rise of the Nile followed by its subsidence, then the time of planting and growth followed by harvest and low water until once again the Nile began to rise and overflow its banks. Gradually primitive man would come to associate some four lunar months with the period of inundation, four more with the season of growth, and four more with harvest and low water. He would also come to notice that the heliacal rising of Sirius (that is, its reappearance in the eastern horizon just before sunrise after it had been invisible for some seventy days because of its proximity to the sun) took place just about the time the Nile began to rise so that he would regard the reappearance of the star as the herald of the inundation. No later than the first dynasty of Egypt (ca. 3100 B. C.) and possibly earlier, all these observations had resulted in the formulation of a well organized and regulated luni-stellar calendar which was kept in place in the seasons by the addition to the year of a thirteenth month when necessary, since twelve lunar months total on the average 354 days. The first lunar month after the heliacal rising of Sirius began the Egyptian year and the year was kept in place by regulating it in such a way that the day and festival of this rising always fell in the last month. Whenever the festival occurred in the last eleven days of the twelfth month, the following year had thirteen months, the first of which was an intercalary one. In this way the year maintained a good relation to the seasons, and these were considered as three of four months each."[371]

As postulated by Parker and generally accepted by most Egyptologists, Sirius's alleged prominence in Egyptian calendrical practices stemmed from the fact that its heliacal rising in July coincided roughly with the annual flooding of the Nile. Insofar as the Egyptian "year" was supposedly timed to mark the annual inundation of the Nile,

---

[371] R. Parker, "The Year in Ancient Egypt," *Journal of Calendar Reform* 25 (1955), p. 81.

Sirius's role as a harbinger of the flood led it to be conceptualized as the star of the New Year.[372]

How, then, did Sirius come to play such an important role in ancient chronology? As is evident from Shaw's quotation at the beginning of the present chapter, Sirius's celebrated status in this regard stems from the fact that scholars have long held out the hope that retrocalculating ancient Sirius observations might provide an accurate means by which to date the different Egyptian dynasties and thereby facilitate the synchronization of the respective chronologies of the ancient Near East (it is commonly agreed that Egyptian chronology forms the linchpin connecting the chronologies of the surrounding regions).[373] James Allen recently offered a succinct summary:

"The Egyptians were avid astronomers, and they kept careful records of their observations of the sun and the stars. One of the more important annual events they noted is called the rising of Sothis (*spdt*, the Egyptian name of the star we call Sirius). Sirius is visible in the Egyptian night sky for most of the year, but during a period of about seventy days in late spring it does not rise above the horizon; then, in mid-July, it reappears above the horizon just before sunrise. This reappearance of Sirius corresponded to the start of the annual inundation of the Nile, and marked the beginning of the year in ancient Egypt.

Ideally, the rising of Sothis should have occurred on 1 Inundation 1, which was the first day of the Egyptian civil calendar. Because that calendar moved backward by one day every four years, however, the rising of Sothis also fell a calendar day earlier every four years. For four years the rising of Sothis might be observed on 1 Inundation 1, but during

---

[372] A. Badawy, "The Stellar Destiny of Pharaoh and the So-Called Air-Shafts of Cheops' Pyramid," *MIO* 10 (1964), p. 203 writes: "Sothis is 'the soul of Isis', whose rising at dawn determined the beginning of the agricultural year with the start of the inundation."

[373] L. Depuydt, "Ancient Chronology's Alpha and Egyptian Chronology's Debt to Babylon," in M. Ross ed., *From the Banks of the Euphrates* (Winona Lake, 2008), p. 35.

the next four years it would fall on Epagomenal Day 5 (the last day of the Egyptian calendar), then on Epagomenal Day 4 for four years, and so forth. It took about 1453 years for the cycle to come full circle; Egyptologists call this span of time the 'Sothic Cycle.' From an observation made in late antiquity, we know that the rising of Sothis actually did occur on 1 Inundation 1 during the four-year period AD 136-139. Calculating backward by the Sothic Cycle, we can determine that it also fell on 1 Inundation 1 during the four-year period from 1320-1317 BC and again in 2774-2771 BC.

If a text records the rising of Sothis on a particular date of the Egyptian calendar in a king's regnal year, it is then a simple matter to calculate the actual date BC of this event (within four years) against these three fixed four-year periods. For pharaonic history there are only three such historical records. Two of these include the regnal year of a king as well as the month and day: on 2 Harvest 1 in Year 9 of Ptolemy III, and on 4 Growing 16 in Year 7 of Senwosret III. The first of these is 94 days before 1 Inundation 1: this dates Year 9 of Ptolemy III to the period between 240 and 237 BC…The second is 140 days before 1 Inundation 1, and places Year 7 of Senwosret III about 1876-1873 BC…Using these dates and other sources, Egyptologists are able to calculate the regnal years of most other Egyptian kings in terms of actual years BC."[374]

Truth be told, however, matters are hardly as clearcut and straightforward as Allen would have his readers believe. In fact, there is no credible evidence that the Egyptians of the Old Kingdom period "kept careful records of their observations of the sun and the stars." Certainly no such records have survived. Indeed, in the thousands of spells from the Pyramid and Coffin Texts describing the sun and stars there isn't a single statement to be found that can be described as a "careful record of observation" (when viewed from the standpoint of modern astronomical science, that is). Otto Neugebauer readily conceded the point: "The only

---

[374] J. Allen, *Middle Egyptian* (Cambridge, 2010), pp. 110-111.

available old-Egyptian astronomical sources are of purely mythological character; only the discovery of an hieratic papyrus could bring new light here."[375]

Indeed, it is highly misleading to speak of "Egyptian astronomy" at all prior to the New Kingdom period. Egyptian astronomy, such as it is, was mostly borrowed second-hand from the Greeks and Babylonians.[376] It is true that there are a number of funerary monuments and coffin lids from the First Intermediate Period and Middle Kingdom that depict various stellar configurations and so-called star clocks, but these monuments have proven notoriously difficult to interpret and hardly testify to sophisticated astronomical practices or a "careful record of observation."[377] Otto Neugebauer, famously, pointed to the "extreme inaccuracy of all aspects of Egyptian astronomy."[378] Parker himself conceded that, during the entire 3000 years of Egyptian history, "there is nothing approaching an astronomical treatise, such as those known from Babylonia, where the movements of the celestial bodies were studied and recorded."[379] Yet a Sothic Calendar of the sophistication imagined by Parker and accepted by so many Egyptologists would seem to require a long and unbroken history of "careful records of observation" extending back well into the third millennium BCE—i.e., some two thousand years before there were any such records in ancient Mesopotamia, the original

---

[375] O. Neugebauer, "Egyptian Planetary Texts," *Transactions of the American Philosophical Society* 32 (1942), p. 236.
[376] G. de Young, "Egyptian astronomy," in H. Selin ed., *Encyclopaedia of the History of Science, Technology and Medicine in Non-Western Cultures* (Norwell, 1997), p. 111: "We have few written records dealing with the heavens, and those that we have are derived from the Greek astronomical tradition and therefore are very late in Egyptian history."
[377] Of the constellations depicted on Senmut's ceiling, Richard Parker, "Egyptian astronomy, astrology, and calendrical reckoning," in C. Gillispie ed., *Dictionary of Scientific Biography, Vol. 16* (New York, 1971-1980), p. 718 observes: "It is just such variations as these, in inclusion or omission of constellations or in their positions relative to one another, that make any attempt at identification of the constellations other than the Big Dipper a hazardous one."
[378] O. Neugebauer, *A History of Ancient Mathematical Astronomy, Vol. 2* (Berlin, 1975), p. 561.
[379] R. Parker, *op. cit.*, p. 706.

homeland of scientific astronomy and the systematic observation of the stars.

The history and relative sophistication of Egyptian astronomy aside, it goes without saying that any and all such attempts to date ancient Egyptian civilization by means of a hypothetical Sothic calendar are entirely dependent upon securely identifying the celestial referent of the star known as Sothis. How confident can we be, then, that the ancient Egyptian skywatchers had Sirius in mind when employing the term *spdt* (the Egyptian word conventionally translated as Sothis)?

For modern Egyptologists there can be no doubt on the matter. With respect to the supposed references to this star in the Pyramid Texts, the astronomer Robert Briggs said that "the identification of the goddess *Spd.t*, Greek Sothis, with the star we call Sirius, is the only one in these texts which is unquestioned."[380] Neugebauer and Parker offered a similar assessment in their monumental compendium of Egyptian astronomy: "That *Spd* and *Spdt* 'Sothis' are both identified with Sirius is one of the rare certainties in Egyptian astronomy."[381] A recent and comprehensive summary of the evidence by Rolf Krauss includes the following pronouncement: "Die Identität von *Spdt*-Sothis mit Sirius (α canis maioris) ist durch eine lange Traditionskette von den PT [Pyramid Texts] bis zu den astrologischen Texten und astronomischen Darstellungen der griechisch-römischen Zeit gesichert."[382] Inasmuch as we have reason to dispute such claims, it is necessary to review the evidence bearing on the matter.

In the analysis to follow, we will focus primarily on the earliest documentary evidence—i.e., that to be found in the Pyramid Texts. The reason for this choice is twofold: (1) the conventional hypothesis holds

---

[380] R. Briggs, "Astronomy," in S. Mercer, *The Pyramid Texts, Vol. IV* (New York, 1952), p. 44.
[381] O. Neugebauer & R. Parker, *Egyptian Astronomical Texts I: The Early Decans* (London, 1960), p. 25.
[382] R. Krauss, *Astronomische Konzepte und Jenseitsvorstellungen in den Pyramidentexten* (Wiesbaden, 1997), p. 146.

that a Sirius-based calendar was already in effect by the early part of the third millennium BCE at least (Krauss would date it to the 28th century BCE[383]), and thus the abundant references to *spdt* and neighboring stars in the Pyramid Texts should support this claim; (2) in order to accurately reconstruct the archaic Egyptian conceptions regarding Sothis and/or Sirius before the intrusion of later extraneous influences which might distort or unduly complicate the situation—Greek astronomical practices, for example, or religious syncretism—it stands to reason that the earliest evidence should be given precedence.

At the outset of our analysis it is necessary to ask: In the absence of any early astronomical texts documenting systematic observations of the heliacal risings of Sirius, upon what factual basis has *spdt* been identified with Sirius? A survey of the vast literature on the subject reveals the following reasons for the identification in question: (1) supposed references in the Pyramid Texts alluding to Sothis's role as a herald of the New Year; (2) supposed references in the Pyramid Texts and elsewhere to Sothis's association with the annual flooding of the Nile; (3) certain passages in the Pyramid Texts which speak of an intimate relation between Sothis and a stellar entity *Sꜣḥ*, the latter conventionally identified with the constellation Orion (the fact that Orion stands in the southern sky like Sirius is commonly thought to support Sothis's identification with the latter star).[384] We will examine each of these arguments in turn.

A number of scholars have claimed to discern an association between Sothis and the New Year in the *Pyramid Texts*. Joachim von Beckerath, for example, writes as if the fact were well-established: "Die Sothis als Bringerin des Jahres und der Tag ihres Frühaufgang als idealer Neujahrstag werden durch zahlreiche Texte bezeugt, zuerst in den

---

[383] R. Krauss, "Egyptian Sirius/Sothic Dates, and the Question of the Sothis-Based Lunar Calendar," in E. Hornung, R. Krauss, & D. Warburton eds., *Ancient Egyptian Chronology* (Leiden, 2006), p. 440.
[384] R. Krauss, *Astronomische Konzepte und Jenseitsvorstellungen in den Pyramidentexten* (Wiesbaden, 1997), pp. 146, 183, 197. This identification goes back to Champollion.

Pyramiden, doch lässt sich nicht sagen, wie alt der betreffende, erstmals bei Phiops I belegte Spruch (Pyr. 965a) ist."[385] In fact, there are but two passages in the Pyramid Texts that even mention the year (*rnpt*) in conjunction with Sothis and they do nothing to substantiate von Beckerath's claim. PT 965, for example, reads as follows: "It is Sothis your beloved daughter who prepares your yearly sustenance in this her name of 'Year' and who guides me when I come to you." Aside from the fact that the epithet *rnpt*, "year," is here applied to Sothis, it is difficult to point to anything that even remotely hints at New Year's rituals, much less to careful astronomical observations or sophisticated calendrical practices.[386]

PT 883 contains a similarly obscure reference to the year: "The sky has borne you [the king as a great star] with Orion, the year has put a fillet on you with Osiris…" As is evident at once, this particular passage—like 965—is sorely lacking in any information that could reasonably be interpreted as a reference to Sirius's heliacal rising and, as such, questions must remain as to the original significance of the appellation "year" (we will offer an extensive analysis of this particular passage below).

Apart from these two references to a goddess known as "Year," very few passages from the Pyramid Texts have even been claimed to have reference to Sirius's heliacal rising at the time of the New Year. Raymond Faulkner cited the following passage as likely alluding to the heliacal rising of Sirius: "The sky is pregnant of wine, Nut has given birth to her daughter the dawn-light, and I raise myself; indeed, my third is Sothis, pure of seats."[387] Yet here, too, it is difficult to recognize an unequivocal reference to the heliacal rising of Sirius. Rather, we seem to be presented with little more than an inference on Faulkner's part, one owing more to that scholar's preconceptions than to a critical analysis of the evidence.

---

[385] J. von Beckerath, "Bemerkungen zum ägyptischen Kalender," *ZÄS* 120 (1993), p. 10.
[386] J. Belmonte and J. Lull, *Astronomy of Ancient Egypt* (Cham, 2023), p. 351 admit that "the direct calendrical meaning is not obvious."
[387] *PT* 1082. R. Faulkner, *op. cit.*, p. 159.

It is certainly true that, at a much later period in Egyptian history, Sothis was considered to have a close connection to the beginning of the New Year, known as *wpt rnpt*. So far as I'm aware, the earliest attested evidence of such a connection in Egyptian literature occurs in the Ebers papyrus from circa 1500 BCE.[388] The Canopus Decree (ca. 239 BCE) offers a clear statement of this traditional belief: "On the day on which the star of Isis rises, which is reckoned in the sacred writings to be the new year."[389] Yet in the absence of similar testimony from the earlier Old Kingdom period, projecting a connection between Sirius and the opening of the calendrical year back to some 500 years before the Pyramid Texts is hardly justified or methodologically sound. I thus find myself in agreement with Anthony Spalinger who, in a discussion of Sirius's possible role in the generation of the ancient Egyptian calendar, offered the following assessment:

"This perspective must remain somewhat debatable although there is little doubt that the star's importance—at least in religious texts—becomes more and more significant in the inscriptions and scenes from the New Kingdom onwards. Data from the Graeco-Roman temples with respect to Sothis must be used with caution as such material does not automatically extend back to earlier periods of time."[390]

Even more problematic are the supposed Old Kingdom references to *spdt*'s connection with the flooding of the Nile. László Kákosy, for example, offered the following summary of the mythology surrounding Sothis:

---

[388] S. Stern, *Calendars in Antiquity* (Oxford, 2012), p. 149: "The Ebers calendar is in fact the earliest source that associates the rise of Sothis with the New Year." See also L. Depuydt, "The Function of the Ebers Calendar Concordance," *Orientalia* 65 (1996), pp. 61-88.

[389] As translated in R. Bagnall & P. Dero eds., *The Hellenistic Period* (Oxford, 2004), p. 266. See also the discussion in J. Belmonte and J. Lull, *Astronomy of Ancient Egypt* (Cham, 2023), pp. 350-351.

[390] A. Spalinger, "Notes on the ancient Egyptian calendars," *Orientalia* 64 (1995), p. 28.

"The flood [of the Nile] was considered as a gift of the goddess, whose appearance [heliacal rise] also initiated a New Year. Already in the Pyramid Texts the goddess was characterized as 'Year'. The connection with the year and the flooding of the Nile remains the outstanding characteristic of Sothis."[391]

Yet on this question the evidence is unequivocal: An association between *spdt*/Sothis and the flooding of the Nile is nowhere to be found in the Pyramid Texts. Inasmuch as the coincidence between Sirius's heliacal rising and the annual inundation of the Nile was the single most noteworthy feature of this star's appearance, emphasized by the Greeks[392] and cited by numerous historians as providing the original empirical basis for the development of a hypothetical Egyptian Sothic-calendar, the absence of *any* testimony on this score in the Pyramid Texts—wherein *spdt* figures prominently and is mentioned in numerous different contexts—must give us some grounds for caution when considering the conventional identification of *spdt* with Sirius.

Equally damning for the conventional hypothesis linking Sirius to the annual inundation of the Nile is the fact that the heliacal rising of the star did not coincide with the inundation during the all-important third millennium—the millennium in which, according to Parker and other Egyptologists—the link between the calendar and the star first became established. Witness the following disclaimer offered by Sacha Stern:

"It is only in the second millennium that Sothis proceeded to the season of the inundation and rose at the beginning of it" (in earlier times it "*preceded* the beginning of inundation in upper Egypt by some days")."[393]

---

[391] L. Kákosy, "Sothis," *Lexikon der Ägyptologie, Vol. 5* (Wiesbaden, 1984), p. 1110. Translation by author.

[392] Plutarch, *De Isid.* 38. J. Quack, "A Goddess Rising 10,000 Cubits into the Air," in J. Steele & A. Imhausen, *Under One Sky* (Münster, 2002), p. 286 speaks of the "intimate connection between the heliacal rising of Sirius and the beginning of the inundation."

[393] S. Stern, *Calendars in Antiquity* (Oxford, 2012), p. 133.

As for the supposed references to Orion in the Pyramid Texts here, too, the evidence does not inspire confidence. The celestial entity identified as Orion is *Sȝḥ*. This asterism, together with *spdt*/Sothis and "Morning Star," is mentioned on several occasions in conjunction with the king's ascension to heaven. A typical passage is the following: "May you ascend to the sky, may the sky give birth to you like Orion."[394]

Upon examination, not one of the references to *Sȝḥ* in the Pyramid Texts provides sufficient information that would confirm an identification of this stellar deity with the modern constellation Orion. This being the case, it is hardly surprising to find that Egyptologists continue to debate whether the Old Kingdom mentions of *Sȝḥ* have reference to the Orion constellation or to some other star situated in the southern sector of the sky.[395] Faulkner, for example, suggested Procyon or Aldebaran as the celestial referent for *Sȝḥ*.[396] Other scholars have pointed to Canopus as being the star in question.[397] Rudolf Anthes, upon examining the references to *Sȝḥ* in the Pyramid Texts, was led to conclude that their subject was Rigel and not a constellation at all.[398] The astronomer Robert Briggs, finally, went so far as to doubt whether an identification was even possible: "Still it is perchance more probable that *Sȝḥ*, like N., was not identified with any one star."[399]

In recent years a number of scholars have returned to this vexing problem. Patrick Wallin, in a thorough review of the evidence from the

---

[394] *PT* 2116.
[395] In a recent summary of supposed references to Orion in the so-called Star Tables, much younger in date than the *PT*, Sarah Simons, "A Star's Year: The Annual Cycle in the Ancient Egyptian Sky," in J. Steele, *Calendars and Years* (Oxford, 2007), p. 23 observes: "The precise extent, composition, and orientation of the ancient constellation *sȝḥ* (that is, which stars formed various parts of the 'figure' of *sȝḥ*) is, however, not known."
[396] R. Faulkner, "The King and the Star-Religion," *JNES* 25 (1966), p. 158.
[397] See the discussion in R. Briggs, "Astronomy," in S. Mercer, *The Pyramid Texts,* Vol. IV (New York, 1952), p. 41.
[398] R. Anthes, "Horus als Sirius in den Pyramidentexten," *ZÄS* 102 (1975), p. 6.
[399] R. Briggs, *op. cit.*, p. 41.

Pyramid and Coffin Texts, stated the obvious when he observed: "It is difficult, however, to determine exactly which stars made up the Egyptian *S₃ḥ*."[400]

In short, the identification of *S₃ḥ* with Orion can hardly be regarded as securely established and thus the argument for identifying *spdt* with Sirius because of the latter's close proximity to Orion falls to the ground.

To summarize our findings to this point: A review of the evidence has confirmed that there is a dearth of references in the Pyramid Texts to *any* natural phenomenon that unequivocally points to the star Sirius as the actual celestial referent of *spdt*. Other testimony from these early texts, moreover, is difficult to reconcile with a Sirius-identification. For example, if *spdt* was Sirius and *Neter Dw₃* Venus, as per the conventional opinion defended by Faulkner and Krauss, how is it possible to account for the fact that these two celestial bodies are occasionally described as cooperating together in some act? Witness the following passage: "I ascend to the sky among the Imperishable Stars, my sister is Sothis, my guide is the Morning Star, and they grasp my hand at the Field of Offerings."[401] Do Sirius and Venus regularly appear together in the same sector of the sky, as if engaging in a stereotypical act? On the contrary, Sirius and Venus *always* occupy different regions of the sky, Venus moving along the ecliptic and Sirius being fixed in the southern sky, some 40 degrees removed from the ecliptic. Indeed, aside from their status as the brightest of the stars and planets respectively, the two celestial bodies would appear to have precious little in common.

In the previously cited passage describing the king's ascension to heaven, moreover, Sothis seemingly accompanies the deceased king in reaching the Field of Offerings amongst the Imperishable Stars. Yet how is it possible to understand a fixed southern star like *spdt* moving in close proximity to the Imperishable Stars in the northern circumpolar skies if

---

[400] P. Wallin, *Celestial Cycles* (Uppsala, 2002), p. 19.
[401] PT 1123.

indeed it is to be identified with Sirius? The obvious conclusion to be drawn from such testimony is that either *spdt* or the Imperishable Stars has been misidentified inasmuch as Sirius has no apparent relation to the northern skies or the circumpolar stars.

## Lifting the Veil on Sothis/Spdt

"Sothis and the Morning Star are free movers. They lead N. to the Marsh of Offerings (1123b)."[402]

"The concept of 'rejuvenation' points to the mystery of cyclical time, which runs back into itself. In fact, there was a close connection between water and time in Egyptian thought, a connection that resulted from the annual Nile inundation. The Egyptian year began (at least theoretically) with the onset of the inundation during the summer. Thus, in Egyptian thought, the concepts of 'year,' 'Nile,' and 'rejuvenation' were closely connected in the sense of reversibility, return, and regeneration. The Egyptian word for 'year' means the 'rejuvenated/rejuvenating one'."[403]

In order to arrive at an evidence-based solution vis a vis the identification of Sothis/*spdt*, it is instructive to review the star-goddess's epithets and attributes in the earliest Egyptian texts. The most important characteristics of *spdt* as represented in the Pyramid Texts may be summarized as follows: (1) personification as a goddess, identified with Isis; (2) mother of a divine child known alternately as Horus or Sopdu; (3) consort of Osiris (*S3ḥ*); and (4) guide to the Egyptian pharaoh in his post-mortem journey to the celestial Hereafter.

The word *spdt*—presumably signifying the "sharp one"[404]—is feminine in nature, as demonstrated by its suffix (t represents the feminine suffix in the Egyptian language). In accordance with this gender *spdt* is regularly identified with the mother goddess Isis.

The decisive key to identifying Sothis/*spdt* is unraveling the celestial context behind her intimate relationship with Horus *spd* as outlined in the Pyramid Texts (see the analysis offered in the previous chapter). As documented earlier, Horus Sopdu is to be identified with the Morning

---

[402] R. Briggs, *op. cit.*, p. 45.
[403] J. Assmann, *Death and Salvation in Ancient Egypt* (Ithaca, 2005), p. 359.
[404] R. Krauss, *op. cit.*, p. 177.

Star. When I first offered this identification in 1994, I was primarily concerned with deciphering the multifarious mythology associated with the planet Mars, identified with the prototypical "Morning Star" by various ancient cultures.[405] In the meantime, other scholars have also proposed that Horus Sopdu should be identified with the Morning Star and additional evidence supporting the equation has come to light.[406] Yet if Horus Sopdu is to be identified with the Morning Star—Venus according to Krauss and Goebs, Mars according to the reconstruction offered here—how are we to account for the specific details of its relationship with Sothis/Sirius?

The Egyptian epithets attached to Horus Sopdu locate the star-god in very close proximity to—or even *within*—Sothis/Isis. The epithet *ḥrw jmj spdt* is representative: "Horus who is in Sothis."[407] Yet the planet Venus *never* closely approaches Sirius and thus it can hardly appear to enter into conjunction with that particular star. In short, it is quite impossible to explain the explicit Egyptian testimony pointing to an intimate relationship between Horus *spd* and Isis/*spdt* from the conventional standpoint.

How, then, are to we to understand the celestial referent of Isis/*spdt*? Most scholars, as we have seen, would identify the star with Sirius.[408] The original historical rationale for this view likely stemmed from Graeco-Roman influence—Plutarch, among others, having identified Isis with Sothis-Sirius.[409] Once the Egyptian hieroglyphs were deciphered, it was possible for Champollion and pioneers in decipherment to lend a measure

---

[405] Such was the case among the Skidi Pawnee of North America, for example. See the discussion in V. del Chamberlain, *When Stars Came Down to Earth* (College Park, 1982), pp. 72-89.
[406] See the discussion in K. Goebs, *Crowns in Egyptian Funerary Literature* (Oxford, 2008), pp. 250-251 and R. Krauss, *op. cit.*, p. 93.
[407] *PT* 632d.
[408] R. Krauss, "The Eye of Horus and the Planet Venus," in J. Steele & A. Imhausen eds., *Under One Sky* (Munster, 2002), p. 202: "Isis...embodies Sirius among the fixed stars."
[409] Plutarch, *De Isid.*, 21, 38, 61; Schol. Arat. 152; Horapollo I:3.

of support for Plutarch's conjecture by referencing various astronomical monuments from the Middle and New Kingdoms which place *spdt* in close proximity to *sꜣḥ*, thereby seemingly supporting an identification of Isis *spdt* with Sirius.

Other ancient commentators, however, identified Isis with the planet Venus. Thus, in his monumental encyclopedia of ancient knowledge, Pliny wrote as follows of the planet Venus: "Now this Planet, in Greatness, exceedeth all the other Stars...And hereupon cometh such great Diversity of the Names thereof; for some have called it Juno, others Isis, and others the Mother of the Gods."[410]

Is it possible that the planet Venus was the original celestial prototype for the goddess Isis-*spdt*? Certainly this identification would make the most sense from the standpoint of comparative religion, insofar as analogous goddesses of various ancient cultures are regularly identified with Venus. The Greeks identified Aphrodite with the planet Venus,[411] for example, and Greek colonists in Egypt identified the celebrated goddess of love with Isis.[412] It is commonly acknowledged, moreover, that Aphrodite's cult stemmed from the ancient Near East, where the Sumerian Inanna and Akkadian Ishtar were each identified with the planet Venus.[413]

That Isis shares a fundamental affinity with these ancient Near Eastern Venus-goddesses is impossible to deny. Egyptian artworks regularly depict Isis suckling the king (see figure Z).[414] Indeed, this is one of the most popular motifs in all of Egyptian art. Here it is possible to point to

---

[410] Pliny, *Natural History* II:VI:37, as translated by P. Holland, *Pliny's Natural History, Vol. 1* (London, 1847/8), p. 41. See also Apuleius *Metamorphoses* 11, 2; Ptolemy, *Tetrabiblos* 2.3.64.
[411] F. Cumont, *Astrology and Religion among the Greeks and Romans* (New York, 1960), p. 27.
[412] W. Helck, "Aphrodite," *Lexikon der Ägyptologie, Vol. I* (Wiesbaden, 1975), col. 337.
[413] W. Heimpel, "A Catalog of Near Eastern Venus Deities," *Syro-Mesopotamian Studies* 4:3 (1982), pp. 9-15. See also the discussion in W. Burkert, *The Orientalizing Revolution* (London, 1992), pp. 97-98.
[414] See the discussion in S. Budin, *Images of Woman and Child from the Bronze Age* (Cambridge, 2011), pp. 87-88.

an exact parallel in ancient Mesopotamia, wherein Ishtar/Venus was depicted in analogous fashion. Simo Parpola, among others, has commented on the prevalence of this motif in the religious iconography of the ancient Near East: "In her capacity as the goddess of love, Ištar had a special relationship to the Assyrian king, who is repeatedly portrayed as her baby."[415] Are we to suppose, then, that Assyrian kings had themselves depicted as being suckled by the planet Venus while Egyptian kings suckled at the teats of Sirius?

The various epithets attached to Isis likewise point to her identification with the planet Venus. The epithet "Queen of the gods of Heaven,"[416] while otherwise unknown in the global nomenclature surrounding Sirius, recalls the terminology associated with Venus, the latter planet being known as the "Queen of Heaven" throughout the ancient Near East.[417] Sothis's recurring epithet *w'bt swt* "pure of places" finds a close parallel in Sumerian lore, wherein Inanna/Venus was known as ki-sikil, literally "pure of place."[418] Inanna's epithet ù.sún.zi.an.na, "exalted Cow of Heaven," likewise, recalls the fact that Isis/Sothis was commonly depicted as a cow in Egyptian iconography.[419]

One of Isis's most prominent attributes, attested already in the Pyramid Texts, found her conceptualized as a goddess of mourning and lamentation.[420] Yet the very same function is ascribed to Inanna and Ishtar. Ishtar-Venus, for example, was invoked as the "star of

---

[415] S. Parpola, "The Assyrian Tree of Life," *JNES* 52:3 (1993), p. 178.
[416] L. Zabkar, *Hymns to Isis in Her Temple at Philae* (Hanover, 1988), p. 130 citing a hymn from Philae.
[417] E. Cochrane, "Aphrodite Urania," *Aeon* 5:2 (1998), pp. 44-47.
[418] P. Lapinkivi, *The Sumerian Sacred Marriage* (Helsinki, 2004), p. 157. On the translation of Sothis's epithet, see R. Hannig, *Ägyptisches Wörterbuch I* (Mainz, 2003), p. 320.
[419] This is the case on the so-called Zodiac of Dendara, for example. See O. Neugebauer & R. Parker, *Egyptian Astronomical Texts, Vol. 3* (London, 1969), p. 80.
[420] *PT* 1004-1005, *PT* 2191-2192. According to Jan Assmann, "Isis," in K van der Toorn et al, *Dictionary of Deities and Demons in the Bible* (Leiden, 1995), col. 857: "The festivals of Osiris…the lamentations by Isis and Nephthys etc. were celebrated in all the religious centers of Egypt." See also J. Bergman, "Isis," in *Lexikon der Ägyptologie, Vol. 3* (Wiesbaden, 1977), col. 188.

lamentation" in an early Babylonian hymn.[421] Babylonian omen texts, likewise, denote the planet Venus as the "star of lamentation" (*Mul ta-nu-qa-ti*).[422]

As noted earlier, Egyptian scribes describe *spdt* as acting as a guide to the dead king during his ascension to the sky. Spell 442 is representative:

"You will regularly ascend with Orion from the eastern region of the sky, you will regularly descend with Orion into the western region of the sky, your third is Sothis pure of thrones, and it is she who will guide you both on the goodly roads which are in the sky in the Field of Rushes."[423]

So far as I'm aware there is no evidence that *any* ancient culture conceptualized Sirius as as a guide for the deceased during a post-mortem ascent to the celestial Hereafter. Yet ancient skywathers around the globe ascribed this very role to the planet Venus. In the New World, for instance, the Pomo Indians of California describe Venus as "a companion to the departing spirit as it travels to the 'happy isles' in the west after death."[424] The fact that the very same belief is found among the Australian Aborigines attests to the archetypal nature of Venus's role as an escort or guide of the departing soul: "When a person dies, his/her spirit is believed to be conducted by the star [Venus] to Bralgu [the Australian netherworld], its last resting place."[425]

It is significant to note that very similar ideas were associated with the Eye of Horus. Thus it is that, during his journey to the celestial Hereafter, the deceased king announces: "The Eye of Horus is my guide."[426] The same idea is evident in the Egyptian New Year's ritual wherein the Eye was invoked as a brilliant "torch" that "illumines the god's, or the

---

[421] F. Stephens, "Prayer of Lamentation to Ishtar," in J. Pritchard, *Ancient Near Eastern Texts Relating to the Old Testament* (Princeton, 1969), p. 384.
[422] E. Reiner & D. Pingree, *Babylonian Planetary Omens, Part Three* (Groningen, 1998), p. 155.
[423] *PT* 821-822.
[424] D. Miller, *Stars of the First People* (Boulder, 1997), p. 144.
[425] R. Haynes, "Aboriginal Astronomy," *Aust. J. Astr.* 4:3 (1992), p. 134.
[426] *CT* II:251g.

deceased's, path wherever he may go."[427] Yet as we documented in a previous chapter, the peculiar traditions attached to the Eye of Horus originated in the extraordinary history of the planet Venus and have nothing whatsoever to do with Sirius.

The uraeus-serpent also served as the "guide" (*sšm*) of the deceased king. An early memory of this tradition is to be found in the Pyramid Texts: "The King's guiding-serpent is on his brow."[428]

The uraeus-serpent is also invoked as a guide to the deceased king in the so-called "Hymns to the Diadem." In these ten hymns celebrating Sobek from the Middle Kingdom, the uraeus-serpent is explicitly identified with the royal crown: "Hier wird die Krone als die Schlange an der Stirn des Herrschers gedacht, die ihn im Kampfe 'leitet'; der gleiche Ausdruck und Gedanke auch Pyr. 396."[429] Most important for our thesis here, however, is the fact that the guiding uraeus-serpent is explicitly identified with Sothis. Witness the following hymn as translated by Adolf Erman:

"Du erwachst in Frieden, die Leitende, die an der Stirn des Horus ist, erwacht in Frieden, das Erwachen deiner Seele ist friedlich. Hoch ist deine Gestalt, Heiße…Machtige, Starke, Flammengeruste, Herrin des Himmels, Herrscherin der beiden Lander, Auge des Horus und seine Leiterin, *Ḥkn-wtt*, Herrin der Ewigkeit. Feurige, Rot, deren Flamme schmerzt, du Schlange des Menschenleiters, Herrin der Flamme, Brennende, Fressende, Feurige(?)…Du erwachst in Frieden, Sothis(?) erwacht in Frieden, dein Erwachen ist friedlich."[430]

But what can it mean that Sothis serves as the uraeus-like headband? Did the ancient Egyptian scribes somehow confuse Sirius with the Eye of Horus, a different star altogether? Obviously puzzled by the passage in

---

[427] H. Nelson, "Certain Reliefs at Karnak and Medinet Habu…," *JNES* 8 (1949), p. 337.
[428] *PT* 396.
[429] A. Erman, *Hymnen an das Diadem der Pharaonen* (Berlin, 1911), p. 32.
[430] *Ibid.*, p. 28.

question, Erman offers the following commentary: "Ob wirklich der Stern Sothis gemeint ist? oder ist es nur eine 'ausgerustete' Schlange?"[431]

Erman's confusion is uncalled for inasmuch as Sothis's intimate connection with the royal crown is attested elsewhere in Egyptian tradition, as documented well over a century ago.[432] A tradition reported by Heinrich Brugsch is instructive in this regard:

"Hathor als Sothisstern, Ra als Sonne gedacht und beide am Neujahrstage in unmittelbarer Nähe eine Stunde vor Tagesanbruch am horizonte emporsteigend, rufen in der bilderreichen Sprache der Denkmäler die mannigfaltigsten Gleichnisse hervor. Die strahlende Morgensonne wird zu einem Löwen, die Sothis zu seiner Tochter...Beide erfassen sich und vereinigen sich am Neujahrstage mit einander. Der Gott steigt in seiner Sonnenbarke zur Lichtsphäre empor, sie nimmt den Vorderplaß im Schiffe wie eine Pilotin ein und erscheint als Diadem (*mehnit*) an seiner Stirn."[433]

It will be noted that Sothis's reunion with and crowning of Ra is said to have occurred at daybreak on the New Year.

The fact that analogous traditions surround Isis underscores her fundamental affinity with Sothis. In the goddess's sacred temple at Philae, for example, Isis was invoked as the diadem atop the head of the ancient sun-god: "Whom Re has raised upon his head, Who shines as the Diadem on his forehead."[434] Here, as elsewhere, the word used to denote "diadem"

---

[431] *Ibid.*, p. 32.
[432] See also the important discussion in J. Darnell, "The Apotropaic Goddess in the Eye," *Studien zur Altägyptischen Kultur* 24 (1997), pp. 46-47.
[433] H. Brugsch, *Religion und Mythologie der Alten Aegypter* (Leipzig, 1890), pp. 318-319. See also the translation of Esna 251 by L. Troy, "Mut Enthroned," in J. van Dijk ed., *Essays on Ancient Egypt in Honour of Herman te Velde* (Groningen, 1997), pp. 311-312.
[434] L. Zabkar, *Hymns to Isis in Her Temple at Philae* (Hanover, 1988), p. 80. Compare a tradition from Aboriginal Australia wherein Venus is described as "Shining on to the fore-heads of all those head-men [i.e., chiefs]." See R. Berndt, "A 'Wonguri'-Mandeikai song cycle of the moon-bone," *Oceania* 19 (1948), p. 35.

is ȝḫt.⁴³⁵ Yet the very same texts identify Isis as the raging uraeus-goddess.⁴³⁶

We will return to the Egyptian tradition describing Sothis as the sun-god's crown below. Here we would simply emphasize the fact that, as guide for the deceased king, Sothis shares an epithet otherwise associated with the uraeus-serpent and the Eye of Horus. There is a perfectly logical reason for this convergence of terminology: Sothis is fundamentally identical with the Eye of Horus *and* the uraeus-serpent. Indeed, the identification is made explicit in the Egyptian sources themselves: Thus a text from Isis's temple at Philae reports that Sakhmet once ascended to heaven as a fiery serpent, on which occasion the name Sothis originated:

"Sakhmet is powerful in Bigge while burning her enemies with her flame. She came forth as fire-serpent into the sky, and so her name 'Sothis' came into being'."⁴³⁷

---

[435] The full text is as follows: *Wṯst Rʿ ḥr tp.f, Psḏt m ȝḫt m ḫnt.f.*
[436] *Ibid.*, p. 131.
[437] *Philae* 1, 69, 6-9 as translated in J. Quack, "A Goddess Rising 10,000 Cubits into the Air," in J. Steele & A. Imhausen, *Under One Sky* (Münster, 2002), p. 289. See also the discussion in M. Smith, *On the Primaeval Ocean* (Copenhagen, 2002), p. 171, who translates the passage in question as follows: "The text concludes: *ḫpr rn=s n Spd.t*, 'Thus came into existence her name of Sothis.'"

## Sothis as Year

We turn finally to consider the epithet *rnpt*, "year," applied to Sothis/Isis throughout the Pyramid and Coffin Texts. As we have seen, it is this epithet that is typically cited by scholars seeking a connection between Sirius and the origins of the Egyptian calendar year. According to Jan Assmann, the word originally denoted rejuvenation or "to make oneself young."[438] A play upon this meaning of the word is evident in Utterance 466 from the Pyramid Texts, wherein the deceased king is described as a "great star":

"O King, you are this great star, the companion of Orion, who traverses the sky with Orion...you ascend from the east of the sky, being renewed at your due season and rejuvenated at your due time. The sky has borne you with Orion, the year has put a fillet on you with Osiris..."[439]

In order to understand the manifold symbolism surrounding the deceased king's post-mortem ascent to heaven and transfiguration, it is necessary to determine what natural events could have inspired the tradition of the Great Star's "rejuvenation" and/or beautification. Identifying the "Great Star" in Utterance 466 is doubtless central to resolving the mystery in question.

In Utterance 466 the Great Star is described as Orion's companion—*rnmwtj*—leading some scholars to identify it with Sothis/*spdt*. Yet as Faulkner pointed out in his commentary on this Utterance, the Great Star in question is masculine in nature and thus its identification with *spdt* is most improbable insofar as the latter star is always feminine. Faulkner himself proposed Procyon or Aldebaran as possible points of reference.[440]

Krauss devotes over 25 pages to a discussion of the Great Star's possible celestial identification, noting that it must have been a "strikingly brilliant star."[441] Like Faulkner, he argues that it is very unlikely that the

---

[438] J. Assmann, *Death and Salvation in Ancient Egypt* (Ithaca, 2005), p. 359.
[439] *PT* 882-883.
[440] R. Faulkner, *The Ancient Egyptian Pyramid Texts* (Oxford, 1969), p. 155. See also his comments in "The King and the Star-Religion," *JNES* 25 (1966), p. 158.
[441] R. Krauss, *op. cit.*, p. 204.

star in question is Sothis/*spdt* insofar as it is clearly described as having been adorned with a fillet (*sšd*) by the latter.[442] Krauss finally settles on Aldebaran as the most likely celestial referent for *sbꜣ ꜥꜣ*, albeit without presenting an iota of substantive evidence in favor of this highly speculative conjecture.[443]

Like all Egyptologists before him, Krauss overlooked a decisive clue with respect to the star's identity—namely, the statement that Sothis adorned the "Great Star" with a *sšd*-fillet. Krauss himself never offers any suggestion as to how we are to understand the headbanding of Aldebaran (or any other star for that matter). Yet this is the single most important datum that must be explained if we are to arrive at a satisfactory identification of the Great Star in question.

The original meaning of the passage, so far as I can determine, is that Year/Sothis "rejuvenates" or transfigures the King (Pepi)—identified here simply as the "Great Star" (*sbꜣ ꜥꜣ*)—by garlanding him with a fillet (*sšd*) or headband. A similar scenario is described in Teti's pyramid, wherein the tying on of the *sšd*-headband "beautifies" the deceased king: "How beautiful is the sight of Teti, with headband [*sšd*] from the Sun's brow, his kilt on him from Hathor, his plumage a falcon's plumage, as he goes forth to the sky among his brothers the gods."[444] Here it must be emphasized that it is the tying on of a *decidedly extraterrestrial sšd-*headband which renders Teti beautiful (*nfrw*) and marks his transfiguration.

A number of Egyptian texts report that the *sšd*-headband was responsible for effecting the deceased king's transfiguration. The following text from the *Book of the Gates* is representative: "The one

---

[442] *Ibid.*, p. 199.
[443] *Ibid.*, p. 206.
[444] *PT* 546 as translated by J. Allen, *op. cit.*, p. 70.

Horus has made for his father Osiris: to transfigure him [$s3ḥ.f$], to restore for him the *sšd*."[445]

The statement that Year/Sothis "has put a fillet" on the king recalls the tradition preserved in PT 1214 wherein Isis equips the deceased king—as the youthful or child-like (*ḥrd*) Horus-star—with a fillet (*mdḥ*). From our vantage point it stands to reason that the youthful Horus, explicitly identified with the Morning Star elsewhere in the same Utterance (1207a), forms a structural analogue to the "rejuvenated" Great Star in PT 883.

In Utterances 220/221, similarly, it is the outfitting of Horus with the Ikhet-headband—the latter explicitly likened to a *sšd*—which renders him as one reborn (see chapter four). If these respective traditions can be viewed as variations upon a common theme—and it is difficult to see how they could be interpreted otherwise—it follows that the garlanding of the Great Star with the fillet by Year/Sothis is best understood in light of the parallels provided by Isis's tying on of Horus's headband and the "crowning" of Horus at the hands of Ikhet the Serpent.

It is Horus, moreover, who represents the "rejuvenated" god *par excellence* in Egyptian tradition. In the Pyramid Texts, as elsewhere, Horus receives the epithet *rnpj*, "rejuvenated."[446] The same idea is evident roughly 1000 years later when King Tut, upon being interred and imagined ascending to heaven, was addressed as "Horus *resurgens*, newly come to the throne."[447] So, too, magical cippi celebrating Horus commonly include the following spell: "The aged god who rejuvenates himself at his season, the old man who becomes a youth."[448] This particular proverb recalls the description of "Great Star" in PT 883: "being renewed at your due season and rejuvenated at your due time."

---

[445] Quoted from S. Collier, *The Crowns of Pharaoh* (Ph.D. Dissertation: University of California Los Angeles, 1996), p. 66.
[446] *PT* 767. See here the discussion in J. Assmann, *Death and Salvation in Ancient Egypt* (Ithaca, 2005), p. 358.
[447] L. Bell, "Luxor Temple and the Cult of the Royal Ka," *JNES* 44 (1985), p. 256.
[448] R. Ritner, "Horus on the Crocodiles," in W. Simpson ed., *Religion and Philosophy in Ancient Egypt* (New Haven, 1989), p. 111.

That the Horus-star formed the celestial prototype for such archaic conceptions is attested already in the Pyramid Texts. Witness Utterance 264:

"The sky's two reedfloats have been placed for Horus, that he might cross on them to the Akhet...to the place where the gods will give him birth, so that he might be fully reborn there, new and rejuvenated."[449]

It will be noted that the phrase translated here as "new and rejuvenated"—*mꜣ rnpw*—is the very expression used in PT 883 to describe the transfiguration of the Great Star.

Yet if the headbanding of the "Great Star" at the hands of the mother goddess Year/Sothis is to be understood by reference to the headbanding of the Horus-star, it stands to reason that the Great Star in question must be identifiable as a Horus-form. There is some evidence supporting this conclusion. Hence it is that, in the Coffin Texts, there is a passing reference to Horus as "the Eyeless One, the great star [*šḥd wr*], joined to Khem."[450] So, too, in the late text known as the *7th Litany of the Sun*, Horus is invoked as *sbꜣ ꜥꜣ*, "Great Star."[451]

If in fact the "Great Star" in PT 882 has reference to the Horus-star, it is obvious that its placement alongside Orion/*sꜣḥ* and Sothis/*spdt* in Utterance 466 finds its closest parallel in Utterance 366, wherein the deceased king—as Horus *spd*—is described as the son of *sꜣḥ* and *spdt* (see our discussion in chapter ten). A possible vestigial memory of the intimate relationship that formerly pertained between these three stellar entities is preserved on the astronomical ceiling at Dendera, whereupon Horus *spd* is placed in close proximity to Orion/*sꜣḥ* and Sothis/*spdt* (see figure one, wherein Horus *spd* is represented as a falcon atop a *wꜣḏ*-pillar).[452] The

---

[449] *PT* 342-344 as translated in J. Allen, *op. cit.*, pp. 78.
[450] *CT* II:117f-g.
[451] K. Goebs, *Crowns in Egyptian Funerary Literature* (Oxford, 2008), p. 21.
[452] O. Neugebauer & R. Parker, *Egyptian Astronomical Texts, Vol. 3* (London, 1969), pp. 80-81. See also J. Lull & J. Belmonte, "The Constellations of Ancient Egypt," in J. Belmonte & M. Shaltout eds., *In Search of Cosmic Order* (Cairo, 2009), p. 182,

image of Horus *spd* atop his papyrus-column, in turn, finds an intriguing parallel in the Coffin Texts, wherein we find an allusion to "the fillet of Horus who is on his papyrus-plant."[453] But this reference merely brings the argument full circle, for the "fillet" (*sšd*) of Horus atop his papyrus-plant naturally recalls the Great Star's *sšd*-fillet in PT 883.

Figure 1

It will be remembered from our analysis in the previous chapter that Horus *spd*—like Horus himself—is to be identified with the Morning Star. If so, it stands to reason that it was this particular star that was conceptualized as the "Great Star" by the Egyptian skywatchers. The fact that indigenous cultures from the New World as well as the Old routinely described the prototypical "Morning Star" by epithets signifying "Great Star" is doubtless germane to the argument at hand.[454]

The reference to the "Great Star" in Spell 466 is not the only such reference in the Pyramid Texts. A "Great Star" is also mentioned in PT 1038, wherein it is described as standing in the "heart" or midst of the east (*ḥrj-jb jȝbt*). In the passage in question, the deceased king aspires to join Nut in heaven:

---

wherein it is noted: "This is the well documented image of Horus-upon-his-pillar *(ḥrw ḥri wȝd.f)* which completes the Osiran triad."
[453] *CT* VI:38y.
[454] The Maya knew the Morning Star as *chak ek*, "Great Star." See S. Milbrath, *Star Gods of the Maya* (Austin, 1999), p. 160. See also the discussion in E. Cochrane, *On Fossil Gods and Forgotten Worlds* (Ames, 2010), pp. 124-138.

"(O Nut), set your hand on me with life and dominion, that you may assemble my bones and collect my members…May I ascend and lift myself up to the sky as the great star in the midst of the East."[455]

It is interesting to note here that some Egyptologists have understood this particular spell to be describing the Morning Star. Samuel Mercer, in his commentary to this passage, observed: "In contradistinction to 882b, however, the star here may be the morning star."[456] Mercer's disclaimer with regard to the reference to the "Great Star" in PT 882 was doubtless influenced by the erroneous assumption that that particular passage had reference to the star's close proximity to Sirius (as Year)—impossible for the Morning Star—and thus he was inclined to see a contradiction between the two traditions when none in fact exists.

To continue with this line of reasoning: It is probable that the information recorded in PT 1048 can shed additional light on the astronomical situation referenced in PT 883 and 1038. Thus, in the passage in question one reads of the "headbanding" of the "Sole Star" (*Sbȝ wʿti*) in the midst of Nut:

"Ho, Pepi!…You will wear the headband as the sole star in Nut's midst."[457]

The fact that the deceased king Pepi is described as "new and rejuvenated" immediately following his "headbanding" in the Utterance in question (1049c) provides a striking parallel to the situation in Utterance 466, thereby confirming that we are justified in comparing the two traditions (in PT 883 the deceased king, as "Great Star," is renewed and rejuvenated as a result of his headbanding at the hands of Year/Sothis).[458] Such parallels, together with the fact that both Utterances represent classic examples of "ascension" hymns, suggest that the "Sole

---

[455] *PT* 1036-1038.
[456] S. Mercer, *op. cit.*, p. 524.
[457] *PT* 1048 as translated in J. Allen, *op. cit.*, p. 134.
[458] See the translation of J. Allen, *op. cit.*, p. 134. It will be noted that the latter part of this passage was not translated by Faulkner.

Star" in PT 1048 is to be identified with the "Great Star" of 1038 and 883. That Horus is called the "Sole-Star" (*sbꜣ wʿti*) in the Edfu texts is certainly consistent with this hypothesis.[459]

To summarize our findings with respect to the astronomical events described in Utterance 466: The passage in question alludes to the archaic Egyptian belief that the mother goddess—here invoked as Year—"rejuvenated" the deceased king (identified explicitly as "Great Star") by adorning him with a fillet (*sšd*) or headband. As we documented in chapter four, it was the tying on of the *sšd*-band that marked the deceased king's transfiguration and rejuvenation as a stellar divinity (as the Horus-star).[460] So, too, it is this singular celestial precedent that explains why the tying on of the *sšd*-headband came to serve as a leading symbol for rejuvenation and rebirth throughout some three thousand years of Egyptian history.[461]

It is evident, moreover, that Year's "crowning" of the Great Star with a *sšd*-headband forms a close parallel to Sothis's crowning of Re in the tradition cited in the previous section, wherein the sun-god's crowning at "daybreak" is explicitly linked to the New Year. Indeed, it is Re/Horus's crowning that marks his accession to the celestial throne and, concomitantly, signals a *new* Year.[462] It is our contention, therefore, that Sothis's intimate connection with the New Year has nothing whatsoever to do with astronomical observations of Sirius during the Old Kingdom—much less with any advanced calendrical computations as imagined by Parker and several generations of Egyptologists. On the contrary, the

---

[459] H. Fairman, "The Myth of Horus at Edfu—I," *JEA* 21 (1935), p. 36.

[460] The *Book of the Dead* alludes to the same basic idea: "The god is born, his fillet is bound on." See 136a as translated in R. Faulkner, *The Egyptian Book of the Dead* (San Francisco, 1994), p. 118.

[461] H. Kocklemann, "Ein neuer funerärer Spruch mit Anrufung der Mumienbinde," in B. Backes, M. Müller-Roth, & S. Stöhr eds., *Ausgestattet mit den Schriften des Thot* (Wiesbaden, 2009), p. 101 writes: "Als Symbole von Wiedergeburt und Erneuerung sind Stoffstreifen, insbesondere das *sšd*-Band, in rituellen und funerären Darstellungen gut bezeugt."

[462] R. T. Clark, *Myth and Symbol in Ancient Egypt* (London, 1959), p. 217: "The appearance of Horus in the sky just before dawn is the mark of the new year."

Egyptian traditions describing the glorious appearance of Horus and/or Sothis at the time of the New Year find their origin in the awe-inspiring and decidedly *catastrophic* astronomical events associated with the Horus-star's headbanding and rejuvenation at the hands of Sothis/Venus at the Time of Beginning—i.e., in *zp tpj*. In this sense, the epithet *Rnpt* most likely describes the planet-goddess Sothis/Isis/Venus as the "rejuvenator" of the Horus-star.

### Summary

Our principal findings in the previous two chapters may be summarized in short order:

(1) A detailed analysis of the references to Horus *spd* in the Pyramid Texts has revealed zero evidence that even hints at the observation or veneration of Sirius. So much for one of the stellar identifications long regarded as "one of the rare certainties in Egyptian astronomy."[463] Rather, as we have documented, Horus *spd*/Sopdu is to be identified with the primordial Morning Star (*Neter Dua*). The Egyptian Morning Star, in turn, was the planet Mars.

(2) The vast corpus of astral traditions preserved within the Pyramid Texts provides precious little evidence for the conventional identification of Sothis/Isis with Sirius. On the contrary, it has been shown that the earliest Egyptian traditions associated with Sothis-Isis are best understood by reference to the planet Venus. This evidence, considered alongside that identifying Horus Sopdu with the Morning Star/Mars, strongly suggests that Egyptologists have erred in their attempt to relate these two star-gods to Sirius. Properly understood, the Egyptian traditions alluding to an intimate relationship or close proximity formerly pertaining between Horus *spd* and Isis *spdt*—far from reflecting ancient conceptions having to do with Sirius—actually have reference to extraordinary natural events involving a "great conjunction" between the planets Mars and Venus.

(3) The sacred traditions surrounding Sothis/Isis in the Pyramid Texts have absolutely nothing to do with arcane workings of a hypothetical Egyptian Sothic calendar as postulated by Richard Parker and several generations of Egyptologists, much less with careful observations of Sirius

---

[463] O. Neugebauer & R. Parker, *Egyptian Astronomical Texts I* (London, 1960), p. 25: "Given the identification of *spd* with Sirius, which is certain."

from the third and fourth millenniums BCE. Rather, such traditions describe and encode the catastrophic astronomical events mythologized as Creation and believed to have occurred *in illo tempore*, wherein the Horus-star appeared to conjoin with Sothis/Venus. As documented here, Sothis's epithet *Rnpt*/Year alludes to Venus's singular role in the headbanding and rejuvenation of the Horus-star, both of which were celebrated in Egyptian New Year's rituals. The statement that Year tied a fillet (*sšd*) or head-band on the "Great Star," in this sense, has specific reference to the catastrophic celestial events wherein Venus/Isis encircled the Horus-star with a comet-like head-band.

In a recent discussion of the astronomical foundations of ancient chronology, Leo Depuydt offered the following observation:

"Chronology is a conceptual structure gradually and incrementally built up from the first principles that serve as its foundations. If the foundations crumble, the whole building comes down."[464]

Having now examined the conceptual structure and evidential basis behind the so-called Sothic calendar, we can say with complete confidence that its foundations have crumbled to the point of being a complete shambles. Simply stated: The Sothic Calendar as envisioned by Richard Parker and his followers is but a figment of their imagination and thus the attempt to reconstruct ancient Egyptian history by means of supposed early references to Sirius is nothing but a fool's errand.

---

[464] L. Depuydt, *op. cit.*, p. 36.

## The Imperishable Stars

> "When viewed from Egypt, the stars surrounding the pole-star are never seen to set. For this reason, the Egyptians called them *iḥmw-sk*, 'the ones that know not destruction'. It was the king's wish to ascend to the circumpolar stars, and the Pyramid Texts…speak of the king doing so by means of a great staircase, providing the king with a very concrete means of ascending to the sky."[465]

The ancient Egyptians "desired to be constellated among the imperishable luminaries of the northern sky."[466]

Numerous passages in the Pyramid Texts implore the deceased king to ascend to heaven and assume a prominent position among the Imperishable Stars—*iḥmw-sk*, literally "those who do not perish."[467] The following passages exemplify this central theme:

"O King, you have not died the death; live among them, the Imperishable Spirits."[468]

"I will cross to that side on which are the Imperishable Stars, that I may be among them."[469]

"May you stand at the head of the Imperishable Stars."[470]

"You shall set me to be a magistrate among the spirits, the Imperishable Stars in the north of the sky."[471]

"O you who are high exalted among the Imperishable Stars, you shall never perish."[472]

---

[465] T. Wilkinson, *Early Dynastic Egypt* (London, 1999), p. 258.
[466] A. Maravelia, "The function and importance of some special categories of stars in the Ancient Egyptian funerary texts, 1," in G. Rosati & M. Guidotti eds., *International Congress of Egyptologists XI* (Oxford, 2017), p. 368.
[467] R. Krauss, *op. cit.*, p. 98. See also F. Friedman, "The Root Meaning of *ȝḫ*: Effectiveness or Luminosity," *Serapis* 8 (1984/5), p. 45.
[468] *PT* 1944b.
[469] *PT* 1222c-d.
[470] *PT* 1926a.
[471] *PT* 1220a.
[472] *PT* 878.

Such passages confirm that the Egyptians recognized a fundamental affinity between the deceased king's desired final resting place and the Imperishable Stars, the latter conceptualized as celestial "spirits." How, then, are we to understand the latter stars from an astronomical standpoint? On this question there would appear to be a general consensus among Egyptologists that the Imperishable Stars are to be identified with the circumpolar stars.[473] Alexander Badawy's judgment is representative:

"The prehistoric Egyptian must have been impressed at a very remote age by those northern stars which, unlike the others, neither rose nor set. They were indeed the ideal abode of the kings who lived eternally in the sky. In the stellar destiny as described in the Pyramid Texts the circumpolar stars, 'the Imperishable Stars' 𓇋𓐍𓅓𓋴𓎡 *iḥm-sk*, 'the imperishable star-gods' 𓇋𓐍𓅓𓋴𓎡 *iḥmw-sk*, so called because they completed their circumvolution in the northern quarters of the sky without disappearing, played the most important role."[474]

The best discussion of Egyptian celestial geography known to me is that by James Allen.[475] Allen summarizes the Egyptian funerary beliefs during the Old Kingdom as follows: "The destiny of the deceased king in the Pyramid Texts is to 'go forth to the sky among the imperishable stars' (Pyr. 1123a) and 'go around the sky like the sun' (Pyr. 130d)."[476] As Allen points out, "for the Pyramid Texts, this celestial vision of the afterlife is a single-minded goal."[477]

Truer words were never spoken. And yet there's a glaring anomaly here, one apparently overlooked by Allen—namely, that it is quite

---

[473] C. Rossi, "Science and Technology: Pharaonic," in A. Lloyd ed., *A Companion to Ancient Egyptian, Vol. 1* (Oxford, 2010), p. 394.

[474] A. Badawy, "The Stellar Destiny of Pharaoh and the So-Called Air-Shafts of Cheops' Pyramid," *MIO* 10 (1964), p. 195.

[475] "The Cosmology of the Pyramid Texts," in W. Simpson ed., *Religion and Philosophy in Ancient Egypt* (New Haven, 1989), pp. 1-28.

[476] *Ibid.*, p. 1.

[477] *Ibid.*, p. 1.

impossible for the deceased king to "go forth to the sky among the imperishable stars" while going "around the sky like the sun." This follows from the fact that, in the current arrangement of the solar system, the Sun is far removed from the circumpolar region at all times (Allen, like virtually every other Egyptologist of note, would understand the Imperishable Stars as the circumpolar stars).[478]

The same contradiction is evident in Jan Assmann's discussion of Egyptian funerary beliefs. Like Allen, Assmann identifies the circumpolar region as the goal of the king's post-mortem ascent to heaven:

"These formulations of the transition to the next world where the idea of a 'physical passage' predominates speak of a path, along which the deceased must proceed. Such texts describe the aspired higher sphere of existence principally as a 'sojourn' in one specific far off place. The Pyramid Texts, our oldest corpus of funerary literature, locate this eternal abode in the northern sky."[479]

Yet in the very same context Assmann speaks of the Old Kingdom's "exclusively cosmic conception of a hereafter ruled by the sun-god Re."[480] The apparent incongruity between a hereafter "ruled" by the sun-god and one located "in the northern sky" is obvious and yet it is never addressed by Assmann. Assmann's most recent statement on the subject of the king's post-mortem ascension to heaven likewise ignores the apparent contradiction in the Egyptians' vision of the afterlife:

"In the Pyramid Texts, the deceased king strove to unite with the sun god. His path led him unequivocally upward, to the sky, to the 'imperishable' stars in the northern sky, the stars that never set."[481]

Absent from Assmann's learned analysis is any discussion of how these two seemingly incompatible ideas can exist side by side; i.e., how

---

[478] *Ibid.*, p. 4.
[479] J. Assmann, "Death and Initiation in the Funerary Religion of Ancient Egypt," in W. Simpson ed., *Religion and Philosophy in Ancient Egypt* (New Haven, 1989), p. 143.
[480] *Ibid.*
[481] J. Assmann, *Death and Salvation in Ancient Egypt* (Ithaca, 2005), p. 149.

is it possible for the deceased king to "unite with the sun god" by traveling *unequivocally upward* to the "imperishable stars" in the northern sky when the present Sun never approaches that particular region of the sky?

The only solution that conventional Egyptologists have offered for this paradox is to propose that, at some point prior to the collection of the respective spells in the Pyramid Texts, there was a conflation of two originally independent and contradictory views regarding the celestial Hereafter—one centered on the northern circumpolar regions of the sky and the other centered on the eastern horizon and the Sun. Indeed, more than one Egyptologist has voiced this very opinion. James Breasted, for example, maintained that the Egyptian scribes were attempting to reconcile two independent and conflicting traditions in the Pyramid Texts: "The place of the Imperishable Stars in the north is pushed over toward the east to harmonize with the doctrine of the eastern sky as the place of the abode of the celestial dead."[482]

Badawy likewise drew a sharp distinction between an earlier "star-based" religion and a later solar-based one: "Students of Egyptian religion are agreed that the conception of the stellar destiny preceded that of the Osirian destiny, itself earlier than the idea of solar destiny."[483] The basic ideology governing the Pyramid Texts, according to this scholar, envisaged the deceased king ascending to heaven along a ladder-like structure and, upon reaching the celestial Hereafter, residing forever thereafter at the forefront of the Imperishable Stars:

"The aim of this ascension was to reach the circumpolar stars, which the deceased would lead (374a) or be in their forefront (537a) and command (2173b). This was the royal destiny as pictured in the stellar religion (656c)."[484]

---

[482] J. Breasted, *Development of Religion and Thought in Ancient Egypt* (Philadelphia, 1912), p. 163.

[483] A. Badawy, "The Stellar Destiny of Pharaoh and the So-Called Air-Shafts of Cheops' Pyramid," *MIO* 10 (1964), p. 193.

[484] A. Badawy, "The Ideology of the Superstructure of the Mastaba-Tomb in Egypt," *JNES* 15 (1956), p. 182.

The pyramids of the Old Kingdom, according to Badaway, were designed in such a manner as to ensure that the entrance corridors to the burial chambers slanted upwards in the direction of the circumpolar stars. After the older stellar religion was supplanted by one focused on the Sun, the pyramids were redesigned—and the Pyramid Texts reworded—to reflect this change in ideology:

"When the sun-god Rēʿ gained the supremacy the Pyramid Texts were reworded, some earlier creeds remodeled and new ones introduced. The burial chamber was no more accessible from the north side of the mastaba but from the east one. It is to be noticed that the entrance to the pyramid was, however, maintained in the north side of the structure during the Old Kingdom. It is only in the Middle Kingdom after Sesostris I that the entrance opens east or west, probably in an attempt to hide it better from robbers rather than on account of some religious ideology. The imperishable stars are now manning the solar boat and the justified souls can sail not only at night with the moon, but in daytime with Rēʿ. This change in religious creed reflects probably some progress in the astronomical conception of the Egyptians about the invisible revolution of the stars in daytime. To adapt both ideologies in the same context did not go without violating the topography of the sky and the compromise complicated the itinerary of Pharaoh: 'The two reed bundles of the sky are placed for N.N. that he mayeth travel over to Rēʿ to the horizon. N.N. will travel till he standeth on the eastern side of the sky, in its northern district among the Imperishable Stars' (1000a-d). Pharaoh is now following Rēʿ as an Imperishable star: 'N., the son of the great sky-goddess who resides in the house of the scorpion-goddess, is an Imperishable star. Rēʿ hath taken N. to himself in the sky that N. may live' (1469a-b)."[485]

Far from being conclusive, Badawy's hypothesis raises more questions than it answers. Is it likely that the ancient Egyptians, justly renowned for their careful attention to the natural world and strict

---

[485] A. Badawy, *op. cit.*, pp. 197-198.

conservativeness in religious matters,[486] would so cavalierly misrepresent the true topography of the sky in order to create an utterly fantastic scenario for the central mystery in their star-based religion—the deceased king's ascension to the celestial Hereafter? And for what purpose would they fashion a celestial landscape so at odds with the familiar appearance and order of the solar system? Certainly it is difficult to conceive of a rationale for going to such extremes or, for that matter, for overturning a circumpolar-based system for one focused on the eastern horizon. In fact, it is our view that a systematic analysis of the Pyramid Texts will reveal that the supposedly distinct stellar (northern) and solar (eastern) strata are, in reality, intimately intertwined and present a coherent vision of the celestial Hereafter, one hitherto misunderstood by all Egyptologists.

Raymond Faulkner, in a comprehensive survey of the earliest Egyptian star religion, postulated that two distinct traditions vis à vis the celestial Hereafter were discernible in the Pyramid Texts:

"We find two distinct strata in the passages quoted above. One stratum is concerned entirely with the circumpolar stars and the northern sky, which appears as the abode of the illustrious royal dead whither the King journeys on his departure from the world…The other stratum is entirely concerned with the constellation of Orion and the star Sothis, the Morning Star and the Lone Star, with only three mentions of the moon. It is noticeable that these two strata overlap very little…"[487]

Faulkner's proposed dichotomy notwithstanding, the "two strata" in question overlap to a considerable degree. Thus it is that the god Horus Duat—explicitly identified with the Morning Star in PT 1207—is described as residing at the forefront of the Imperishable Stars. PT 1301

---

[486] Henry Fischer "Hieroglyphen," *Lexikon der Ägyptologie, Vol. 2* (Wiesbaden, 1977), col. 1190 speaks of "their well-known predilection for the permanent and unchanging aspects of all things."

[487] R. Faulkner, "The King and the Star-Religion in the Pyramid Texts," *JNES* 25 (1966), pp. 160-161.

is explicit: "May you go up as Horus of the Netherworld who is at the head of the Imperishable Stars."[488]

The same idea is evident elsewhere in the Pyramid Texts. Witness the following passage, wherein the deceased king is likened to Horus as the Morning Star and placed among the Imperishable Stars:

"Rēˁ summons you into the zenith(?) of the sky as the Jackal, the Governor of the Two Enneads, and as Horus *Ḫnty-mnit-f*; may he set you as the Morning Star in the midst of the Field of Rushes. The door of the sky at the horizon opens for you, the gods are glad at meeting you as the star which crosses the sea below the under-part of the sky in this dignity of yours which issued from the mouth of Rēˁ. May you sit on this iron throne of yours as the Great One who is in On, may you lead the spirits and propitiate the Imperishable Stars."[489]

Horus is here said to "lead the spirits" (*akhu*) and propitiate the Imperishable Stars as the Morning Star, thereby challenging Faulkner's pronouncement that the Pyramid Texts rarely mingle the stellar strata with that involving the Morning Star. Insofar as it is quite impossible for the current Morning Star—i.e., the planet Venus—to journey to the northern heavens and sojourn among the circumpolar stars, it stands to reason that something is seriously amiss with the conventional identifications of the various asterisms mentioned in the Pyramid Texts.

The Imperishable Stars are elsewhere said to aid Re in his daily circumambulation about the sky. This idea is evident in the following passage:

"My father [the deceased king] ascends to the sky among the gods who are in the sky; he stands at the Great Polar Region and learns the speech of the sun-folk. Rēˁ finds you [the deceased king] on the banks of the sky as a waterway-traveler who is in the sky…Be pure; occupy your seat in the Bark of Rēˁ, row over the sky and mount up to the distant ones;

---

[488] *PT* 1301.
[489] *PT* 1719-1722.

row with the Imperishable Stars, navigate with the Unwearying Stars…"⁴⁹⁰

The deceased king is here described as ascending to the *wrt*—the "Great Polar Region," according to Faulkner's translation, "great shin" according to Allen's—whereupon he learns the speech of the sun-folk and rows in the Bark of Re together with the "Imperishable Stars." One could hardly ask for a more explicit statement with respect to the intimate association between the ancient sun god and the Imperishable Stars, yet the relationship in question is plainly preposterous from the conventional standpoint that would understand Re as the current Sun and the Imperishable Stars as the circumpolar stars. Preposterous or not, an intimate relationship between the ancient sun-god and the Imperishable Stars is attested in other hymns as well. Witness the following passage:

"If you [the sun god] prevent me from coming to the place where you are. Your crew of the Imperishable Stars will be prevented from rowing you."⁴⁹¹

A close affinity between the Imperishable Stars and Re is also evident in another passage from the Pyramid Texts:

"The King shall go aboard the bark like Rēʿ on the banks of the Winding Waterway, the King shall be rowed by the Unwearying Stars and shall give orders to the Imperishable Stars."⁴⁹²

Such traditions attest to the intimate and indissoluble connection thought to exist between the Imperishable Stars and the daily cycle of the ancient sun god. Yet the question remains to be answered: What can the circumpolar stars possibly have to do with the daily cycle of the present Sun? The circumpolar stars are *never* visible during the day. The Sun itself, in turn, is *never* visible together with the circumpolar stars, much less in their immediate vicinity, as implied in the Pyramid Texts.⁴⁹³

---

⁴⁹⁰ *PT* 1168-1171.
⁴⁹¹ *PT* 1438-1439.
⁴⁹² *PT* 2172-2173.
⁴⁹³ J. Gwyn Griffiths called attention to the apparent astronomical anomaly many years ago. See his "Review of 'The Imperishable Stars of the Northern Sky in the Pyramid

In order to decipher how the Egyptian skywatchers conceptualized the Imperishable Stars, it is necessary to resolve how they understood the boats of the Sun. It is to that millennia-old mystery that we now turn.

---

Texts'," *JEA* 80 (1994), p. 232, wherein he writes: "The case of Re seems more difficult, for if he is the sun-god and the sun plainly sets every evening, how can he belong to the 'never-setting stars', which is the Egyptian phrase for the Circumpolar Stars?"

## The Boats of the Sun

> "The supreme beatification in the Pyramid Texts was to join the Sun God's boat or to become 'one of those dwellers in the light.'"[494]

> "The iconography of the sun's course had—or acquired in the course of its development—more than a paradigmatic status in the whole of Egyptian religion: it became a sort of formulation of the cosmos, the central idea in the Egyptian picture of the world."[495]

> "The most frequently recurring themes are the sun-god's voyages across the sky in the day-barque and across the inverted vault of the netherworld in the night-barque."[496]

> "The Egyptian conception of solar barks and solar motion is apparently a not inconsiderable part of the cosmology that is to a large extent the framework of Egyptian religion."[497]

The failure of conventional Egyptology to account for the most basic facts of Egyptian celestial geography and funerary religion is nowhere more evident than when it comes to explaining the manifold traditions surrounding the boats of the sun, the so-called "day-boat" ($m'nd.t$) and "night-boat" ($mskt.t$). Despite the fact that the solar boat(s) form(s) one of the most prominent themes in all of Egyptian religion, modern scholars are unable to point to a tangible celestial prototype behind the imagery in question. Indeed, in his monumental study of Egyptian astral religion Rolf Krauss speaks simply of an "imagined" ship.[498] James Allen has defended a similar view:

---

[494] R. T. Clark, *Myth and Symbol in Ancient Egypt* (London, 1978), p. 141.
[495] J. Assmann, *The Search for God in Ancient Egypt* (Ithaca, 2001), p. 109.
[496] H. Stewart, *Traditional Egyptian Sun Hymns of the New Kingdom* (London, 1967), p. 38.
[497] E. Thomas, "Solar Barks Prow to Prow," *JEA* 42 (1956), p. 79.
[498] R. Krauss, *Astronomische Konzepte und Jenseitsvorstellungen in den Pyramidentexten* (Wiesbaden, 1997), p. 145 writes: "Das imaginierte Sonnenschiff selbst liesse sich im entsprechenden stellaren Bereich suchen."

"The Egyptians understood the solar circuit as a circumnavigation of the world by boat...The sky was seen as the surface of the cosmic ocean where it met the atmosphere, and the sun's daily journey through the sky therefore required a boat, known as the Dayboat."[499]

A survey of the extensive literature on the subject will fail to reveal a single coherent explanation of how the solar boats are to be conceptualized from the standpoint of natural science or modern astronomy.[500] Instead one finds vague allusions to abstract symbolism and/or figurative interpretations of the sun's daily movements from east to west—as if this could ever inspire a rich tradition of a solar boat manned by clearly identified stars.

The solar boat's central importance in Egyptian religion forms a recurring theme in Samuel Mercer's four-volume commentary on the Pyramid Texts. In an attempt to come to grips with the archaic tradition that the Imperishable Stars rowed the day-boat, Mercer offered the following observation:

"Among the earliest regular boats were the two famous boats of the sun already mentioned, which were of such great importance that they were sometimes rowed by the stars, the imperishable stars rowing the *m'nd.t*, or day boat (1439a, 1171c), and the indefatigable rowing the *mskt.t*, or night boat (2173a, 1171d), for perhaps, the *m'nd.t*-boat had to take a southern course in order to reach the West, and the *mskt.t*-boat a northern one to reach the East due to the teaching of the stellar tradition

---

[499] J. Allen, *The Ancient Egyptian Pyramid Texts* (Atlanta, 2005), p. 9.
[500] For previous studies of the Egyptian traditions of the solar bark, see K. Sethe, "Altägyptische Vorstellungen vom Lauf der Sonne," *Sitzungsberichten der Preussischen Akademie der Wissenschaften* (Berlin, 1928), pp. 259-284; H. Altenmüller, "Aspekte des Sonnenlaufes in den Pyramidentexten," in F. Daumas ed., *Hommages à Françoise Daumas* (Montpellier, 1986), pp. 1-15; R. Anthes, "Die Sonnenboote in den Pyramidentexten," ZÄS 82 (1957), pp. 77-89; O. Firchow, "Königsschiff und Sonnenbarke," WZKM 54 (1957), pp. 34-42; W. Westendorf, *Altägyptische Darstellungen des Sonnenlaufs auf der abschüssigen Himmelsbahn* (Berlin, 1966); E. Hornung, *Die Nachtfahrt der Sonne* (Zurich, 1990).

still influential, which doubtless preceded the rise and influence of the solar teaching of Heliopolis."[501]

In his fourth and final volume Mercer offered a diagram depicting the Egyptian universe wherein the respective movements of the two boats are modeled (see figure one).[502] Like all other Egyptologists, Mercer takes it for granted that the day boat moves from east to west overhead during the day, while the night boat travels from west to east while out of sight beneath the Earth during the night. As we will discover, however, such movements are impossible to reconcile with the express testimony of the earliest Egyptian texts.

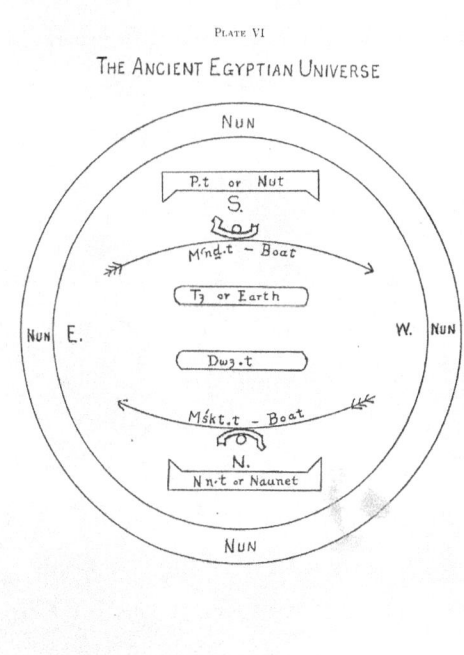

Figure 1

---

[501] S. Mercer, *op. cit.*, Vol. 4, p. 71.
[502] Plate VI, reproduced here as figure one.

Jan Assmann was arguably the world's foremost authority on Egyptian solar religion. If anyone was in a position to offer some guidance in elucidating the Egyptian conceptions attending the solar boats, it should have been him. For Assmann the archaic beliefs about the solar boats reflected an abstract symbolism associated with the familiar cycle of day and night:

"The two boats are symbolic of day and night/east and west, which comprise the total movement of the sun. The sun god travels during the day in the *Mꜥnḏt* boat (east-west) and at night in the *Msktt* boat (west-east). The change of vessel takes place in the morning and at night. But in the hymns this detailed conception of solar movement is unimportant. The duality of boats, moreover, stems from the basic structure of Egyptian thinking in polar opposite pairs or 'dual units', which expresses an abstract and complex higher concept of 'unification' of two concrete and complementary partial concepts. What is expressed in the two boats and all pair symbols relating to the day-night cycle is a concept of periodicity and perpetuity characterizing the Egyptian concept of cosmic time as eternal movement circling within itself."[503]

How exactly Assmann's highly speculative hypothesis helps us to understand the constellation of detailed traditions surrounding the solar boat(s) remains unclear. In what sense can "a concept of periodicity and perpetuity" with respect to time as eternal movement help to explain the role of the Imperishable Stars as rowers of the day-boat?

In his entry on the sun god in the *Lexikon der Ägyptologie*, Assmann offered a diagram of the movements of the two boats (see figure two).[504] Like Mercer, Assmann has the day-boat traveling in the southern sky while the night-boat travels in the northern sky. How, then, are we to

---

[503] J. Assmann, *Egyptian Solar Religion in the New Kingdom* (London, 1995), p. 50.
[504] J. Assmann, "Sonnengott," *Lexikon der Ägyptologie* VI (Wiesbaden, 1984), col. 1088. It should be noted that, in a recent discussion of the solar cycle, Silvia Zago, *A Journey through the Beyond* (Columbus, 2022), p. 5 offers a schematic representation all but indistinguishable from that of Assmann.

explain the Egyptian report that the Imperishable Stars—consistently said to reside in the north—man the day-boat?

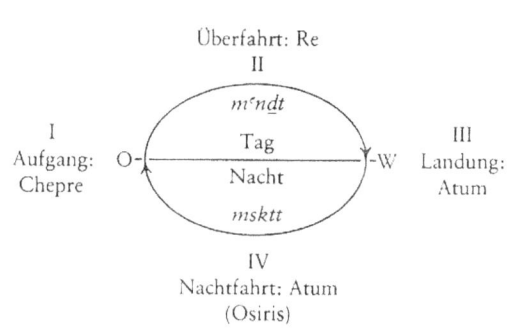

Figure 2

As proved to be the case with regards to the ultimate decipherment of the Egyptian hieroglyphic script itself, it was an outsider who pointed the way to a solution. In a masterful analysis first published in 1988, David Talbott argued that Egyptian traditions describing the ship of heaven originated in a perfectly concrete astronomical phenomenon—specifically, a luminous crescent which revolved around the ancient sun god (not the present sun). According to Talbott's historical reconstruction, the Earth participated in a polar configuration wherein it shared axial alignment with a number of other planetary bodies during the prehistoric period (more on this later). During the brief but memorable period in question—likely measured in hundreds of years—the inclination of this configuration's axis with respect to our current Sun was such that the latter's light illuminated only one side of the ancient sun god, causing a crescent to be projected onto the latter body. The crescent circled around the circumpolar heaven with the daily revolution of the Earth about its axis. This crescent would have been described as as a ship, among other metaphors. Figure three illustrates the primary phases of the crescent-ship's revolution as reconstructed by Talbott.[505]

Figure 3

In the model depicted above, the movement of the crescent proceeds in a counterclockwise manner around the central orb. As the crescent descended to the left of the illuminated orb(s) it gradually increased in brilliance until it reached its brightest phase immediately below the planetary orb in question (as in the second illustration in figure three). Thereafter the crescent gradually dimmed until it reached the uppermost position over the central orb (as in the fourth illustration of figure three). According to Talbott, it was the periodic illumination and dimming of the crescentine "ship" that constituted the cycle of day and night during the period in question.[506]

It will be noted that Talbott's model would turn that of Mercer on its head, as it were, placing the *Mʿnḏ.t*-boat at the base of heaven (north) and the *Mskt.t*-boat at the apex (south). The direction(s) traveled by the respective boats, similarly, are reversed in this model as opposed to those of Mercer and Assmann (counterclockwise as opposed to clockwise). Most important, perhaps, is the fact that, in Talbott's model, the solar boat's entire range of motion occurs in plain view in the circumpolar region overhead while in the models offered by the two Egyptologists the nocturnal voyage of the *Mskt.t*-boat occurred *under* the Earth and thus out of sight of Egyptian skywatchers. Each of these unique features of Talbott's model leads to a number of specific and *testable* deductions

---

[505] D. Talbott, "The Ship of Heaven," *Aeon* 1:3 (1988), pp. 57-96.
[506] *Ibid.*, p. 59: "It is my claim that all aspects of the primitive daily cycle derive their meanings from the appearance and behavior of the polar configuration."

which, should they be confirmed, have profound ramifications for a proper understanding of Egyptian celestial geography, to say nothing of modern astronomy.

As a case in point, Talbott's model requires that the solar boat travel *downwards* during the "day" phase and *upwards* during the "night." This unique feature of the model stands in dramatic contrast to what would naturally be expected given the conventional view, wherein the sun "climbs upwards" during the day and "descends" below the western horizon at night. What, then, do the earliest Egyptian texts have to say on the matter?

A survey of the relevant passages from the Pyramid and Coffin Texts describing the movements of the solar boat provides dramatic confirmation of Talbott's thesis while revealing one anomaly after another for the conventional model. Consider the following verse from Spell 18 from the Coffin Texts: "You shall go up upon the great west side of the sky and go down the great east side of the earth."[507] This passage prompted Raymond Faulkner to lodge the following protest:

"This unexpected reversal of the points of the compass is incomprehensible. We would expect the deceased to go up on the east and down on the west as does the sun. Perhaps we have here a blunder in an early copy which no-one has noticed or at least attempted to correct."[508]

If we return to the model of the Egyptian cosmos depicted in figure three, it will be seen that the solar boat gradually becomes more illuminated on the "left" side of the polar configuration and dims on the right side. The ancient Egyptians understood the first phase as "going down the great east side of the earth." The opposite phase—the third illustration here—the Egyptians understood as "going up upon the great west side of the sky."

---

[507] *CT* I:55.
[508] R. Faulkner, *The Ancient Egyptian Coffin Texts* (Warminster, 1973), p. 11. See here the discussion of D. Talbott, "The Ship of Heaven," *Aeon* 1:3 (1988), p. 85.

Far from being an isolated example of "confusion" on the part of Egyptian scribes, the same downward motion of the day-boat is reported elsewhere in the Egyptian texts. Witness the following passage from Spell 44 of the Coffin Texts: "You travel upstream in the *Msktt* Boat You travel downstream in the *M'ndt* Boat."[509] Although it is difficult to understand such statements by reference to the motion of the present Sun, which appears to travel upwards and east to west by day and west to east (or downwards) by night, it is perfectly descriptive of the movements of the solar boat in Talbott's model.[510]

Significantly, Faulkner offered a slightly different translation of Spell 44 from the Coffin Texts: "May you sail southward in the Night-bark and northward in the Day-bark."[511] How are we to explain this choice by Faulkner? In order to make sense of such traditions with respect to the solar boat(s) it must be remembered that, according to the conventional view, the ancient Egyptians oriented themselves toward the south—i.e., the region associated with the source of the Nile.[512] The Nile itself flowed towards the north. In Spell 44 quoted above, the statement "You travel downstream in the *M'ndt* Boat" naturally implied traveling northwards. John Wilson emphasized this point in his pioneering essay on the nature of the Egyptian cosmos:

"It is now time to consider the terms in which the Egyptian viewed the physical universe, of which his land was the focal centre. First of all, he

---

[509] J. Assmann, *Egyptian Solar Religion in the New Kingdom* (London, 1995), pp. 61-62.

[510] It will be noted that the very same anomaly is evidently attested in ancient India. See the discussion in G. Nagy, *Greek Mythology and Poetics* (Ithaca, 1990), p. 96: "Savitr, who goes *pravat-* 'downstream' during the day; come sunset, Savitr reaches the dreaded second sky of the lower world, where he travels *udvat-* 'upstream' during the night."

[511] *CT* I:184-185 as translated by R. Faulkner, *op. cit.*, p. 36.

[512] L. Lesko, "Ancient Egyptian Cosmogonies and Cosmology," in B. Shafer ed., *Religion in Ancient Egypt* (Ithaca, 1991), p. 117 writes: "The Egyptians' geographical orientation was toward the south—the source of the Nile. Accordingly, Upper Egypt was in the south and Lower Egypt in the north, while one word meant both 'west' and 'right' and another both 'east' and 'left.'"

took his orientation from the Nile River, the source of his life. He faced the south, from which the stream came...On his left was the east and on his right the west. The word for 'east' and 'left' is the same, and the word for 'west' and 'right' is the same."[513]

Returning to the model of the Egyptian cosmos depicted in figure three, it stands to reason that if the illuminated first (left) phase represents the "east" and the third (right) phase the "west," then the second or *lowermost* phase should represent the "north" and the fourth or *uppermost* phase the "south" (It will be noted that, in this sense, Talbott's model agrees with that of Mercer, wherein the cardinal directions are similarly ordered).[514] The second phase, as noted earlier, was that associated with the greatest illumination of the day boat, while the fourth phase was that associated with the dimming of the night-boat. Taking Talbott's model as our guide, it follows that as the day-boat began descending to the left of the sun god it was conceptualized as traveling "downstream" or "northward"—this in accordance with the situation in Egypt whereby boats on the Nile journeyed downstream from the south towards the Delta in the north. As the solar boat traveled to the right of the sun god, on the other hand, it was thought to move "upstream" or "southward" towards the apex of the celestial watercourse. In short, the testimony from the Coffin Texts to the effect that the day-boat travels "northward" or "downstream" during the day and the night-boat "southward" or "upstream" during the night—while impossible to reconcile with the Sun's current movements or the models of Mercer and Assmann—agrees in every respect with Talbott's model depicted in figure three.

---

[513] J. Wilson, "Egypt," in H. Frankfort et al eds., *Before Philosophy* (Baltimore, 1946), p. 51.
[514] D. Redford, "Egypt and the World Beyond," in D. Silverman ed., *Ancient Egypt* (London, 1997), p. 40 noted that "south" connoted "up": "For the ancient Egyptians, the south was 'up'; the word for west was cognate with the West Semitic word for 'right hand'; and places south were at the 'forefront'. This southward orientation betokened a cultural and political fact: for most of its history until the New Kingdom, Egypt was far more interested in its African roots than any relationship with Asia."

Especially telling is the fact that the day-boat is apparently never represented with a sail or mast. This is doubtless because it was conceptualized as traveling *downstream towards the north*.[515] The night-boat, on the other hand, *is* depicted with mast and sails, presumably because it was thought to travel *upstream* or against the current, thereby requiring a sail. Wilson emphasized this point many years ago:

"Navigation on the Nile employed the power of the current in moving north. In moving south, boats raised the sail in order to take advantage of the prevailing north wind, which would push them against the current. Since this was normal, it became the ideal for any world, including the afterlife. Into their tombs the Egyptians put two model boats, which might be projected by magic into the next world for navigation there. One boat had the sail down, for sailing north with the current on the waters of the other world; one boat had the sail up for sailing south with that north wind which must be normal in any proper existence, here or hereafter."[516]

Equally significant is the fact that the Coffin Texts report that the sun shines while traveling "downstream" to the north. Witness the following passage from Spell 129:

"To know the paths to the sky. I have opened the paths in the sky, the sun has shone when going downstream to the north from the south."[517]

Suffice it to say that passages such as this and the others quoted above will never be explained by reference to the familiar movements of the current Sun. Yet the earliest Egyptian testimony accords perfectly with the reconstruction advanced here, wherein the solar boat becomes increasingly illuminated as it moves downwards, or downstream, from the south to the north and dims as it climbs the sky to the south.

Yet with each mystery resolved, additional questions present themselves. To return to the vexing problem which Sethe and several

---

[515] J. Assmann, *op. cit.*, p. 50 writes: "I know of no representation of a Day Boat with a mast and sail; but cf. the two boats on the picture of sunset in the Book of Night."
[516] J. Wilson, *op. cit.*, p. 46.
[517] *CT* II:150.

generations of Egyptologists struggled to explain: How are we to understand the Egyptian testimony to the effect that the Imperishable Stars in the north could man the day-boat?[518]

---

[518] Kurt Sethe, "Altägyptische Vorstellungen vom Lauf der Sonne," *Sitzungsberichten der Preussischen Akademie der Wissenschaften* (Berlin, 1928), p. 283: "Hier sind es also ganz unzweideutig wirklich die Sterne Nordhimmels, die im Tagesschiff den Sonnengott begleiten, die des Südhimmels, die im Nachtschiff bei ihm sein sollen."

# Localizing the Imperishable Stars in the Egyptian Cosmos

> "Here it should be remembered that groups of stars may be envisaged as the 'crew' rowing or towing the solar barque, even though they may not be visible to the human onlooker."[519]

In a previous chapter we noted that the ancient Egyptian testimony with regard to the Imperishable Stars poses seemingly insurmountable problems for Egyptologists and astronomers alike. For if the Imperishable Stars are to be identified with the circumpolar stars, as most Egyptologists would have us believe, it is difficult to understand why they would be described as manning the day-boat of the Sun. This follows directly from the readily observable fact that the circumpolar stars are *never* visible together with the Sun during the daytime. Indeed, the circumpolar stars do not move in close proximity to the ecliptic—the apparent path of the Sun across the sky.

Especially puzzling are statements to the effect that the Imperishable Stars are to be found in the "Lower Sky" (Naunet). In Spell 570 from the Pyramid Texts, for example, the following speech is attributed to the deceased king:

"I am a star which illumines the sky...I live beside you, you gods of the Lower Sky, the Imperishable Stars."[520]

If the Imperishable Stars are to be identified with the circumpolar stars, it seems unfathomable that the Egyptian skywatchers would describe them as occupying the lowermost portion of the sky. Such a statement is patently absurd from the conventional understanding of the Imperishable Stars, wherein the latter—by definition—occupy the circumpolar region some 30 degrees removed from the horizon as visible at Cairo.

---

[519] K. Goebs, *Crowns in Egyptian Funerary Literature* (Oxford, 2008), p. 92.
[520] *PT* 1455-1456.

How, then, are we to make sense of the Egyptian traditions describing the Imperishable Stars? What is needed, it would appear, is a solution that accounts for the intimate relationship between the Imperishable Stars and the day-boat of the sun-god while also explaining their relationship to the *lowermost portion of heaven*—not to mention their proverbial location in the north.

Turning now to the model outlined in figure one, it can be seen that the day-boat is to be identified with the illuminated (and upturned) crescent at the base of the Egyptian cosmos. If we are to take the Egyptian statements at face value, it follows that the Imperishable Stars must be located in close proximity to this crescentine boat. And this, in fact, is precisely where our model would place them.

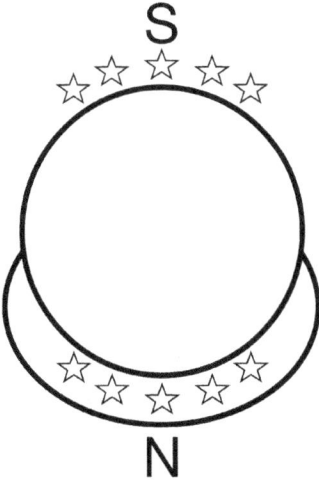

Figure 1

Keys to Figure 1:
   (1) The lower stars are the Imperishable Stars (*iḥmw-sk*).
   (2) The upper stars are the Unwearying Stars (*iḥmw-wrḏ*).
   (3) The lower crescent is the day bark (*Mꜥnḏt*).
   (4) The region labeled A is the lower sky (Naunet) or north.
   (5) The region labeled B is the upper sky or south.

What, then, are we to make of the testimony offered by PT 1456b, wherein the Imperishable Stars are said to reside in the Lower Sky? Simply put, it makes perfect sense in terms of the model outlined here: The Imperishable Stars—as rowers of the day boat—*occupied the "lower" portion of the visible Egyptian cosmos*. It is for this reason, presumably, that the word *nn(w)t*, "Lower Sky," is determined with an upturned crescent-like form, understood by Egyptologists to represent an "inverted" sky sign.[521]

It will be noted, moreover, that the Pyramid Texts specifically locate the lower sky *in the north*.[522] This, too, is a decisive datum for, as noted earlier, our model agrees with that of Mercer in placing the "north" in the lowermost portion of the Egyptian cosmos—i.e., in the very region associated with the day-boat. Thus it follows that, as inhabitants of the day-boat, the Imperishable Stars *must have been localized in the northern or lowermost portion of the Egyptian cosmos*.

An additional clue to deciphering the original celestial context behind Egyptian references to the Imperishable Stars is the fact that they are occasionally named in opposition to the *iḥmw-wrḏ*, "the Unwearying Stars."[523] PT 1171, quoted earlier, is typical in this regard: "Occupy your seat in the Bark of Rēʿ, row over the sky and mount up to the distant ones; row with the Imperishable Stars, navigate with the Unwearying Stars."

Having defined the Imperishable Stars as those satellites that occupied the lowermost portion of the Egyptian cosmos, how would we propose to understand the so-called Unwearying Stars? As complementary stellar counterparts to the Imperishable Stars, it stands to reason that the Unwearying Stars most likely correspond to those satellites that occupied

---

[521] *PT* 149, as elsewhere.
[522] *PT* 1691b.
[523] H. Beinlich, "Sterne," *Lexikon der Ägyptologie, Vol. 6* (Wiesbaden, 1986), cols. 12-13 writes as follows of the Imperishable Stars: "Sie dienen zusammen mit den Nicht-Zirkumpolarstern (*jḥmw-wrḏ*, Dekanen und Planeten) als Besatzung der Sonnenbarke, wobei die *jḥmw-sk* den Sonnengott in seiner Tagesbarke, die *jḥmw-wrḏ* ihn in seiner Nachtbarke begleiten."

the uppermost portion of the Egyptian cosmos (i.e., the "southernmost" stars[524] labeled 2 in figure one). If so, it is to be expected that the Unwearying Stars would man the solar boat during its "evening" phase—i.e., during that period when the crescentine boat is associated with the phase of growing dim. In fact, this is exactly where the Egyptian texts place them.[525] The latter idea is attested in a text dating to the New Kingdom:

"You take your place in the day boat, [m]anned by the 'indestructibles'…Re sets in the night boat, Manned by the 'inexhaustible ones'."[526]

In this context it is telling to note that the Egyptian scribes employed two different terms to describe the precise means of propelling the solar boat during its daily circumambulations. In the passage above (1171), describing the rowing of the Imperishable Stars in the day boat, the verb employed is *ḫn,* written with a pictograph depicting two arms engaged in rowing with a paddle ( ). Yet in the complementary passage describing the behavior of the Unwearying Stars in the night-boat, the verb is *sqdj*, denoting sailing "with the wind," determined with the following pictograph: .[527] Here, too, there would appear to be a perfectly rational basis for the scribes' choice of verbs, for it is only within the night-boat

---

[524] J. Allen, *The Ancient Egyptian Pyramid Texts* (Atlanta, 2005), p. 9 would identify the Unwearying Stars with the stars of the south in contrast to the Imperishable Stars in the north.

[525] P. Wallin, *Celestial Cycles* (Uppsala, 2002), p. 119: "It has been emphasized that the Imperishable Stars were identified with the crew of the day bark and that the Unwearying Stars were equated with the crew of the night bark as early as the Old Kingdom." See also R. Krauss, *op. cit.*, pp. 142-145.

[526] Berlin 7316 as translated in J. Assmann, *Egyptian Solar Religion in the New Kingdom* (London, 1995), p. 44. With reference to this text, A. Blackman, "The Stela of Nebipusenwosret," *JEA* 21 (1934), p. 5 wrote as follows: "According to an inscription in the Berlin Museum…dating from the New Kingdom, the Imperishable Stars (*iḥmw-sk*) man the sun-god's day-boat (*mʿndt*), while the Unwearying Stars (*iḥmw-wrḏ*) man the night-boat (*msktt*)."

[527] R. Hannig, *Ägyptisches Wörterbuch I* (Mainz, 2003), p. 1247.

that a sail would be needed—i.e., as we noted earlier, it was only when traveling during the night that the boat was going towards the south, or "upstream" and thus against the current, thereby requiring a sail. Evidently the Egyptian scribes employed the verb *ḫn* when describing rowing with the current and *sqdj* when sailing with the wind against the current. In short, while such fine points of language have no conceivable point of reference in the modern skies, wherein a "night-boat" is nowhere to be found and the Unwearying Stars remain a subject of endless conjecture, the language in question accurately describes the *perceived* behavior of the respective satellites in the model depicted in figure one, wherein the Imperishable Stars "row" downstream towards the north, seemingly with the current, while the Unwearying Stars sail upstream to the south with the prevailing north wind.

It should also be noted that the reconstruction offered here stands in dramatic contrast to what would ordinarily be expected from the perspective of conventional Egyptology, in which the voyage of the solar boat commemorates the movement of the Sun around the Earth. As Allen points out, Egyptologists understand the Lower Sky to be that invisible portion of the sky *beneath the Earth*:

"During the day, the sun sailed in his 'day-boat' across the waters of the sky. At night he transferred to the 'night-boat' and sailed through the Duat, across the waters of the under-sky (Naunet), while the stars emerged to sail across the sky above the earth."[528]

Yet as we have documented above, the Lower Sky (Naunet) is explicitly identified as that portion of the sky wherein reside the Imperishable Stars as rowers of the day-boat—i.e., the very opposite of what would be expected from Allen's understanding (it is also the very opposite of what would be expected in Mercer's model, wherein the day boat occupied by the Imperishable Stars travels overhead, in the *south*). It

---

[528] J. Allen, *Middle Egyptian* (Cambridge, 2010), p. 22.

is the Upper Sky, in fact, which is associated with the voyage of the night boat.

Even more problematic for Egyptologists is the fact that the Egyptian texts are quite clear that the Lower Sky is that region of the sky wherein the gods live and grow brilliant. Recall again the passage quoted above: "I am a star which illumines the sky…I live beside you, you gods of the Lower Sky, the Imperishable Stars."[529] Elsewhere the deceased king is said to "descend to the Lower Sky…to the place where the gods are."[530] Are we to believe, then, that the gods live and grow brilliant on the other side of the Earth, where they remain invisible to Egyptian skywatchers? Such an interpretation is not only an affront to common sense—it is at odds with the express testimony of the Egyptian scribes themselves. Properly understood the Egyptian testimony is perfectly straightforward: *The Lower Sky is a perfectly visible celestial structure which figured prominently in the daily cycle associated with the ancient sun god.*

---

[529] *PT* 1455-1456.
[530] *PT* 1275.

## Horus and the Ship of Heaven

"Ancient Egypt has served as a kind of Rorschach test on which each generation has imposed its own image."[531]

A recurring theme in Egyptian texts from all periods finds the Horus-star being located in close proximity to the solar bark. The testimony from the *Book of the Dead* is representative: "I am Horus who flew up, I have lighted on the vertex of Re in the prow of his bark which is in the Primordial Water."[532]

Similar conceptions are evident in the Coffin Texts, wherein it is implied that Horus became King of the Gods at the very moment he entered into the celestial bark. In Spell 760, for example, the falcon-god is invoked as follows:

"[He] who is in the bow of the bark which her word brought into being on his account in the presence of the Sole Lord...It goes well with Horus son of Isis since he went in; he has become lord of the bark and he has inherited the sky. He has become the double of the Lord of All since he entered into it, and it is this Horus son of Isis who rules all the skies and their gods who are in them."[533]

In Spell 148, similarly, the Horus-star is stationed in the solar bark at the time of his accession to the throne as King of the Gods. In the Coffin Text in question Isis addresses Horus as follows: "I ask that you shall be always in the suite of Rēʿ of the horizon in the prow of the primeval bark for ever and ever."[534]

Horus's intimate relation to the solar bark figures prominently in the so-called "Legend of the Winged Disk," inscribed on the walls of the god's temple at Edfu, completed in the third century BCE.[535] In the

---

[531] A. Stille, "Perils of the Sphinx," *New Yorker* (February 10, 1997), p. 62.
[532] Spell 66 in "The Theban Recension," as translated in R. Faulkner, *The Ancient Egyptian Book of the Dead* (Austin, 1990), p. 107.
[533] VI:390.
[534] II:222.
[535] The text in question traces to the New Kingdom but doubtless reflects more archaic traditions.

opening lines of the text Horus is addressed as follows: "*Thou alightest on the prow of the barque of Rē'-Ḥarakhte.*"[536] Elsewhere in the same text it is said: "*Come, let us hasten to the Pool of Horus, that we may see the Falcon in his ship, that we may see the son of Isis in his war-galley, like Rē' in the Bark of the Morning.*"[537] Yet another passage reads: "*Come and see Horus in the prow of his ship, like Rē' when he shineth in the horizon…*"[538]

Far from being a product of later priestly speculation or syncretism, Horus's intimate connection with a celestial bark is evident already at the dawn of history. Thus, a comb from the First Dynasty reign of King Djet shows a falcon perched within a bark (see figure one).

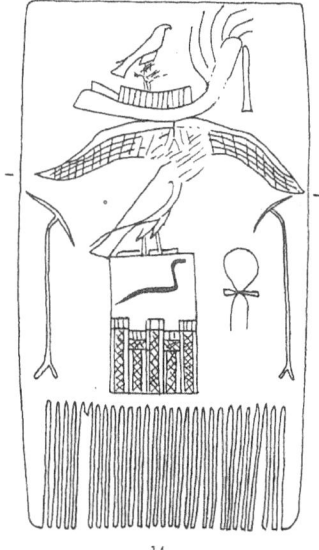

Figure 1

---

[536] H. Fairman, "The Myth of Horus at Edfu—I," *JEA* 21 (1935), p. 27.
[537] A. Blackman & H. Fairman, "The Myth of Horus at Edfu—III," *JEA* 29 (1943), p. 6.
[538] *Ibid.*, p. 10.

The Pyramid Texts likewise place Horus in close proximity to a giant celestial boat. Thus in Spell 519 we read that the Horus-star appeared in front of a celestial boat at the time of Creation:

"O Morning Star, Horus of the Netherworld, divine Falcon, *wȝḏȝḏ*-bird whom the sky bore…give me these your two fingers which you gave to the Beautiful, the daughter of the great god, when the sky was separated from the earth, when the gods ascended to the sky, you having a soul and appearing in front of your boat of 770 cubits which the gods of Pe bound together for you, which the eastern gods built for you."[539]

Insofar as the Egyptian pharaoh was considered to be the human incarnation of the Horus-star, it comes as no surprise to find that he hoped to secure a place within the celestial bark upon his death. This wish was the subject of several spells from the Pyramid and Coffin Texts. In Spell 45 from the Coffin Texts the deceased king was invoked as follows: "You have appeared at the bow of the Bark and you have authority over the starboard side."[540] Spell 61 makes a similar claim: "You sit on the mat(?) of turquoise at the bow of the Bark of Rēʿ."[541] In Spell 366, finally, the deceased king prays that he might follow Horus's example and be raised up by Isis: "I am raised up by Isis, just as she established her son Horus in the bow of the bark of Rēʿ which he raised up."[542]

As noted earlier, Horus is said to have acceded to the throne as King of the Gods upon entering the celestial bark. Spell 295 is representative: "Horus is commander of the sacred bark, and his father's throne has been given to him."[543] Here, too, the deceased king hopes to emulate Horus: "See, you are at the bow of the Bark, and a throne in the shrine is given to you; see, you are king of the sky."[544]

---

[539] *PT* 1207-1210.
[540] I:196f-g.
[541] *CT* I:260f.
[542] *CT* V:28.
[543] *CT* IV:49.
[544] *CT* I:224-5.

Given its conspicuous role in Egyptian cosmogonical tradition, it stands to reason that Horus's "throne" within the celestial bark would have left its mark on the architecture and/or artifacts of Egyptian temples. Egyptian temples, in fact, typically included a miniaturized bark not unlike that associated with Horus's primordial accession to the throne:

"Most Egyptian temples follow a common plan, with an open-air courtyard in front, a columned hall in the middle, and a small sanctuary at the back housing the god's image…The sanctuary itself was normally a small, dark, room, with a pedestal in its middle. The pedestal held a miniature bark in the form of a papyrus skiff, carrying a closed shrine (represented by the hieroglyph ⛵). The god's image was housed in this shrine, usually in the form of a gold statue."[545]

Having now surveyed Egyptian texts spanning a period of well over 2000 years, it is evident that they testify to a stubborn belief that Horus's bark was a prominent fixture of the archaic sky. Asked to provide a natural reference for the solar bark, Krauss points to the eastern horizon:

"The notion of the god [Seth as Mercury] standing in the bow of the solar barque can be understood as Mercury seen at dawn on the eastern horizon. For the ancient Egyptians who imagined that the sun god travelled in a barque, it was evident that Mercury-Seth stood in the prow of the solar barque."[546]

Amazingly, Krauss argues that the mere fact that the present Sun rises in the eastern horizon is enough to produce the persistent belief that the ancient sun-god moved across the skies in a celestial bark distinguished by Mercury standing in its prow—an invisible prow in an invisible bark, as it were. Such an hypothesis strains credulity to its limit and flies in the face of everything we know about the Egyptians' preference for concrete imagery. A scientific approach to the ancient Egyptian astronomical traditions should be able to do better than ad hoc wild guesses such as this.

---

[545] J. Allen, *Middle Egyptian* (Cambridge, 2010), p. 57.
[546] R. Krauss, "The Eye of Horus and the Planet Venus," in J. Steele & A. Imhausen eds., *Under One Sky* (Munster, 2002), p. 198.

## Horus of the Daybreak

> "Whoever wishes to understand ancient Egyptian culture, and especially its religion and way of thinking, must learn the language of images."[547]

A cornerstone of modern Egyptology holds that the earliest Egyptian texts are primarily devoted to describing the daily cycle of the current sun.[548] If so, it should be a relatively easy matter to point to early literary passages that clearly and unequivocally describe the familiar sunrise in readily recognizable imagery and terminology. Yet such references are nowhere to be found in the Pyramid Texts. What we find instead are numerous references to towering doors or gates within which the Horus-star was wont to appear. Utterance 325 from the Pyramid Texts is representative:

"The doors of the sky [are opened], The doors of the firmament are thrown open at dawn for Horus of the Gods, He goes up into the Field of Rushes, He bathes in the Field of Rushes. The doors of the sky are opened, The doors of the firmament are thrown open at dawn for Harakhti…The doors of the sky are opened, The doors of the firmament are thrown open for Horus of Shezmet."[549]

The same basic text occurs in Utterances 479 and 563 as well, albeit with some minor variations. Utterance 479 reads as follows:

"The doors of the sky are opened, The doors of the firmament are thrown open for Horus of the Gods; He goes forth at dawn and bathes in the Field of Rushes. The doors of the sky are opened, the doors of the firmament are thrown open for Horus of the East; He goes forth at dawn and bathes in the Field of Rushes. The doors of the sky are opened, The

---

[547] E. Hornung, "Ancient Egyptian Religious Iconography," in J. Sasson ed., *Civilizations of the Ancient Near East, Vol. 3/4* (Farmington Hills, 1995), p. 1729.
[548] W. Westendorf, "Horizont und Sonnenschiebe," *Studia Aegyptiaca* 1 (1974), p. 389 writes: "Das tägliche Auf- und Untergehen der Sonne, vor allem ihre regelmässige Wiederkehr im Osthorizont, ist für den Agypter zu einer eingängigen Symbol des sich zyklisch erneuernden Lebens geworden."
[549] *PT* 525-528.

doors of the firmament are thrown open for Horus of Shezmet; He goes forth at dawn and bathes in the Field of Rushes."[550]

Spell 563, finally, reads as follows:

"The doors of the sky are opened, The doors of the firmament are thrown open for Horus of the Gods, That he may ascend and bathe in the Field of Rushes. The doors of the sky are opened for me, The doors of the firmament are thrown open for me, That I may ascend and bathe in the Field of Rushes. The doors of the sky are opened, The doors of the firmament are thrown open for Horus of Shezmet, that he may ascend and bathe in the Field of Rushes."[551]

Such references are so commonplace in the Egyptian texts that it is quite easy to overlook the obvious fact that there are no "door"-like structures in close proximity to the Sun that would provide a ready tangible reference for such imagery, at once rich in detail and recurring across three millennia of Egyptian history. How, then, are we to understand the "doors/gates of heaven" from the standpoint of natural science?

---

[550] *PT* 981-983.
[551] *PT* 1408-1416.

### The Doors of Heaven

A decisive clue to the archaic imagery is provided by the fact that the Egyptians ascribed a bovine form to the doors/gates in question. In the Pyramid Texts, for example, the double doors of heaven are celebrated as follows: "The King opens the double doors, the King attains the limit of the horizon…"[552] In the passage in question the word translated by Faulkner as "double doors" is *ḫnswy*, determined with a double bull set next to two door-leaves (see figure one). In his commentary on this passage, Samuel Mercer observed: "The word *ḫns* means 'door' (WB. III 300) and refers to the heavenly double-bull…and here means the door of heaven with two leaves."[553]

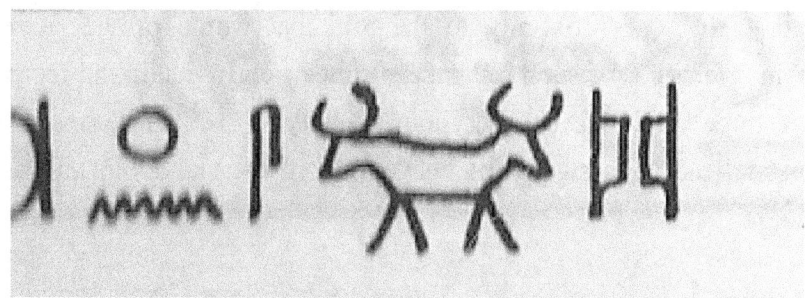

Figure 1

Mercer's analysis is doubtless correct, so far as it goes, but his "explanation" begs the question: Where in all of heaven is a double-bull to be found?

Allusions to a double bull in the sky are also to be found in the Coffin Texts. Spell 260 offers a case in point: "I am this double bull who is on the vertex of Rē', who makes brightness in the East."[554]

---

[552] *PT* 416.
[553] S. Mercer, *The Pyramid Texts in Translation and Commentary, Vol. 2* (New York, 1952), p. 193.
[554] *CT* III:381.

The double bull in question is here explicitly linked to the "brightness" (*ḥḏ*) associated with the onset of daybreak. This is an important clue to the original celestial context of the imagery, as we will discover below.

What are we to make of such traditions? Why would the literal-minded Egyptian skywatchers describe the single most important natural event in their astral religion as occurring within two seemingly invisible celestial entities—in this case, two "doors" or bulls set end-to-end? This question, in turn, begs another: Are we to understand the Egyptian imagery attached to the double doors/bulls as figurative in nature, or as a relatively accurate characterization of the prehistoric skywatcher's experience of the Horus-star's glorious epiphany?

Aside from pointing out the obvious—namely, that early Egyptian descriptions of the "sunrise" regularly feature the double doors or bulls—Egyptologists themselves have had virtually nothing substantive to say with regards to the possible natural origins or celestial counterpart of the double bull.[555] Doubtless most scholars would attribute the bovine imagery to creative imagination and/or metaphor. Yet there is every reason to believe that this default position is erroneous. Indeed, the mere fact that the double bull appears already on predynastic artworks (circa 3300-3100 BCE) suggests that its function in the Pyramid and Coffin Texts is akin to that of an *aide-de-mémoire* describing a familiar—*and perfectly visible*—structure or constellation in the skies overhead (see figure two).[556]

---

[555] John Baines, "Origins of Egyptian Kingship," in D. O'Connor & D. Silverman eds., *Ancient Egyptian Kingship* (Leiden, 1995), p. 112 suggested the double bull was a symbol of kingship.
[556] Adapted from the so-called *Hunter's Palette* (cat. 115) as depicted in *Visual Encyclopedia of Art: Egypt* (Florence, 2009), p. 25.

Figure 2

The same conclusion is bolstered by the fact that archaic cylinder seals from Mesopotamia describe the solar epiphany in analogous fashion. Thus, a popular scene on Akkadian cylinder seals depicts the sun-god as appearing between two celestial doors or gates (see figure three).[557]

Figure 3

---

[557] Adapted from W. Ward, *The Seal Cylinders of Western Asia* (Washington, 1910), p. 89.

Given the fact that there are no readily visible celestial structures in the immediate vicinity of the current Sun that would provide an objective reference for the "doors/gates" in question, scholars have been inclined to view such scenes as imaginary in nature. Such was the opinion offered by William Ward, a pioneer in the study of archaic Mesopotamian art: "No class of cylinders better illustrates the poetic imagination of a primitive people than those which give us the representation of the Sun-god Shamash emerging from the gates of morning and rising over the Eastern mountains."[558]

It is relevant to note, moreover, that in ancient Mesopotamia as in Egypt, the horns of a bull (or bulls) occasionally substitute for the double doors as the locus of the sun-god's epiphany (see figure four).[559] Of such scenes in Mesopotamian art, Elizabeth van Buren observed:

"The Sun-god with rays stands as in the earlier representations, pressing down with a hand on each side, but here it is not upon mountains but on the heads of two recumbent bulls whose bodies merge into the other, for they are supposed to be lying back to back to support the rising Sun-god…Here the bulls were substituted for the mountains for they were themselves the embodiment of the mountains."[560]

Figure 4

---

[558] *Ibid.*, p. 87.
[559] Adapted from R. Boehmer, *Die Entwicklung der Glyptik während der Akkad-Zeit* (Berlin, 1965), figure 397. See also figure 2:9 in P. Amiet, *La glyptique mésopotamienne archaique* (Paris, 1961), pp. 39-41.
[560] E. Douglas van Buren, "The Sun-God Rising," *Revue d'Assyriologie* 49 (1955), p. 13.

Why two bulls placed end-to-end would come to be conceptualized as the "embodiment of the mountains" is left unexplained by van Buren.

Christopher Woods recently returned to this iconographic motif in a series of important articles. Like Ward and van Buren before him, Woods' default position holds that the archaic images of the bovine figures marking the locus of sunrise are best understood as a figment of the Mesopotamian skywatchers' imagination: "No region of the cosmos plays upon the imagination like the horizon."[561]

Of the cylinder seals depicting a double bull at the site of sunrise, Woods writes: "On several Sargonic seals Šamaš is depicted climbing over a pair of kneeling bison-men—an emblematic variation of the common Sargonic motif in which Šamaš climbs the eastern mountains to begin his daily journey."[562] As for how or why this artistic motif originated, the best Woods can do is refer readers to Frans Wiggermann's suggestion that it was inspired by the bovine fauna native to the Mesopotamian landscape: "As suggested by Wiggermann, the association of the bison-man with Šamaš stems, in all probability, from the bison's natural habitat in the hilly flanks and mountainous regions east of Mesopotamia, 'distant countries traveled only by the sun.'"[563]

Are we to imagine, then, that a similar congregation of *Bos tauri* on mountains to the east of Egypt gave rise to analogous bovine imagery in that part of the world? On the contrary, the very fact that this archaic Mesopotamian image forms a precise counterpart to the Egyptian concept of the *ḫnswj* or double-bull marking the locus of sunrise tends to confirm the likelihood that some readily visible, tangible structure in the celestial landscape inspired the imagery in question (That is, of course, unless one is willing to propose that diffusion gave rise to the appearance of these analogous images and traditions in both cultures.)

---

[561] C. Woods, "At the Edge of the World: Cosmological Conceptions of the Eastern Horizon in Mesopotamia," *JANER* 9:2 (2009), p. 185.
[562] C. Woods, "The Sun-God Tablet of Nabû-apla-iddina Revisited," *JCS* 56 (2004), p. 55.
[563] *Ibid.*, p. 55.

Especially significant for the historical reconstruction offered here is the fact that Akkadian texts stress an explicit connection between the celestial bulls and the radiance of the ancient sun-god. Witness the following passage from an Early Dynastic Shamash hymn: "The bisons of Shamash make visible (his) divine radiance."[564] It will be noted at once that this archaic literary tradition offers a striking parallel to the passage from the Coffin Texts, cited earlier, wherein the double bull makes the "brightness" of the ancient sun-god: "I am this double bull who is on the vertex of Rēʿ, who makes brightness in the East."[565] To point out the obvious: Imaginary celestial structures do not shine forth in beacon-like fashion, signaling the locus of sunrise. Nor, for that matter, do they perform specific and multiple functions in ancient myth and cosmography as if on cue.

---

[564] P. Steinkeller, "Early Semitic Literature and Third Millennium Seals," in P. Fronzaroli ed., *Literature and Literary Language at Ebla* (1992), p. 266.
[565] *CT* III:381.

### Horus in utero

To return to the Egyptian traditions purportedly describing the prototypical daybreak: The first point to be emphasized is that it is the star-god Horus which is the subject of these archaic hymns. The second point that deserves underscoring is that the deceased king, as the Horus-star, is described as ascending to heaven through the doors and bathing in the Field of Rushes. Yet this is the very destination associated with the Morning Star. Utterance 461 is exemplary in this regard:

"O King, may you ascend as the Morning Star…The doors of the sky are opened for you, the doors of the firmament are thrown open for you, that you may travel by boat to the Field of Rushes, that you may cultivate barley, that you may reap emmer and prepare your sustenance therefrom like Horus the son of Atum."[566]

But we are not yet done exploring the exquisitely detailed imagery included in these archaic accounts of the prototypical "daybreak." It is notable that, in each of the three Utterances quoted above, the Horus-star is said to impregnate the sky-goddess receiving him. Utterance 325 reads as follows:

"The sky's doorway has been opened, the Cool Waters' door has been pulled open, for Horus Shezmet at daybreak…The sky's belly has swollen with the force of the [god's] seed that is in it. Behold Teti: Teti is the god's seed that is in it."[567]

Here Teti is identified with the Horus-star as the seed of the mother goddess. Utterance 563 offers a similar scenario:

"The sky's door has been opened, the Cool Waters' door has been pulled open, to Horus of Shezmet, that he might emerge and become clean in the Marsh of Reeds…Your belly, Nut, will swell with the god's seed that is in you; in fact, Pepi is the god's seed that is in you, Nut."[568]

Utterance 479, finally, offers yet another close analogue:

---

[566] *PT* 871-874.
[567] *PT* 528-532 as translated in J. Allen, *op. cit.*, p. 68.
[568] *PT* 1409-1416 as translated in J. Allen, *op. cit.*, p. 174.

"The sky's door has been opened, the Cool Waters' door has been pulled open, for Horus of Shezmet, that he might go forth at daybreak, having become clean in the Marsh of Reeds…Nut's belly has become impregnated with the seed of the akh who is in her."[569]

The peculiar testimony with regards to the stellar seed within the womb of Nut has drawn only passing mention from Egyptologists. In his commentary on the Pyramid Texts, Samuel Mercer noted the parallels but did not elaborate, much less elucidate:

"According to 532 a-b and 1416c-1417a, the seed 'which shall be' in Nut is the deceased king, which is divine, and here [990a] it is said that the seed which shall be in Nut is the seed of the spirit, therefore the 'divine seed' and the 'seed of the spirit' are one and the same, which is the king."[570]

In what sense, pray tell, does the present Sun give the impression that it is impregnating some other celestial body during its daily epiphany? Yet as we have documented here, this is *precisely* the action attributed to the Horus-star as the sharp star (*spd*). Recall again the passage quoted earlier:

"Your sister Isis has come to you, around [for] love of you. You have put her on your phallus so that your seed might emerge into her, sharp as Sothis, and sharp Horus has emerged from you as Horus in Sothis."[571]

And just as the deceased king is commonly identified as Horus *spd* during his prototypical epiphany so, too, is the deceased king expressly identified with a "star with sharp front" during the ascent to heaven. The two traditions are best viewed as variations upon a single theme. Encoded in both traditions is the memory that the Horus-star (Mars) appeared to enter into, or "impregnate," the mother goddess (Venus) as it ascended to heaven during its prototypical appearance.

---

[569] *PT* 983-990 as translated in J. Allen, *op. cit.*, pp. 280-281.
[570] S. Mercer, *The Pyramid Texts, Vol. II* (New York, 1952), p. 501.
[571] *PT* 632-633 as translated in J. Allen, *op. cit.*, pp. 81-82.

## Horus: Star of the Corporation

"As long as there are individuals who are struck by evident disharmonies, all is not yet lost."[572]

In previous chapters we have presented a wealth of evidence from the ancient historical record that seemingly points to a radically different solar system prevailing during the relatively recent prehistoric period. Among the most compelling testimony are the numerous references to a corporation of stellar satellites associated with the Horus-star in the earliest Egyptian texts. Archaic stamp seals recording royal domain names from the Early Dynastic period in the third millennium BCE (circa 2990-2600) describe the Horus-star as accompanied by an entourage or "corporation"—*ḫt*—the latter clearly understood as an assemblage of stars. Examples from the first two dynasties include *Ḥr-sbꜣ-ḫt*, "Horus, star of the corporation;" *Ḥr-tpi-ḫt*, "Horus, first of the corporation (of gods);" and *Ḥr-dsr-ḫt*, "Horus, holy of the corporation."[573]

The same idea figures prominently in the nomenclature borne by the pharaohs from the first three dynasties, who adopted names incorporating the idea of Horus as accompanied by an assembly. Examples include Semerkhet, "companion of the corporation"; Netjerikhet "(most) divine of the corporation"; and Sekhemkhet "(most) powerful of the corporation."[574]

Analogous traditions are also reflected in cosmogonic myth. In an account of creation preserved in the Pyramid Texts, the deceased king announces himself as "I am one of this great company which was born aforetime in On."[575] Here the word translated as "company" is *ḫt*. So, too, Spell 80 from the Coffin Texts includes a passage referencing the period

---

[572] H. von Dechend, "Bemerkungen zum Donnerkeil," *Prismata: Festschrift für Willy Hartner* (Wiesbaden, 1977), p. 96.
[573] See the discussion in T. Wilkinson, *Early Dynastic Egypt* (London, 1999), pp. 120-121.
[574] *Ibid.*, p. 173.
[575] *PT* 1041.

"before the first generation had been born," wherein "first generation" is the aforementioned *ḫt*.[576] A Coffin Text referencing the "First Company of Re" (*ḫt Rˁ*) confirms the celestial background of such phraseology.[577]

The stellar assembly was known by a number of different names in ancient Egypt. In the Pyramid Texts the related word *ḫt* describes the stellar "suite" accompanying the sun-god Re: "I belong to those who are in the suite of Rēˁ, who are before the Morning Star."[578] Here, too, the "suite" of Re is clearly conceptualized as an assembly of stars located in the immediate vicinity of the sun-god.

The divine assembly was also known as the "sun-folk"— *ḥnmmt*.[579] Spell 305 from the Coffin Texts describes Horus's rise to power:

"The god grows, the god rises up from his nest, he flies and soars to the underside of the sky as that great falcon, sharp of talon, long of plume, of seven cubits along his back, his wings being of greenstone…I [Horus] have shaken out my plumage on the bank of the Winding Waterway;…I have assembled the sun-folk, and all the great gods come to me bowed down."[580]

The Horus-star is here said to have "assembled the sun-folk" at the time of his epochal flight to heaven. The statement that "all the gods come to me bowed down" is a sure sign that the Divine Assembly has been convened and acknowledges the new King of the Gods.

Conclusive evidence that the so-called sun-folk are stellar in nature can be found in the Coffin Texts. Thus, in one passage a god boasts that he appears with the "sun-folk about me, about me, like Rēˁ when he was

---

[576] *CT* II:34d.
[577] *CT* V:232i.
[578] *PT* 132b. Analogous traditions appear in the Coffin Texts. See *CT* II:116; III:317; VII:146 and VII:217.
[579] N. Billing, *Performative Structure* (Leiden, 2018), p. 285 observes of the *ḥnmmt*: "A divine assembly, basically located in the sky."
[580] *CT* IV:58-59.

born."[581] Notice the specific reference to the gathering of the stellar assembly at the time when Re "was born."

Analogous traditions are evident in ancient Mesopotamia. Thus, the Great Shamash Hymn invokes the sun-god as follows: "At your rising, the gods of the land assemble."[582] The same basic scenario is evident in an Old Babylonian fable known as *The Tamarisk and the Palm*, wherein the introduction harks back to the circumstances attending Creation:

"In former days...the gods of the land, Anu, Enlil, and Ea, convened an assembly...In their midst Šamaš was seated."[583]

In short, the testimony from ancient Mesopotamia is in essential agreement with that from ancient Egypt and elsewhere: The sun-god's prototypical appearance or "birth" at the time of Creation occurred in conjunction with the dramatic appearance of a Divine Assembly. Implicit in these archaic cosmogonic traditions is the memory that the nascent sun stood in the midst of a circle or corporation of stars.

In seeking to understand these archaic accounts of a Divine Assembly attending the prototypical appearance of the sun-god, we would suggest that the most methodologically sound approach is to simply allow the archaic artworks to illuminate the cosmogonical traditions. The Mesopotamian cylinder seal depicted in figure one likely offers the very clue that we are looking for.[584]

---

[581] *CT* IV:122.
[582] Line 47 from the Great Shamash Hymn as translated by W. Lambert, *Babylonian Wisdom Literature* (Winona Lake, 1996), p. 129.
[583] Lines 1-5 as translated in *Ibid.*, p. 163.
[584] Adapted from figure 6 in L. Werr, *Studies in the Chronology and Regional Style of Old Babylonian Cylinder Seals* (Malibu, 1988), figure 26.

Figure 1

The resemblance between this image and that presented in Figure 2 is obvious at once: Indeed, the two images are virtually identical except for the fact that figure one includes an assemblage of dots or "satellites" about the central star—the Divine Assembly in our historical reconstruction. Note further the presence of the crescent adorning the so-called sun. Although there is nothing about this image that suggests that the ancient artists were trying to depict the present sun, the presence of the crescent recalls countless images of the ancient sun on Mesopotamian cylinder seals.

Figure 2

Occam's razor rears its head at this point: Granted that the Old Babylonian cylinder seal illustrated in figure one offers a relatively realistic representation of the prehistoric sky, it stands to reason that the circle of satellites around the central star would be conceptualized as an "assembly" or entourage of stellar gods circling about the primordial sun. Yet once grant this possibility and the floodgates are suddenly thrust open, revealing at once a veritable plethora of pictographic images that suggest that modern astronomy's view of the solar system's recent history is seriously flawed.

## The Star at the Front of the Sky

"It has taken years to produce preliminary translations of the huge corpus of Egyptian religious literature, and these translations often defy logical interpretation and encourage wild speculation. It is often discouraging to find that translations of the edited texts of the pyramid's inner chambers (Pyramid Texts), coffin interiors (Coffin Texts), and the papyri called the Book of the Dead contain some grammatically and lexicographically lucid passages interspersed with what can be described only as gibberish. The ancient Egyptians themselves had considerable difficulty understanding their texts, as is demonstrated by, for example, the widely differing interpretations preserved in the glosses appended regularly to chapter 17 of the Book of the Dead."[585]

Throughout the Pyramid Texts the Horus-star is described as being stationed at the "front" or forefront of a number of prominent structures in Egyptian cosmic geography. In PT 1209a, for example, Horus Duat is stationed at the "front" (ḫnt) of the solar bark. In the spell in question the falcon-god is explicitly identified as the Morning Star:

"O Morning Star, Horus of the Netherworld...you having a soul and appearing in front of your boat of 770 cubits which the gods of Pe bound together for you, which the eastern gods built for you."[586]

Horus Duat is elsewhere described as standing at the front (ḫntj) of the Imperishable Stars: "You shall emerge as Horus of the Duat at the fore of the Imperishable [Stars]."[587] This epithet recalls the third-dynasty domain name, cited in a previous chapter, describing Horus as sbꜣ ḫntj pt: "star at the front of the sky."

The fact that such Horus-epithets recur repeatedly throughout the earliest texts confirms that they had a profound significance for the

---

[585] L. Lesko, "Ancient Egyptian Cosmogonies and Cosmology," in B. Shafer ed., *Religion in Ancient Egypt* (Ithaca, 1991), p. 88.
[586] *PT* 1207-1209.
[587] *PT* 1301 as translated in J. Allen, *op. cit.*, p. 117.

Egyptian scribes and their royal audience. That each of these epithets is also employed to describe the desired destination of the deceased king points to the same conclusion and provides additional support for our hypothesis that the post-mortem ascent to heaven was expressly modeled upon the mythological career of the Horus-star.

Far from describing the familiar solar system, the epithets in question reference a radically different celestial landscape—namely, that which formerly prevailed during the prehistoric period prior to the unification of Egypt. Especially significant are those texts which imply that the Horus-star remained fixed at the "front" of the sky. In PT 1948, for example, the deceased king is implored to "endure" as Horus Duat at the "front" (*ḫnt*) of the sky: "Make the sky clear and shine on them as a god; may you be enduring at the head of the sky as Horus of the Netherworld."[588] The word *mn*, translated as "enduring" by Faulkner, literally means to "remain" or "be permanent."[589] James Allen, in fact, translates this particular phrase as follows: "Permanent at the fore of the sky as Horus."[590] Yet what can it mean that a particular star remains "permanent" at the front of the sky? Certainly such a statement is extremely difficult to reconcile with the current motions of the Sun or Venus insofar as neither celestial body occupies the same general place for more than a few hours at most.

Curiously enough, however, the Horus-star is described in similar terms again and again throughout the Egyptian texts. Much the same idea is evident in PT 1301, wherein Horus Duat is likened to the *djed*-pillar—the latter representing the classic Egyptian symbol of permanence and stability:

---

[588] *PT* 1948.
[589] R. Hannig, *Ägyptisches Wörterbuch I* (Mainz, 2003), p. 526.
[590] J. Allen, *The Ancient Egyptian Pyramid Texts* (Atlanta, 2005), p. 326.

"May you go up as Horus of the Netherworld who is at the head of the Imperishable Stars…May you be long-lasting as the ḏd-pillar for ever and ever."[591]

If we are to remain faithful to the literal meaning of the Egyptian passages in question, and leaving modern astronomical theory aside for the moment, it would appear that the scribes were celebrating the Horus-star's singular capacity for remaining in one particular spot in the sky for a prolonged period of time. Insofar as the deceased king sought to emulate the Horus-star he, too, hoped to "endure" (mn) in the celestial Hereafter. Thus it is that, upon ascending to heaven and being invoked as Horus spd, the deceased king is implored to "endure" at the front (ḫnty) of the celestial spirits (i.e., the Imperishable Stars[592]): "Endure, endure, O enduring Bull, that you may be enduring at the head of them and at the head of the spirits for ever."[593] It will be noted that this is the very same celestial locus ascribed to the Horus-star in PT 1301—namely, at the front of the Imperishable Stars.

A similar prayer is preserved in PT 945, wherein a command that the King "long endure" (mn) is repeated four times. The Cannibal Hymn preserves the same basic idea: "While the King is this one who ever appears and endures."[594] In the passage in question, the words translated as "appears" (ḫʿ) and "endures" (jmn) are doubled in order to provide emphasis.

The very same stability and permanence is emphasized with respect to the Horus-star's placement within the solar bark. Thus, in Spell 148

---

[591] It will be noted that the word translated here as "long-lasting" by Faulkner is ḏd, whence the phrase ḏd-pillar. See also *PT* 2107c, wherein the king is implored: "May you live…stable as a ḏd-pillar." On the symbolism in question, see Hartwig Altenmüller, "Djed-Pfeiler," *Lexikon der Ägyptologie, Vol. 1* (Wiesbaden, 1975), col. 1103. On Horus's intimate connection to the ḏd-pillar, see H. Frankfort, *Kingship and the Gods* (Chicago, 1978), p. 178.

[592] See *PT* 656 and *PT* 1220, wherein the identification of the spirits with the Imperishable Stars is made explicit.

[593] *PT* 481c-d.

[594] *PT* 414a.

from the Coffin Texts, cited previously, Isis addresses Horus as follows: "I ask that you shall be always in the suite of Rēʿ of the horizon in the prow of the primeval bark for ever and ever."[595] Yet if the Horus-star in question is the Morning Star, as attested by Spell 519 from the Pyramid Texts, what can it mean that a planet will reside forever at the prow or "front" of the solar bark, however the latter is to be conceptualized?

The inference to be drawn from such spells, repeated throughout the Pyramid and Coffin Texts like so many magical mantras, is that the Horus-star assumed a conspicuous *and seemingly permanent* position at the "front" of a celestial bark in the wake of its glorious manifestation *in illo tempore*. It will be noted, moreover, that this placement locates the Horus-star "at the front" of the Imperishable Stars, the rowers of the bark in question.

Such epithets have elicited precious little discussion or analysis from Egyptologists. This should not surprise us, given the fact that it is exceedingly difficult to discern what possible significance these peculiar epithets attached to the Horus-star can have from the standpoint of modern astronomy. For Krauss, as we have seen, the solar bark is an imaginary construct and thus it would seem to follow that, for him, the various spells describing the Horus-star as residing at its "front" must be considered imaginative or fantastic in nature and, as such, essentially devoid of any astronomical or cosmographic import. From the standpoint of conventional Egyptology, similarly, in which the Imperishable Stars represent the circumpolar stars, it is patently absurd to even entertain the possibility that the Horus-star—whether identified as the Sun or Venus—remained fixed at their "front."

Equally notable is the fact that, given the currently prevailing view in which the ancient Egyptian celestial landscape is virtually indistinguishable from that at present, each and every statement about the Horus-star residing at the "front" of this or that celestial structure can only

---

[595] *CT* II:222.

have a temporary or transient meaning; i.e., regardless of which star Horus is to be identified with, it can only *occasionally* reside at the "front" of the solar bark or Imperishable Stars and even then only for a very brief period (measured in minutes or hours at most). Why, then, did the Egyptian scribes make a special point of emphasizing the "permanence" of the Horus-star with respect to these all-important celestial structures?

From the conventional standpoint, moreover, whatever is said about the Horus-star should also apply to a number of other planets and stars. Thus, if the Horus-star is to be identified with Venus, as per Krauss, one should expect to find similar statements about Seth/Mercury since it presumably visits the same celestial loci as a "Morning Star." Yet such statements are very hard to come by in the Pyramid Texts. In short, from the standpoint of modern Egyptology the aforementioned epithets describing the Horus-star as remaining "fixed" at the "front" of the solar bark and/or Imperishable Stars are relatively insignificant in nature and, if not entirely fanciful or meaningless, can hardly be unique to the star in question.

From the unique vantage point offered by our historical reconstruction, in contrast, such epithets serve to describe the Horus-star in such a manner that its position can be precisely pinpointed in the prehistoric Egyptian cosmos (during a particular phase in the polar configuration's evolutionary history, that is). The statement that the Horus-star resided at the front of the Imperishable Stars implies that it was stationed in close proximity to the day-boat *at some point between those particular stars and the Earth*.[596] Each and every one of these epithets, moreover—far from being mutually exclusive— describes the Horus-star in specific relation to the respective structures mentioned and is therefore best understood as being complementary and analogous in informational

---

[596] It will be noted that the epithet *ḫnt*, in addition to denoting "before" or "in front of" also implies the first in position. In this sense, then, this epithet likely preserves the memory that Horus/Mars was the closest star to Earth and, as such, stood first in line in the polar configuration—i.e., in front of the other stars. See J. Allen, *Middle Egyptian* (Cambridge, 2014), p. 109.

content. Thus, if the Horus-star was described as remaining fixed at the "front" of the solar bark as well as at the "front" of the Imperishable Stars, this implies that the latter stars were themselves formerly located in very close proximity to the solar bark. In this sense the two statements "Horus Duat stands at the front of the solar bark" and "Horus Duat stands at the front of the Imperishable Stars" are functionally analogous in nature and ultimately have reference to the same uniquely ordered celestial landscape—albeit a landscape that is impossible to reconcile with the one known to modern astronomers.

## The Horus-pillar

> "Research of Rolf Krauss on astronomical aspects of the Pyramid Texts may suggest that more allowance should be made for stellar beliefs than has been done."[597]

A number of epithets identify Horus as a pillar or pillar-like form. The epithet *Jwn-Mwt.f*, for example, describes the god as the "pillar of his mother."[598] In the Coffin Texts Horus is invoked as a son of Isis: "My son, Pillar shining of horn."[599] Yet another passage from the same corpus speaks of "the circle of the Pillar of Horus which is north of the opening of darkness."[600]

It is also relevant to note that the stellar Horus was depicted atop a pillar on various Egyptian astronomical monuments. This is the case on the Zodiac of Dendera, for example, wherein the falcon-god is perched atop a *wȝḏ*-pillar (see figure one in chapter ten). The antiquity of such conceptions is confirmed by the fact that the Coffin Texts likewise invoke the falcon-god as *Ḥr ḥr wȝḏ.f*, "Horus who is on his pillar."[601]

In the Pyramid Texts, as noted in a previous chapter, the Horus-star was invoked in conjunction with the *djed*-pillar. Thus PT 1301 identifies the deceased king with the Horus-star and likens him to the *djed*-pillar: "You shall emerge as Horus of the Duat at the fore of the Imperishable [Stars]...alive as the Beetle lives and stable as the *djed*-pillar for the course of eternity."[602] As is evident from the spell in question, the *djed*-pillar was a proverbial symbol of stability and endurance.[603] This symbolism doubtless reflects the fact that the *djed*-pillar was thought to

---

[597] J. Baines, "Egyptian Myth and Discourse," *JNES* 50 (1991), p. 97.
[598] *PT* 1593a. R. Hannig, *Ägyptisches Wörterbuch I* (Mainz, 2003), p. 58.
[599] *CT* I:115 as recorded on B2Bo. See the discussion in R. Faulkner, *The Ancient Egyptian Coffin Texts* (Warminster, 1973), p. 23.
[600] *CT* VII:214.
[601] *CT* II:348.
[602] J. Allen, *The Ancient Egyptian Pyramid Texts* (Atlanta, 2005), p. 117.
[603] H. Altenmüller, "Djed-Pfeiler," *Lexikon der Ägyptologie I* (Wiesbaden, 1975), col. 1103.

uphold or otherwise support heaven, a point emphasized by Rundle Clark many years ago:

"The word *Djed* meant 'stable' or 'durable'. If this is taken into consideration it is easy to see why the column could be used as a cosmic pillar or sky support as well as a symbol of revival...In more formal settings, such as the elaboration of the royal protocol, the royal name has to fill the world below the sky vault. To show this the top of the name enclosure is always formed by a sky sign and the ends of it rest on cosmic supports. As early as Khasekhemui of the Second Dynasty a well-known stele has a support made from a composite column formed of a *Djed* and, underneath, a strange object known as a *Tit*, a knot of cloth or leather. This was the emblem of Isis or of the Mother Goddess in general."[604]

As the testimony of PT 1301 evinces, the deceased king aspired to attain the stability and permanence of the *Djed*-pillar upon ascending to the celestial Hereafter. Much the same sentiment is expressed in PT 1559, wherein the king prays to Horus that he "may endure in the sky like a mountain, like a support." The Egyptian word *ḏw*, translated as "mountain" here, denotes a twin-peaked mountain—⛰. As is well-known, the ancient sun god was believed to appear in conjunction with—or within—a twin-peaked mountain, an idea that was given concrete expression in the hieroglyph *akhet*, which depicts the sun-disc in conjunction with the *ḏw*-mountain—⛰.

The word translated as "support" in PT 1559—*sḫnt*—is employed in the Coffin Texts to denote "the great prop which separates the earth from the sky."[605] In that particular passage, as elsewhere, the word is determined with the following glyph: 𓊃.[606] Such traditions recall ancient

---

[604] R. T. Clark, *Myth and Symbol in Ancient Egypt* (London, 1959), pp. 236-237.
[605] *CT* III:209.
[606] In B1BO. In *CT* I:263f and 264a the word is used in the sense of "post" or support(s) of the sky.

conceptions associated with the World Pillar, commonly believed to uphold the sky and have the form of a forked-pole.[607]

Such widespread and enduring traditions are exceedingly difficult to explain by reference to the modern sky, needless to say, inasmuch as a tangible pillar-like structure is nowhere to be seen. Yet early Egyptian artworks depict pillar-like forms in conjunction with celestial bodies. Witness the following image from a prehistoric ivory-handle (Figure 1):

Figure 1[608]

Although largely overlooked by the current generation of scholars, the multifaceted symbolism attached to the World Pillar pervades Egyptian religion.[609] As a case in point, consider the Egyptian artworks wherein the pharaoh, in an apparent attempt to emulate Shu's role as World Pillar, is depicted upholding heaven.[610]

---

[607] M. Eliade, *Patterns in Comparative Religion* (Lincoln, 1996), pp. 271-300. See also the extensive discussion in M. van der Sluijs, *Traditional Cosmology, Vol. Three* (London, 2011), pp. 161-190.
[608] Adapted from figure two in R. Anthes, "Die Sonnenboote in den Pyramidentexten," *ZÄS* 82 (1957), p. 83 showing the so-called Gebel el-Arak knife believed to date from 3500-3200 BCE.
[609] D. Kurth, *Den Himmel stützen* (Brussels, 1975).
[610] E. Hornung, "Ancient Egyptian Religious Iconography," in J. Sasson ed., *Civilizations of the Ancient Near East, Vol. 3/4* (Farmington Hills, 1995), p. 1727. See also M. Weyersberg, *op. cit.*, pp. 132-137.

Egyptian traditions attesting to the memory that Horus was thought to uphold the sky in Shu-like fashion bring the argument full circle.[611] Thus the "Myth of Horus at Edfu" states with respect to the falcon-god: "He is like Shu who 'lifts up heaven'."[612] Elsewhere in the same text Horus is invoked for his role in establishing the four supports of heaven: "Horus hath flung (his missile) with his hand, he whose arm was strong from the first, when he established the sky upon its four supports."[613]

To summarize our findings in this chapter: When the Egyptian pharaoh prayed that he might "endure in the sky like a mountain, like a support" this can only mean that he wished to emulate the towering Pillar which, during the tumultuous events attending Creation, became established at the front of the sky like a mountain or pole-like support (properly understood, the words $\underline{d}w$ and $s\underline{h}n.t$ are simply two complementary terms for the World Pillar as conceptualized in ancient Egypt). Like the *Djed*-pillar itself, which was likewise thought to uphold the sky,[614] the celestial mountain ($\underline{d}w$) and $s\underline{h}nt$-pole were symbols of endurance, strength, and stability *precisely because they were synonymous with the World Pillar which propped up and supported the Egyptian cosmos*. In the final analysis, then, the sentiment expressed in PT 1559 is simply a variation upon that which finds the deceased king praying that he will endure like the Horus-star at the front of the sky. Recall again PT 1948, quoted earlier: "May you be enduring at the head of the sky as Horus of the Netherworld."

---

[611] The identification of Horus and Shu was commonplace in ancient Egypt. See H. Willems, *The Coffin of Heqata* (Leuven, 1996), p. 316.

[612] A. Blackman & H. Fairman, "The Myth of Horus at Edfu—III," *JEA* 29 (1943), p. 27.

[613] A. Blackman & H. Fairman, "The Myth of Horus at Edfu—III," *JEA* 29 (1943), p. 12.

[614] H. Schäfer, "Weltgebäude der alten Ägypter," *Die Antike* 3 (1927), pp. 117-119.

## The Horus-Bull

> "Thematically the Cannibal Hymn begins with a greeting to the appearance of the king, manifest as the Bull of the Sky in a moment of cosmic disruption. It salutes the immanence of the risen king, so that performance as a hymn might indeed be envisaged as just such a ritual invocation."[615]

In his classic study of Egyptian religion—*Kingship and the Gods*—Henri Frankfort noted that the concepts "pillar and bull are often interchangeable in Egyptian imagery."[616] This being the case, and given the evidence presented in the previous chapter attesting to the intimate relationship between Horus and a pillar-like form, it stands to reason that the Horus-star might have been likened to a bull by the Egyptian skywatchers. In fact, this is a recurring motif in Egyptian literature. The pharaoh, conceptualized as the great god incarnate, is frequently invoked as "Horus the mighty bull" (*Ḥr kꜣ nḫt*).[617]

Analyses of this familiar epithet have rarely, if ever, considered the possibility that there might be a celestial basis for the imagery in question. Yet an examination of the earliest Egyptian texts confirms that the bovine imagery attached to Horus owes much to celestial determinants. In the Coffin Texts, for example, Horus recounts his birth as follows: "I have issued from between the thighs of Isis as Horus, I have measured out(?) my flesh in the sky as a great and young wild bull."[618] If we are to take the testimony of this passage at face value, it can only mean that, at the time of his "birth" from Isis/Venus, the Horus-star presented the

---

[615] C. Eyre, *The Cannibal Hymn* (Liverpool, 2002), p. 60.
[616] H. Frankfort, *Kingship and the Gods* (Chicago, 1948), p. 381. See also G. Wainwright, "Some Celestial Associations of Min," *JEA* 21 (1935), p. 163: "The sky-pole *wḫ* was personified by a bull (p. 168). Thus, a pillar and a bull (generally 'the Bull of the Sky') form quite an ordinary combination."
[617] L. Zabkar, *Hymns to Isis in Her Temple at Philae* (Hanover, 1988), p. 25.
[618] *CT* II:50b.

appearance of a young wild bull *in the sky overhead*, presumably as a bovine-shaped pillar.[619]

Elsewhere in the Coffin Texts Horus is likened to a White Bull standing at the front of heaven on the day of his accession to the throne as King of the Gods:

"I am Horus on the day of his accession…who navigates in front of the stars of the sky on the belly of my mother Nut…I am the White Bull who presides over the field."[620]

The localization of the Horus-star "in front of the stars of the sky" recalls that star's placement at the "front" of the sky in Djoser's domain name, as elsewhere. Such traditions, in our opinion, commemorate the dramatic appearance of Horus/Mars at the front of heaven in pillar-like form—an event remembered as being coterminous with Horus's accession to the throne as King of the Gods.

The express goal of the deceased Egyptian king, as attested in PT 1948 and other passages, was to "endure" (*mn*) at the front (*ḫnt*) of heaven like Horus Duat. Inherent in such spells is the archaic belief-system that the pharaoh would come to stand *as stable and permanent* (*mn*) as the World Pillar propping up heaven. Not surprisingly, the very same symbolism attaches to the Bull of the sky. Thus it is that, upon ascending to heaven, the deceased king—expressly invoked as Horus Sopd—is implored to "endure" (*mn*) as a bull at the front *(ḫnty)* of the celestial spirits (i. e., the Imperishable Stars): "Endure, endure, O enduring Bull, that you may be enduring at the head of them and at the head of the spirits for ever."[621] Here the celestial Bull is urged to stand at the very locus otherwise associated with the Horus-star—namely, "at the head of the spirits." Absolutely essential to a proper understanding of the symbolism in

---

[619] Compare also Chester Beatty IV, Recto IX.4: "O Horus, thou art made young again. For thou has been conceived by Nut during the night and thou art born as a young bull."
[620] *CT* III:263.
[621] *PT* 481c-d.

question is the fact that the deceased king, as a bovine form *but also as the star spd*, assumes a seemingly *permanent* place at the front of the Imperishable Stars, the latter stars themselves being renowned for their inherent stability and permanence.

That the Bull of the sky was fundamentally identical with the World Pillar is stated in no uncertain terms by the Egyptian scribes. PT 792, for example, addresses the deceased king as follows: "May you ferry over by means of the Great Bull, the Pillar of the Serpent-nome, to the Fields of Rē· which he loves." Here the celestial Bull is explicitly identified with the Pillar of Wadjet (*jwn wȝḏt*).[622]

The homology between the Bull of the sky and the World Pillar is also evident in Utterance 254 from the Pyramid Texts, wherein the deceased king is made to announce: "I am the Unique One, the Bull of the sky."[623] Elsewhere in the same spell, however, the Bull in question is identified with the Pillar of Kenzet: "For they have seen the Pillar of Kenzet, the Bull of the sky."[624]

How else, apart from the tacit identification of the Bull of the sky with the World Pillar, is it possible to understand such rich and multilayered symbolism?[625] And how else, apart from some sort of celestial prototype, is it possible to explain the Egyptian traditions alluding to the Horus-star residing at the front of heaven as a pillar-like form or Bull of the sky? Far from being conflicting images, the Horus-pillar and "great and young wild bull" have reference to the

---

[622] The same identification occurs in *CT* VII:35. See here the insightful discussion of G.A. Wainwright, "Some Celestial Associations of Min," *JEA* 21 (1935), pp. 163ff.
[623] *PT* 293.
[624] *PT* 280.
[625] D. Talbott, *The Saturn Myth* (New York, 1980), pp. 260-269. Here it is important to note that ancient scribes regarded the signs X and T as interchangeable. See here the discussion in A. Mace & H. Winlock, *The Tomb of Senebtisi at Lisht* (New York, 1916), p. 87.

same celestial apparition—a brilliant star set atop a pillar-like structure at the front of heaven (see figure one).[626]

Figure 1

Analogous images depicting a sun or star atop a pillar-like object will be found around the globe. The iconographic motif is especially prevalent in ancient Mesopotamia (see figure two).[627] It is significant that the pole is held by a bull-man, a none-too-subtle clue to the bovine nature of the World Pillar upholding the sun. Figure three depicts a similar image.[628]

---

[626] Adapted from figure two in R. Anthes, "Die Sonnenboote in den Pyramidentexten," *ZÄS* 82 (1957), p. 83 showing the so-called Gebel el-Arak knife believed to date from 3500-3200 BCE.
[627] Adapted from plate 23 in G. White, *The Religious Iconography of Cappadocian Glyptic in the Assyrian Colony Period and its Significance in the Hittite New Kingdom* (1993), a Dissertation submitted to the University of Chicago, p. 452.
[628] Adapted from Ibid., plate 59b. See also plates 28, 31, and 47 from the same source.

Figure 2

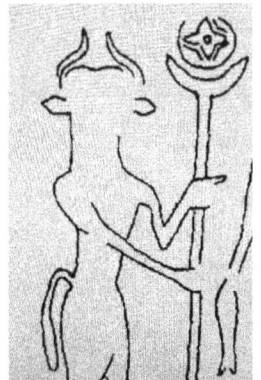

Figure 3

## The Separation of Heaven and Earth

"The most important event of the creation: the separation of heaven and earth."[629]

"The origin of the created world in a process of diversification, of the separation of elements that were previously united, dominates Egyptian ideas of creation. Earth and sky, which were originally united, are separated by Shu; light comes forth from darkness; land emerges from the primeval water; the creator god 'divided (*wpj*) the nature of the one from that of the other,' thus endowing every being with its unmistakable individuality."[630]

In previous chapters we have documented that the prototypical appearance of the Horus-star was said to have occurred in conjunction with the separation of heaven and earth, the latter remembered as a pivotal event in Creation. The present chapter seeks to flesh out some of the details pertaining to this thematic pattern in Egyptian cosmogonic myth.

The Pyramid and Coffin Texts employ a number of different terms to denote the dwelling-place of the Horus-star. The most common is the *akhet*, the subject of chapter eight. In Utterance 456, the locus of the ever-enduring Horus-star is described by the phrase *wpt pt*, translated as "zenith of the sky" by Faulkner:

"Hail to you, Unique One, who daily endures! Horus comes, the Far-strider comes, he who has power over the horizon comes, (even) he who has power over the gods. Hail to you, Soul who are in your blood, Unique One of whom your father spoke, Wise One of whom the gods spoke, who takes his place at the zenith of the sky, in the place where you are content."[631]

In order to decipher this particular passage, it is essential that we gain a basic understanding of the Egyptian term *wpt*. According to Maria

---

[629] E. Hornung, "Ancient Egyptian Religious Iconography," in J. Sasson ed., *Civilizations of the Ancient Near East, Vol. 3/4* (Farmington Hills, 1995), p. 1717.
[630] E. Hornung, *Conceptions of God in Ancient Egypt* (Ithaca, 1982), pp. 171-172.
[631] *PT* 853-854.

Betró, the word *wpt* has reference to the sagittal line of the cranium and this circumstance accounts for the word's semantic connection with "forehead, summit, the beginning."[632] James Allen, presumably following a similar line of reasoning, translates the phrase *wpt pt* as "sky's brow."[633] At no point, however, does this esteemed scholar explain how we are to understand this physiological metaphor from the standpoint of Egyptian celestial geography.

Samuel Mercer, following a suggestion by Kurt Sethe, argued that the phrase *wpt pt* had reference to the site where heaven was separated from earth at the time of Creation.[634] This hypothesis has a great deal of merit.

The verb *wpt* (𐊠▫⌒) was employed to describe the separation of heaven and earth in a decisive passage from the Pyramid Texts recounting the prototypical appearance of the Horus-star, quoted previously: "When the sky was separated from the earth, when the gods ascended to the sky."[635]

The same term describes the separation of heaven and earth in the Coffin Texts: "The great prop which separates [*wpt*] the earth from the sky."[636] The word translated as "great prop" here is *shnt*, determined with the following hieroglyph—𓉾—which, as we documented in chapter twenty, is homologous with the Bull of the sky. The underlying idea, evidently, was that the separation of heaven and earth was inextricably connected with the appearance (or erection) of a bovine-shaped pillar.

It is relevant to note that the word *wpt* can also denote the horns of a bull or cow.[637] Indeed, a recurring theme in later Egyptian accounts of creation finds the mother goddess adopting the form of a cow in order to carry the sun-god (as Re or Horus) to the sky at the time of the primeval

---

[632] M. Betró, *Hieroglyphics* (New York, 1996), p. 119.
[633] J. Allen, *The Ancient Egyptian Pyramid Texts* (Atlanta, 2005), p. 119.
[634] K. Sethe, *Übersetzung und Kommentar zu den altägyptischen Pyramidentexten, Vol. III* (Glückstadt, 1962), pp. 11-13.
[635] *PT* 1208c.
[636] *CT* III:209.
[637] R. Hannig, *Ägyptisches Wörterbuch I* (Mainz, 2003), p. 332, entry 7264.

separation of heaven and earth. In the *Book of the Heavenly Cow*, for example, one reads: "Thus heaven and earth were separated, and the sun-god remained on the back of the heavenly cow."[638] Mark Smith cited an analogous account from the Book of Fayyum: "There, too, he [Horus/Re] mounts upon the back of his mother, who ascends heavenward and transforms herself into the sky, thereby completing the process of separating the earth and heaven."[639]

In the Carlsberg Papyrus, we read that the celestial cow sought to protect her son by placing him between her two horns (*wpy*).[640] So, too, in the Neith cosmogony preserved at Esna, the sun-god is whisked away to heaven by his bovine mother and placed between her horns for safety: "When she [Neith in the form of the Akhet-cow] had saved her son Ra from the hands of his children, she placed him between her horns and she swam on the water while carrying him."[641] In other accounts from the same temple the sun-god is alternately placed *ḥr wp.t*, "on the brow," or *imy-tw wp.t=s*, "between her horns."[642]

Such cosmogonic traditions naturally call to mind the Egyptian artworks depicting Horus as a small child sitting between the horns of the Hathorian cow.[643] Equally relevant are other artworks showing the Hathor-cow supporting a red disk between her horns (see figure one).[644]

---

[638] W. Muller, "Egyptian Mythology," in L. Gray ed., *The Mythology of All Races, Vol. 12* (Boston, 1918), p. 78. See also the discussion in M. Smith, "P. Carlsberg 462: A Fragmentary Account of a Rebellion Against the Sun God," in P. Frandsen & K. Ryholt eds., *A Miscellany of Demotic Texts and Studies* (Copenhagen, 2000), p. 96.
[639] M. Smith, *op. cit.*, p. 109.
[640] *Ibid.*, p. 105.
[641] B. Richter, *The Theology of Hathor of Dendera* (Atlanta, 2016), p. 72.
[642] M. Smith, *op. cit.*, p. 105.
[643] S. Mercer, *The Pyramid Texts in Translation and Commentary, Vol. 2* (New York, 1952), p. 347.
[644] E. Hornung, *Der ägyptische Mythos von der Himmelskuh* (Freiburg, 1982), pp. 99-100.

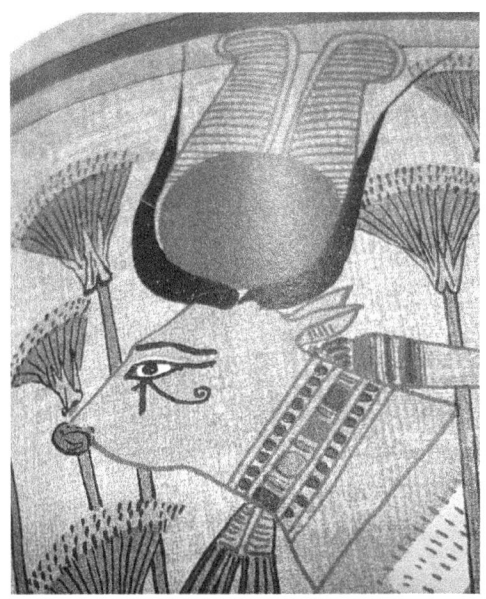

Figure 1[645]

The Egyptian artworks depicting a sun-like object between bovine horns recall a passage in the Coffin Texts alluding to the placement of the sun (*jtn*) upon horns (*ꜥbw*) at the dawn of time: "Before the sun was firm on the horns."[646] In addition to attesting to an inherent connection between the ancient sun-god and celestial horns, the tradition in question naturally implies that there was a time *before* the sun-disk was "firm on the horns."

Although modern astronomers will be hard-pressed to point to any visible "horns" in the immediate vicinity of the present sun, the idea that the sun-god (Horus or Re) formerly stood in close proximity to a pair of bovine horns is a commonplace in Egyptian cosmography. Recall again the following passage from the Coffin Texts: "You are the Double Bull, the Great One who is on the vertex of Rēʿ."[647] The word translated as

---

[645] Adapted from plate 37 in R. Faulkner, *The Egyptian Book of the Dead* (San Francisco, 1994).
[646] *CT* IV:181. See also the discussion in J. Assmann, "Schöpfung," *Lexikon der Ägyptologie 5* (Wiesbaden, 1984), col. 677.
[647] *CT* III:400.

"vertex" here by Faulkner is *wpt*, and thus we evidently have yet another reference to bovine "horns" in conjunction with the ancient sun-god.

Figure 1

In the previous passage from the Coffin Texts the word translated by Faulkner as "Double Bull" is *ḫnz*, determined with a double bull set next to two door-leaves (see figure one). The same word appears in PT 416, wherein it serves to denote the double-doors associated with the Pharaoh's post-mortem ascent to heaven: "The King opens the double doors, the King attains the limit of the horizon…"[648] In his commentary on this passage, Samuel Mercer observes:

"The word *ḫns* means 'door' (WB. III 300) and refers to the heavenly double-bull…and here means the door of heaven with two leaves. The deceased king opens the double doors, and proceeds to one of the limits of the horizon."[649]

As is evident from this Pyramid Text, the double bull not only substitutes for the double doors as the site of the sun-god's glorious epiphany, it serves to demarcate the desired destination of the deceased king in heaven, thereby paralleling the situation with respect to the Horus-star's localization in the *wpt pt* in PT 854.

The vertex (*wpt*) of Re is elsewhere identified as the dwelling place of the Horus-star. Witness the following passage from the *Book of the Dead*: "I am Horus who flew up, I have lighted on the vertex of Rēꜥ in the prow of his bark which is in the Primordial Water."[650]

---

[648] *PT* 416.
[649] S. Mercer, *The Pyramid Texts in Translation and Commentary, Vol. 2* (New York, 1952), p. 193.
[650] "The Theban Recension," as translated in R. Faulkner, *The Ancient Egyptian Book of the Dead* (Austin, 1990), p. 107.

Horus's "lighting" on the *wpt* of Re naturally recalls the passage quoted at the outset of this chapter, wherein the Horus-star "takes his place" at the *wpt pt*. The fact that the Horus-star was said to "endure" (*dd*) there every day suggests that this particular station was likewise conceptualized as being permanent in nature:

"Hail to you, Unique One, who daily endures! Horus comes, the Far-strider comes, he who has power over the horizon comes, (even) he who has power over the gods. Hail to you, Soul who are in your blood, Unique One of whom your father spoke, Wise One of whom the gods spoke, who takes his place at the zenith of the sky, in the place where you are content."[651]

The Egyptian traditions adduced above with respect to bovine-shaped structures associated with the locus of the ancient sun-god prompt the following question: Is it possible to reconcile the archaic symbolism attached to the sun-god's "horns" with Sethe's suggestion that the term *wpt* has reference to the locus of the primeval separation of heaven and earth? Here it will be remembered that the primeval separation (*wpt*) of heaven and earth was coterminous with the erection of the *shnt*-pole: "The great prop which separates the earth from the sky."[652] And insofar as the inaugural appearance of the *shnt*-pole evidently signaled the separation (*wpt*) or "pillaring apart" of heaven and earth, it stands to reason that the bovine horns (𐤍) serving as the logogram for *wp* likely originated with, and referenced, the crescentine horns atop the pillar-like pole. Likewise, it is by reference to these singular events attending "Creation" that we find a ready explanation for the semantic situation in which the word *wpt* came to signify "the Beginning": For it was in *zp tpj*— literally the "First Time" or Beginning—that the bovine "horns" (*wpt*) suddenly appeared at the very place (*wpt pt*) where heaven was separated (*wpt* or *wpj*) from earth.[653]

---

[651] *PT* 853-854 as translated by R. Faulkner, *op. cit.*, p. 152.
[652] *CT* III:209.
[653] Jan Assmann, *Egyptian Solar Religion in the New Kingdom* (London, 1995), p. 117 translates *zp tpj* simply as "beginning."

And if we are to believe the abundant Egyptian testimony with regards to the extraordinary circumstances attending the Horus-star's primordial ascent to heaven, it was on those very same horns that he became established (*mn*) as King of the Gods. The Egyptian scribes, upon witnessing the triumphant sun-god safely ensconced within the horns of his celestial mother, described him as being truly content or at *rest* (*ḥtp*)—i.e., the very term otherwise employed to describe the restoration of cosmic order after the primeval disaster associated with the departure of the Eye of Horus.[654]

---

[654] It will be noted that the disaster associated with the Eye forms the historical/mythological backdrop for the primeval appearance of the celestial cow in the *Book of the Heavenly Cow* and other Egyptian writings.

## Identifying Thoth

"In a struggle, Seth gouged out Horus's eye. The wounded eye went missing, but the moon god Thoth returned it to Horus and made it whole again. Because of the planetary association attested for Seth [Mercury, in Krauss's view] and the proposed association of Horus with Venus, it is feasible that the myth about the eye, first wounded and afterwards healed, reflects astronomical observations centering on Mercury, Venus and the moon."[655]

"It is very doubtful if any star in the PT [Pyramid Texts] can be accurately identified with any particular star as known to the ancient Greeks and now to ourselves."[656]

The Egyptian god Thoth figures prominently in the Pyramid and Coffin Texts and, in a rare consensus, Egyptologists are seemingly unanimous in understanding the god as a personification of the Moon.[657] Yet as we intend to document, there is little justification for the conventional identification in the earliest texts.

The Pyramid Texts provide a wealth of information regarding Thoth's particular role in the pivotal events attending Creation. This testimony will prove decisive as we attempt to discover the god's original celestial referent and reconstruct his role and mythological function in Egyptian cosmogonic myth and cosmography. Utterance 257, purportedly describing the prototypical appearance of the Horus-star during the immediate aftermath of the primeval separation of heaven and earth, is especially instructive:

"There is tumult in the sky; 'We see something new', say the primeval gods. O you Ennead, Horus is in the sunlight, the possessors of forms

---

[655] R. Krauss, "The Eye of Horus and the Planet Venus: Astronomical and Mythological References," in J. Steele & A. Imhausen eds., *Under One Sky* (Münster, 2002), pp. 194-195.
[656] S. Mercer, *The Pyramid Texts, Vol. 2* (New York, 1952), p. 156.
[657] Mark Smith, *On the Primaeval Ocean* (Copenhagen, 2002), p. 94 writes: "Thoth was the pre-eminent lunar deity in ancient Egypt." See also P. Boylan, *Thoth* (London, 1922), pp. 62-75; R. Krauss, *op. cit.*, pp. 76-79.

make salutation to him, all the Two Enneads serve him, for he sits on the throne of the Lord of All. The King takes possession of the sky, he cleaves its iron…The King shines anew in the East, and he who settled the dispute will come to him bowing. Make salutation, you gods, to the King, who is older than the Great One, to whom belongs power on his throne…Rejoice at the King, for he has taken possession of the horizon."[658]

The passing reference to "he who settled the dispute"—*jwt n.f wp hnnw*—serves to identify Thoth in his familiar role as the god who "judged" (*wp*) or otherwise resolved the theomachy between Horus and Set *in illo tempore*.[659] A central message of Utterance 257, therefore, is that Thoth appeared in close proximity to the Horus-star during the singular events attending the separation of heaven and earth.

How, then, are we to understand the mythological events remembered as a "dispute" between Horus and Set? In the passage before us the word translated as "dispute" is *hnnw*.[660] An important clue to the historical context of the natural events in question is provided by the first line from the same Utterance, wherein the phrase "tumult in the sky" is *hnnw m pt*.[661] This particular choice of words suggests that the dispute mediated by Thoth is somehow related to the tumultuous events which surrounded Horus's inaugural hierophany and accession to the celestial throne *in illo tempore*.[662]

---

[658] *PT* 304-307.
[659] K. Goebs, "*Niswt nhh*—Kingship, Cosmos, and Time," in Z. Hawass ed., *Egyptology at the Dawn of the Twenty-first Century, Vol. 2* (Cairo, 2003), p. 253. See also S. Quirke, *Going out in Daylight* (London, 2013), p. 19: "Separator of the two rivals (Horus and Seth) is an epithet of the god Thoth."
[660] *PT* 306c.
[661] *PT* 304a.
[662] J. Allen, *Grammar of the Ancient Egyptian Pyramid Texts, Volume 1: Unis* (Winona Lake, 2017), p. 333 translates the passage as "he who parted chaos." According to P. Boylan, *op. cit.*, p. 55, *hnnw* denotes a prodigious storm—specifically "the phenomena of storm-clouds which were the enemy of the sun-god." There he cites the following passage from the *Book of the Dead* as evidence for this view: "For I am Seth, who can raise a tumult of storm in the horizon of the sky like one whose will is destruction."

Utterance 570 provides additional insight into the catastrophic natural events conceptualized as ḫnnw. There one finds reference to the primeval disaster wrought by the raging Eye of Horus:

"Which was born before anger came into being; which was born before noise came into being; which was born before strife came into being; which was born before tumult came into being; which was before the Eye of Horus was gouged out(?), before the testicles of Seth were torn off."[663]

The word translated here as "tumult" is ḫnnw—the very same word used to describe the "dispute" resolved by Thoth. Thus it seems logical to conclude that the "dispute" in question had some relationship to the cosmic upheaval precipitated by the displacement of Horus's Eye *in illo tempore*. The same conclusion is supported by a passage from Utterance 486, wherein we learn that the disaster associated with the raging Eye was likened to turmoil (ḫnnw) or strife (šnṯt), albeit in the most allusive language[664]:

"Hearts were pervaded with fear, hearts were pervaded with terror when I was born in the Abyss before the sky existed, before the earth existed, before that which was to be made firm existed, before turmoil existed, before that fear which arose on account of the Eye of Horus existed."[665]

This allusion to cosmic upheaval during the Time of Beginning (*zp tpj*) is far from unique or isolated. Indeed, Egyptian texts are replete with references to an apocalyptic storm that plunged the world into darkness and chaos during Creation.[666] Commonly described as a terrifying meteorological disturbance of epochal proportions, the storm in question

---

[663] *PT* 1463-1464.
[664] K. Goebs, *Crowns in Egyptian Funerary Literature* (Oxford, 2008), p. 131 introduces this passage as follows: "There follows a difficult section whose general theme seems to be tumult and strife in the sky."
[665] *PT* 1039-1040.
[666] H. Grapow, "Die Welt vor der Schöpfung," *ZÄS* 67 (1931), pp. 34-38. See also E. Hornung, "Chaotische Bereiche in der geordneten Welt," *ZÄS* 81 (1956), pp. 28-32.

is often attributed to a quarrel between Horus and Seth over the Eye. Equally often, however, the Ur-storm is ascribed to the fiery "wrath" of the Eye itself. Witness the following passage from the Pyramid Texts, quoted in chapter four:

"I [Horus] will put flame in my eye, and it will encompass you and set storm among the doers of (evil) deeds, and its fiery outburst among these primeval ones. I will smite away the arms of Shu which support the sky."[667]

The same apocalyptic situation is evidently alluded to in the Coffin Texts, wherein we read of a storm associated with the raging Eye-goddess: "The storm of Her who is mighty of dread, Mistress of the land, is quelled (?)."[668] Here, as in the previous passage from the Pyramid Texts, the storm attributed to the raging Eye is denoted by the term *nšn*. That the Egyptian scribes recognized a fundamental affinity between the two terms *ḫnnw* and *nšn* is confirmed by a passage from the Louvre statue wherein the apocalyptic *nšn*-storm is set in apposition to the *ḫnn*-tumult associated with Thoth's intervention: "This hand of Atum which drives away the disturbance (*nšni*) at heaven, the disorder by his eye (*ḫnn m ir.t.f*)."[669]

As noted in an earlier chapter, Thoth was credited with playing a decisive role in quelling the storm associated with the raging Horus-eye.[670] This episode is the subject of a passage in the Coffin Texts, later incorporated into Spell 17 from the *Book of the Dead*, wherein the god is made to announce: "I raised up the hair from the Sacred Eye at the time of its wrath."[671] Although exactly how Thoth managed to quell the storm associated with the raging Eye is never spelled out in detail, he was apparently conceptualized as having played some part in lifting (*ts*) or

---

[667] *PT* 298-299.
[668] *CT* VII:36.
[669] J. Borghouts, *The Magical Texts of Papyrus Leiden I 348* (Leiden, 1971), p. 117.
[670] A later text refers to Thoth as "who pacifies the Raging One." See L. Zabkar, *Hymns to Isis in Her Temple at Philae* (Hanover, 1988), p. 81.
[671] *CT* IV:238.

otherwise dispelling its "hair" (It is to be noted that the Egyptian word *ts* also denotes the dispelling of a storm; here one naturally thinks of the modern English expression of a storm being "lifted").[672] The end result of Thoth's intervention, in any case, is that Horus's Eye was "pacified" and restored to its owner—originally Horus[673]—thereby averting cosmic disaster (see Chapter X). This idea is evident in Spell 167 from the *Book of the Dead*:

"Thoth has fetched the Sacred Eye, having pacified the Eye after Re had sent it away. It was very angry, but Thoth pacified it from anger after it had been far away."[674]

An account preserved in the Edfu texts is of similar import: "He [Thoth] removed its raging, he cooled its fire."[675]

That Thoth had something of a reputation as a dispeller of storms is abundantly attested in the Egyptian texts. Witness the following passage from the Coffin Texts, wherein the god is invoked as he "who splits open the firmament [*bjꜣ*] and dispels cloudiness [*ḥꜣtj*] in his realm."[676] Spell 183 from the *Book of the Dead* offers corroborating testimony: "I am Thoth…who dispels darkness and clears away the storm."[677] Elsewhere in the same Spell, moreover, Thoth is described in his customary role as banisher of the apocalyptic "tumult" attending the primeval *Götterdämmerung*: "He [Thoth] has pacified the Rival gods for you, he has stopped the raging and the tumult for you."[678]

The dispelling of the cosmos-engulfing storm *in illo tempore* constitutes an archaic and recurring motif in Egyptian accounts of Creation. The same motif was incorporated into the myth of the deceased

---

[672] As in *CT* VII:110, for example. On the various meanings of *ts*, see R. van der Molen, *op. cit.*, pp. 771-773.
[673] J. Griffiths, *The Conflict of Horus and Seth* (Chicago, 1969), p. 29.
[674] R. Faulkner, *The Ancient Egyptian Book of the Dead* (Austin, 1990), p. 162.
[675] *Ibid.*, p. 186 apparently citing *Edfu* II, 16.
[676] *CT* VII:393c.
[677] *Ibid.*, p. 184.
[678] R. Faulkner, *The Ancient Egyptian Book of the Dead* (Austin, 1990), p. 184.

king's post-mortem ascent to heaven. In PT 326d, for example, Unis is described as splitting (*wp*) the storm/tempest (*nšn*).[679] The very same idea is expressed in Papyrus Gardiner III: "I am he who divides (*wp*) the storm."[680] It will be noted that the word used to describe the "dividing" or "splitting" of the apocalyptic storm is *wp*—i.e., the very verb employed to denote Thoth's "judging" or "settling" the quarrel between Horus and Seth. This convergence of sacred terminology can scarcely be a coincidence.

It is possible to be more specific here. It will be remembered that Horus's ascension to heaven and enthronement occurred in conjunction with the separation of heaven and earth, the latter event being denoted by the verb *wp*. Insofar as the prehistoric ascent of the Horus-star likely formed the mythological prototype for Unis's post-mortem ascent described in PT 326, quoted above, the language of the respective accounts suggests that the separation (*wp*) of heaven and earth *in illo tempore* is either coterminous with or identical to the parting of the primeval storm. That the Egyptian scribes recognized this to be the case is indicated by the fact that the parallel passage for PT 326d in the Coffin Texts substitutes "I separate the sky from the earth"—*jnk wp(w) p.t r tʒ*—for "splitting the storm/tempest."[681]

The same conclusion is suggested by the description of the events attending the Horus-star's ascent to heaven in Utterance 519. There, too, we read that a dispelling of a storm was coterminous with the primeval separation of heaven and earth:

"O Morning Star, Horus of the Netherworld, divine falcon, *wʒdʒd*-bird whom the sky bore...and which dispel the storm for the sake of (?) peace; give me these your two fingers which you gave to the Beautiful, the

---

[679] Note: A variant Spell in Pepi's pyramid is translated as follows in J. Allen, *op. cit.*, p. 149: "[Pepi is the one] who parts the tempest."
[680] R. Faulkner, *The Ancient Egyptian Coffin Texts* (Warminster, 1973), p. 216 note 9.
[681] *CT* IV:40g.

daughter of the great god, when the sky was separated from the earth, when the gods ascended to the sky."[682]

Although more than a little obscure in its terminology and meaning, this archaic Utterance would appear to preserve a wealth of valuable information about the state of the cosmos at the time of Creation. The phrase translated as "dispel the storm for the sake of peace" by Faulkner is *ḥsrw sšn n ḥtpw*. The verb *ḥsrw* is commonly employed to denote the clearing away of an apocalyptic storm occluding the sky during pre-Creation times. Indeed, Egyptian texts imply that the dispelling of the primeval storm formed a prelude or necessary precondition for the awe-inspiring "appearance" of the Horus-star. PT 1449 is suggestive: "Be ascended to this Pepi in your identity of [the Sun] and dispel the sky's blanket (of darkness) for Horus [of the Akhet]."[683] It is doubtless relevant to the present discussion to find that the very same expression used here to describe the dispelling of the storm obscuring the Horus-star—*ḥsr(w) ḥ3tj*—is elsewhere applied to Thoth's intervention: "who splits open the firmament and dispels cloudiness in his realm."[684]

Equally significant is the fact that Thoth's role in judging (*wp*) the dispute between Horus and Seth is specifically mentioned in conjunction with a "clearing" of the sky at Creation. Witness the following passage from the Coffin Texts:

"The sky is cleared, the Horizon-dwellers rejoice, when Rēʿ arises from the Double Gates…See, you are at the bow of the Bark, and a throne in the shrine is given to you; see, you are king of the sky…magic and protection are knit together about you within the Sacred Booth…O god who judged between the contestants, whom I have placed upon this great

---

[682] *PT* 1207-1209.
[683] As translated in J. Allen, *op. cit.*, p. 177.
[684] *CT* VII:393c.

height, says the Lord of the Ennead…I am Thoth…the god who judged between the contestants; do not hold yourself back from me."[685]

The traditions adduced above enable us to clarify Thoth's role in the catastrophic events attending Creation as perceived by the Egyptian skywatchers. Horus's accession, as we have documented, was attended by Thoth and occurred during the singular events associated with the separation of heaven and earth. This pivotal event was described by the term *wp/wpt* and determined by bovine horns—the latter, in our view, a clear reference to the luminous crescent in the northern circumpolar heavens. Insofar as Thoth is specifically associated with the very same term as "judge" of the combatants (Horus and Seth) *and* as queller of the primeval storm associated with the raging Eye of Horus, it stands to reason that he was involved in the separation of heaven and earth as well. If so, it follows that Thoth must bear an intimate relationship to the crescent itself, insofar as the appearance of the bovine horns (*wp*) signaled the separation of heaven and earth. It is our opinion, in fact, that Thoth himself was fundamentally indistinguishable from the heaven-spanning crescent which first appeared during the dramatic events attending the prototypical appearance of the Horus-star *in illo tempore*. The crescent in question, it must be emphasized, has nothing whatsoever to do with the present lunar orb.

It is significant to note that Egyptian texts trace Thoth's inaugural appearance to the tumultuous events surrounding the primeval Theomachy. Thus, a passage from the Pyramid Texts reports that Thoth is to be identified with "the sharp knife which came forth from Seth."[686] The Turin Papyrus evidently references the same tradition when it describes Thoth by the epithet "sprung from the forehead," wherein

---

[685] *CT* I:223-230. The word translated here as "cleared" by Faulkner is *ḏsr*. That the same word is elsewhere employed to describe the separation of heaven and earth at Creation is doubtless germane to the thesis advanced here. See *PT* 1778b; *CT* III:49e; VI:310; VII:199ff.

[686] *PT* 1999. Thoth is also associated with a "sharp knife" in *CT* III:337g.

forehead is *wpt*.⁶⁸⁷ Although frustratingly opaque in nature, the original import of such passages seems to be that Thoth himself first appeared during the cataclysmic natural events surrounding the dispute between Horus and Seth.

Alison Roberts is one of the few Egyptologists who has recognized the cosmogonic import of such traditions. As she observed, the reference is to the restoration of cosmic order after the disaster attending the "dispute" between Horus and Seth:

"This victory of Horus over Seth has profound meaning within the cosmic order. The re-emergence of light from Seth's head, in the form of the crescent moon-disk, is interpreted in texts as the birth both of Thoth, 'the cutter', and of each month's new moon."⁶⁸⁸

Given the fact that Horus's triumphant appearance as King of the Gods occurred in the immediate aftermath of the primordial *Götterdämmerung* remembered as the victory of the powers of light over the forces of darkness and chaos, it is readily understandable that the Egyptian skywatchers would draw the inference that the brilliant "light" associated with Thoth's crescent played a pivotal role in "clearing" (*ḏsr*) the sky and/or dispelling (*ḥsr/ts*) the apocalyptic storm (*nšn, ḫnnw*) that characterized the nascent cosmos. If so, it can be deduced that the inaugural appearance of the luminous crescent—as the celestial god Thoth—was conceptualized as playing a decisive role in ending the cosmic tumult (*ḫnnw*) which attended Creation. By the same logic, Thoth's crescent was credited with having contributed to the restoration of cosmic order—hence the god's dual function as a dispeller of storms and as Horus's ally in the reordering of the cosmos.

---

⁶⁸⁷ P. Boylan, *op. cit.*, p. 186.
⁶⁸⁸ A. Roberts, *Hathor Rising* (Devon, 1995), p. 110.

## The Bull of the Stars

> "There is no question that at the very beginning of their history, about 3000 B.C., the Egyptians were aware that the concept of the sky could not be understood directly by means of reason and sensual experience. They were conscious of the fact that they were employing symbols to make it understandable in human terms. As no symbol can possibly encompass the whole essence of what it stands for, an increase in the number of symbols might well have appeared enlightening rather than confusing."[689]

A wealth of evidence can be adduced to show that Thoth and the primordial crescent are one and the same. The crescent in question was commonly conceptualized as the luminous "horns" of the Bull of the sky (*kꜣ pt*), the latter identified as a colossal pillar upholding heaven. It is for this reason, presumably, that Thoth was described by the epithet "Bull of the stars."[690] The same god was elsewhere invoked as the "Great Bull." Witness the following passage from the Coffin Texts: "Thoth is the great Bull who sees the sun-folk and who attacks those who belong to the Netherworld with his arms outstretched."[691]

As argued earlier, it is our opinion that the Thothian crescent originated in conjunction with the tumultuous events associated with the primordial separation of heaven from earth. The prototypical appearance of the crescent was at once extraordinary and awe-inspiring in nature and, as such, has absolutely nothing to do with regularly recurring events such as the monthly appearance of the lunar crescent.

To take but one of several arguments that could be advanced in this regard: In Spell 50 from the Coffin Texts, quoted above, Thoth is described as being placed "upon this great height"—*kꜣꜣ*.[692] Insofar as the

---

[689] R. Anthes, "Mythology in Ancient Egypt," in S. Kramer ed., *Mythologies of the Ancient World* (Garden City, 1961), pp. 21-22.
[690] *CT* VII:367a.
[691] *CT* VII:25h-j.
[692] *CT* I:230b. In a note appended to the spell, Faulkner translates "*kꜣꜣ (pn) kꜣ*."

Egyptian term $k_{33}$ also denotes the Primeval Hill which congealed at Creation,[693] this tradition implies that Thoth appeared at the summit of the Ur-Hill at some point during the tumultuous events *in illo tempore*, presumably in the form of a crescent.[694] In fact, this is exactly where our model would place the crescent.

An analogous situation is described in early Sumerian traditions of celestial geography. Witness the following passage, wherein the crescent-formed Sin is described as being stationed atop the Primeval Hill:

"Come out, O Sin…Be present, O Sin, on the hill of the pure sky! And may be present with you the [great] gods! May be present with you the gods, the judges! And may be present with you the gate of the [sky]!"[695]

As the Primeval Hill of Creation, the Sumerian $Du_6$ (or Du-ku) offers a precise structural analogue of the Egyptian $k_{33}$.[696]

Like the Egyptians and other cultures around the globe, the cultures of ancient Mesopotamia sought to incorporate every major feature of celestial geography into their monumental structures such as temples or ziggurats. It is for this reason that ziggurats commonly featured a set of luminous horns set atop their apex. Thus it is that Gudea (circa 2140 BCE) boasts of the towering "horn" adorning his magnificent temple dedicated to Ningirsu:

"One makes the house grow upwards like a mountain…makes it lift its horn like a bull…in heaven and on earth the house has raised its head to heaven like a mountain."[697]

---

[693] As in *PT* 1652, for example. See here K. Martin, "Urhügel," *Lexikon der Ägyptologie*, *Vol. 3* (Wiesbaden, 1977), cols. 873-875.
[694] R. Hannig, *Ägyptisches Wörterbuch I* (Mainz, 2003), p. 1327.
[695] As translated in P. Steinkeller, "On Stars and Men…," in A. Gianto ed., *Biblical and Oriental Essays in Memory of William L. Moran* (Rome, 2005), p. 28.
[696] On the primeval hill in ancient Mesopotamia, see S. Maul, "Die altorientalische Hauptstadt—Abbild und Nabel der Welt," in G. Wilhelm ed., *Die orientalische Stadt* (Halle, 1997), pp. 109-124. See also B. Hruška, "Zum heiligen Hügel in der altmesopotamischen Religion," *WKZM* 86 (1996), pp. 161-175, who observes: "Die Heilige Hügel war eigentlich eine der wichtigsten kosmischen Hierophanien."
[697] Lines 19-23 of Gudea Cylinder A as quoted in D. O. Edzard, "Deep-Rooted Skyscrapers and Bricks: Ancient Mesopotamian Architecture and its Imagery," in M.

In his extensive survey of horned buildings in ancient cultures, Professor Dan Potts calls attention to their former prevalence. At the same time, Potts confessed his inability to explain their symbolic significance:

"The use of wild animal horns in elevated, conspicuous positions in both religious and secular architecture in the Near East is more widespread, both spatially and temporally, than has generally been acknowledged…Even if the specific rationale behind such displays generally eludes us, it is clear that the symbolism involved is one of long standing, which must, I think, be bound up ultimately with notions of divine power and protection."[698]

Yet from the unique vantage point offered by the historical reconstruction advanced here, the mystery regarding the original inspiration for the horned monumental structures in the ancient Near East and around the globe is readily explained: Such structures model or materialize the unique celestial geography that formerly prevailed in prehistory, during which a Primeval Hill featuring a luminous crescent dominated the sky, the upturned horns of which naturally presented the image of bovine horns shining far and wide.

If our historical reconstruction has merit, it must be expected that ancient pictographs will depict analogous forms—albeit anomalous from the standpoint of astronomical reality. A prehistoric pictograph from Neolithic China likely offers a snapshot into how the polar configuration appeared during this particular phase in its evolution (figure one).[699]

---

Mindlin et al eds., *Figurative Language in the Ancient Near East* (Jerusalem, 1987), p. 15.

[698] D. T. Potts, "Notes on Some Horned Buildings in Iran, Mesopotamia and Arabia," *RA* 84 (1990), p. 40.

[699] Adapted from W. Boltz, *The Origin and Early Development of the Chinese Writing System* (New Haven, 1994), p. 45. Scholars estimate that the glyph in question traces to around 3000 BCE.

Figure 1

If it be granted that the five-peaked structure at the base represents a hill-like object—and Chinese sources identify the five-peaked mountain with the Primeval Hill—it can be seen at once that the crescent rests upon it, exactly as described in the Coffin Text quoted above. While stationed in this particular position, the crescent formed the "twin peaks" of the World Mountain, celebrated in ancient mythological traditions from around the globe and encoded in the classic Egyptian *akhet* logogram: ⚊, which juxtaposes the sun-glyph (N5) and the mountain-glyph (N26). An early Egyptian pictograph from circa 3000 BCE seemingly offers a close parallel to the Chinese pictograph (see figure two).

Figure 2[700]

---

[700] Adapted from figure 16.8 in J. Baines, "Sources of Egyptian Temple Cosmology," in D. Ragavan ed., *Heaven and Earth* (Chicago, 2013), p. 413. The image appears on a tag from the reign of Djer, circa 3000 BCE.

To return to the Sumerian hymn linking Sin to the Primeval Hill, quoted above: It will be noted that the "gate" of the sky is expressly linked to Sin's appearance, thereby recalling the situation described in Spell 50 from the Coffin Texts, wherein Thoth is said to appear atop the great height in conjunction with the celestial Double Gate and the ancient sun-god. The inherent structural *and* functional relationship between Sin and the heavenly gate(s) is preserved in an ancient Sumerian proverb: "Sin, as you become visible you open the doors of heaven."[701] As this passage states in no uncertain terms, it was the *illumination* of Sin's crescent which signaled the opening of the heavenly doors associated with the locus of the prototypical sunrise. Properly understood, this Sumerian tradition forms a perfect complement to the aforementioned Egyptian traditions reporting that the double-bull(s) (ḥns) formed the gate attending the glorious epiphany of the ancient sun-god. And much as the illumination of Sin's crescent opens the doors of heaven so, too, is the double-bull indissolubly connected with the appearance of light: "I am this double bull who is on the vertex of Rēʿ, who makes brightness in the East."[702] Indeed, there is every reason to believe that the disparate accounts from Egypt and Mesopotamia are describing the same extraordinary celestial events from two different vantage points—namely, the inherent relationship between the luminous crescent atop the Primeval Hill and the bulls/"gates" of heaven.[703]

---

[701] *RA* 12 (1915) 191:3 as quoted in W. Heimpel, "The Sun at Night and the Doors of Heaven," *JCS* 38/2 (1986), p. 134.

[702] *CT* III:381.

[703] Comparable is the archaic tradition reported in *PT* 496: "[She] will open the door of the Akhet for the emergence of the Dayboat."

# Creation Ideology in Ancient Egypt

"To judge from the surviving texts, the process of creation, in all its ramifications, was the dominant interest of Egyptian cosmogony."[704]

"Egyptian interest in nature and the resulting style of cognition and theorizing was religious in its orientation; put more precisely, it was a solar theology. The actual locus of Egyptian 'natural history' and cosmography was the cult of the sun, which was the source of the iconological principles and the concrete models for the reliefs that we admire in the tombs."[705]

"The birth of the sun is actually the culmination of creation in the Heliopolitan system, as it is in the early myth of the primeval mound. The sun's first rising into the newly created world-space marks the end of creation and the beginning of the eternal cycle of life."[706]

"The origin and repetition of creation is the event which, also because of its funerary significance (due to the implicit regeneration that it entails), seems to interest the Egyptians the most."[707]

The Pyramid Texts tell us that the glorious appearance of the Horus-star atop a Primeval Hill comprised the supreme moment of Creation and signaled the triumph of light over the forces of darkness. These singular events, in turn, were endlessly celebrated and inform virtually every aspect of Egyptian life, including coronation rituals, New Year's celebrations, and funerary practices. It thus stands to reason that if one is going to reconstruct the ideological wellsprings behind the origin of Egyptian civilization—its *raison d'être*, so to speak—one must seek to

---

[704] J. Allen, *Genesis in Egypt* (New Haven, 1988), p. 58.
[705] J. Assmann, *The Search for God in Ancient Egypt* (Ithaca, 2001), p. 55.
[706] J. Allen, *Middle Egyptian* (Cambridge, 2014), p. 177.
[707] J. Belmonte & J. Lull, *Astronomy of Ancient Egypt* (New York, 2023), p. 47.

understand the natural history and, if possible, rationale behind their conception of Creation.

How, then, are we to explain the astronomical events encoded in Egyptian cosmogonic myth? According to the current consensus, the ancient Egyptians developed their creation account by carefully observing the day-to-day movements of the solar orb and speculating about its genesis. Indeed, a central premise of modern Egyptology holds that cosmogonic myth is primarily a human construct. Witness the recent summary of Lucia Gahlin:

"Myths were constructed in order to provide explanations for the fundamentals of human existence. Creation mythology contains a range of carefully constructed metaphors and provides a window into the Egyptian mind."[708]

Confronted with the archaic tradition reporting that the prototypical sun-god emerged from a primeval ocean, wherein it had lain in inertness and darkness for a prolonged period of time, Egyptologists assure us that this is little more than fantasy.[709] James Allen, for example, points out that most Egyptian accounts of creation make the primeval sun "appear" from out of the cosmic waters—*this despite the fact that these waters have never been seen by mortal man*:

"Before the world was created the universe was a limitless ocean, whose waters stretched to infinity in all directions…Although no one had ever seen this universal ocean, its features could be imagined by contrast to the created world. It was water (*nwj*), while the world contains dry land and air. Where the created world is active, it was inert *(n(j)n(j)*…While the world is lit by the sun, it lay in perpetual darkness (*kkw*). And in

---

[708] L. Gahlin, "Creation Myths," in T. Wilkinson ed., *The Egyptian World* (London, 2007), p. 296. See also J. Assmann, *The Search for God in Ancient Egypt* (Ithaca, 2001), p. 7: "The deities and their actions, to whose reality human activity responds, are a cultural creation."

[709] S. Zago, *A Journey through the Beyond* (Columbus, 2022), p. 47: "The primeval ocean represented everything that was beyond human knowledge."

contrast to the tangible and knowable world, it was hidden (*jmn*) and lost (*tnm*)."[710]

In short, in addition to imagining the universal ocean the Egyptian scribes evidently felt free to invent a pre-Creation world of perpetual darkness, inertness, and hiddenness.[711]

Together with creative imagination and metaphor, analogical reasoning is also believed to have played an important role in guiding the Egyptian scribes in developing their myths of creation. The archaic belief in the Primeval Hill—a central theme in Egyptian creation accounts—is thought to reflect the annual spectacle of the Nile's flooding and the ensuing formation of verdant hillocks:

"The first texts that deal with Egyptian ideas about the universe and its creation appear nearly a thousand years after the beginnings of recorded Egyptian history. For earlier concepts, we are dependent on pictorial and architectural images, and on what later texts tell us these may have meant. One of the earliest notions seems to have been that of the primeval hill, the first 'place' to emerge from the infinite waters, over which the sun first arose. It is tempting to see in this image a reflection of the environment experienced by Egypt's first settlers: watching the highest points of fertile land emerge as the annual Nile flood receded, these early farmers could easily have pictured the world gradually appearing in the same way at creation. Whatever its origins, the image of the primeval hill remained potent throughout Egyptian history. Some temples contained, in their sanctuaries, a mound of earth or sand evoking it. The tombs of Egypt's first dynasties were

---

[710] J. Allen, *Middle Egyptian* (Cambridge, 2014), pp. 159-160, hieroglyphs deleted.
[711] J. Belmonte & J. Lull, "Cosmogonies: The Formation of The Ancient Egyptian Universe," in J. Belmonte & J. Lull, *Astronomy of Ancient Egypt* (Cham, 2023), p. 2: "This pre-creation realm of the world is expressed by a primordial ocean, the Nun, characterized by its extreme darkness, its stillness, and its silence."

marked by a similar mound, promising a new creation and rebirth to those buried below it."[712]

And so it is that, with each additional geographical feature or recurring theme of Egyptian cosmogonic myth, the list of hypothetical imaginings increases incrementally. Alongside the imaginary cosmic waters and primeval hill, we are assured that the Egyptian scribes saw fit to conjure up a solar boat and heaven-spanning waterway when describing the nascent sun's appearance and circumambulations.[713] Such, in essence, is the Egyptian creation myth as *imagined* by modern scholars. According to this view, the genesis of ancient cosmogonic myth is essentially a fictional enterprise, akin to composing a great novel, whereby the Egyptian scribes drew freely upon creative imagination, analogy, and whimsical punning in developing a plotline.[714]

Fundamental to the conventional position is a correlate thesis: Namely, that the ancient Egyptians were so impressed by this fictional construct that they made it the cornerstone and mythological charter for their daily existence, whereby they ordered their personal behavior, religious rituals, and monumental architecture around the sun god's imagined behavior at the time of creation. In accordance with this

---

[712] J. Allen, "The Celestial Realm," in D. Silverman ed., *Ancient Egypt* (London, 1997), p. 120.
[713] S. Zago, *A Journey through the Beyond* (Columbus, 2022), p. 42: "The Egyptians imagined that a *mr-ḫ3*, commonly translated as 'winding canal' or 'winding waterway', existed in the sky." See also R. Krauss, "The Eye of Horus and the Planet Venus: Astronomical and Mythological References," in J. Steele & A. Imhausen eds., *Under One Sky* (Münster, 2002), p. 198: "For the ancient Egyptians who imagined that the sun god traveled in a barque…"
[714] Witness the statement of Rohit Manglik, *op. cit.*, col. 41: "The movements of the firmament are fascinating and give rise to a desire to translate celestial events into stories. The emergence of such stories has something of cloud gazing. If one stares long enough, forms appear, faces of people, animals, and so on. But different people tend to see different shapes, even if one can be persuaded to see a certain form. Likewise, the Pyramid Texts are full, I believe, of scenarios imagined by one or more authors in the star sky. It is no longer possible to reconstruct fully what these authors saw and why they saw it, just as it is not clear why someone sees a certain shape in a certain cloud. This may account for the frustrating incomprehensibility of much of the Pyramid Texts."

worldview of "as above, so below," each and every feature of celestial geography was encoded within religious structures. The Egyptian temple, according to this view, was expressly modeled upon the Primeval Hill from which the sun-god first arose:

"In Egypt the creator was said to have emerged from the waters of chaos and to have made a mound of dry land upon which he could stand. This primeval hill, from which the creation took its beginning, was traditionally located in the sun temple at Heliopolis…Each Holy of Holies throughout the land could be identified with the primeval hill. Thus it is said of the temple of Philae, which was founded in the fourth century B.C.: 'This [temple] came into being when nothing at all had yet come into being and the earth was still lying in darkness and obscurity.' The same claim was made for other temples…The equation with the primeval hill received architectural expression also. One mounted a few steps or followed a ramp at every entrance from court or hall to the Holy of Holies, which was thus situated at a level noticeably higher than the entrance. But this coalescence of temples with the primeval hill does not give us the full measure of the significance which the sacred locality had assumed for the ancient Egyptians. The royal tombs were also made to coincide with it. The dead, and, above all, the king, were reborn in the hereafter. No place was more propitious, no site promised greater chances for a victorious passage through the crisis of death, than the primeval hill, the center of creative forces where the ordered life of the universe had begun. Hence the royal tomb was given the shape of a pyramid which is the Heliopolitan stylization of the primeval hill."[715]

If the prototypical sunrise was thought to occur within the doors/gates of heaven so, too, did the daily ritual incorporate this imaginary structural feature: "The temple-gate was identified with the cosmic gate in the east

---

[715] H. & H.A. Frankfort, "Myth and Reality," in H. Frankfort et al eds., *Intellectual Adventure of Ancient Man* (Chicago, 1946), pp. 21-22.

and the two towers of the pylon represented the mountains of the borderland (*akhet*), between which the sun rose."⁷¹⁶

If the prototypical sun was believed to travel about the sky in a celestial bark, a boat was provided in the temple as well: "To every sun temple belonged the model of a large boat built in stone."⁷¹⁷ What was true of the solar boat and celestial gates was also true of the primeval waters, the falcon's nest at Chemmis, and *akhet*, each of which was carefully modeled in Egyptian temples.⁷¹⁸

The same belief-system governed coronation rites. Thus it is that the pharaoh was invested with the very same crowns that the nascent sun had received at the time of Creation. Witness the comments of Katya Goebs: "The paraphernalia he receives are explicitly said to be those of Re (often 'on the occasion of creation', *sp tpy*), and he thus assumes on earth both, the outer appearance of the sungod in his various manifestations, and his role."⁷¹⁹

Indeed, the correspondence between daily life and cosmogonic myth was so inextricably intertwined and deeply ingrained that even the Pharaoh's wars against foreign powers were conducted in such a manner as to evoke the catastrophic natural events in *zp tpj*. Thus it is said of Ramses II that, during his war against the Hittites, he fought "like Sekhmet in the moment of her fury."⁷²⁰ So, too, during the New Year's ritual it was believed that the king waged an apocalyptic war against the powers of chaos led by Apophis. Henri Frankfort emphasized this point in his analysis of royal ideology:

---

⁷¹⁶ J. Zandee, "Prayers to the Sun-god from Theban Tombs," *Jaarbericht ex Oriente Lux* 16 (1964), pp. 49-50.
⁷¹⁷ A. von Lieven, "The soul of the sun permeates the whole world," *Pandanus* 10 (2010), p. 31.
⁷¹⁸ See the helpful illustration in figure 1:19 in J. Belmonte & J. Lull, *Astronomy of Ancient Egypt* (Cham, 2023), p. 48.
⁷¹⁹ K. Goebs, "King as God and God as King," in R. Gundlach & K. Spence eds., *Palace and Temple* (Wiesbaden, 2011), p. 95.
⁷²⁰ J. Assmann, *The Mind of Egypt* (Cambridge, 2002), p. 260.

"The verse says of the enemies of the king: 'They shall be like the snake Apophis on New Year's morning.' The snake Apophis is the hostile darkness which the sun defeats every night on his journey through the nether world from the place of sunset in the west to the place of sunrise in the morning. But why should the enemies be like Apophis on New Year's morning? Because the notions of creation, daily sunrise, and the beginning of the new annual cycle coalesce and culminate in the festivities of the New Year."[721]

In short, there was nary an aspect of Egyptian daily life that was not ordered in accordance with, or *measured* against, the divine blueprint provided by the myth of creation, wherein the sun-god made its prototypical appearance in heaven.

To return to the question posed on nearly every page of this monograph: Whence derives this seemingly single-minded fixation on the sun? The consensus view evidently takes it for granted that the prehistoric Egyptian skywatchers were so enthralled by the rising and setting of the solar orb that they were compelled to make this familiar event the focal point of their cosmogonic myth. This seems more than a little strange on its face. After all, if the present sun has been appearing and disappearing in the same precise manner since time immemorial why speak of a creation at all? Would it not make more sense to simply assume that the indomitable sun has always been there and always will be?

The conventional position seems to imply that, after countless millennia of observing the sun rise in the east and set in the west, an Egyptian scribe woke up one day and felt inspired to invent a grand myth of creation in which this daily "miracle" held the secret to all existence and set the normative standard for all human behavior. Such a hypothesis seems more than a little absurd and illogical when spelled out in such plain terms.

---

[721] H. and H. A. Frankfort, "Myth and Reality," in R. Segal ed., *Philosophy, Religious Studies, and Myth* (London, 1996), p. 164.

The conventional position becomes infinitely more difficult to maintain once one proceeds to examine the specific details of the Egyptian creation account(s). Upon making its daily appearance, according to Egyptian texts, the sun sailed along in a day-boat across the sky, this while fending off attacks from the ever-lurking Apophis serpent, the latter of whom threatened to bring back the primeval night and plunge the world into darkness and chaos.[722] Manning the solar bark were the so-called Imperishable Stars which, Egyptologists assure us, are to be identified as the circumpolar stars. Together with the *ḥnmmt*—conventionally identified as "sun-folk" or "mankind"—the Imperishable Stars form an entourage (*ḫt*) accompanying the sun during its daily journey across the sky.[723] To add to the spectacle, a menagerie of baboons and other creatures was described as rejoicing and dancing in order to celebrate the sun-god's glorious epiphany and triumph over the forces of darkness. Harry Stewart, the translator of the Theban solar hymns, offered the following commentary on this archaic cosmogonical theme:

"The sun-god's triumphant emergence into the upper world is celebrated joyfully by his crew, the gods, mankind, and all living creatures, sometimes typified by apes, whose chattering heralds the sunrise. Of all the themes this universal acclamation greatly predominates in the hymns."[724]

There is just one problem with this story: It is at loggerheads with the empirical reality of the current sun's daily behavior. Where, exactly, is the oft-mentioned solar boat to be found? Where is a serpent-dragon threatening to impede the sun's progress across the heavens? Where are

---

[722] See the discussion in J. Zandee, *Der Amunhymnus des Papyrus Leiden I 344, Verso, Vol. 1* (Leiden, 1992), pp. 160-163.

[723] N. Billing, *The Performative Structure* (Leiden, 2018), p. 285 observed of the *ḥnmmt*: "A divine assembly, basically located in the sky." See also J. Assmann, *Egyptian Solar Religion in the New Kingdom* (London, 1995), p. 52: "It is part of the idea of the boat journey as a royal journey that the sun god is surrounded by a 'court' (*šnjt*)."

[724] H. Stewart, "Traditional Egyptian Sun Hymns of the New Kingdom," *Bull. Inst. Arch.* 6 (1967), p. 39.

we to find a stellar entourage raucously celebrating the sunrise, raising a din? In what sense is it possible for the circumpolar stars, as denizens of the northern circumpolar region of the sky, to man the solar boat? The mere fact that the circumpolar stars are never visible together with the Sun makes this conflation of imagery incongruous to say the least.

Especially problematic for the conventional position is how to account for the explicit catastrophic elements in the Egyptian account of creation. How are we to explain the forcible separation of heaven and earth, which itself serves as the mytho-historical backdrop for the appearance of the Horus-star and the unfolding of creation (see the discussion in chapter A)? Equally pressing questions surround the natural disaster associated with the prototypical sunrise, in which the heavens shake and stars are disturbed. Are these archaic mythological traditions, like those telling of the cosmic waters and the sudden emergence of the Primeval Hill from the chaotic darkness, to be attributed to imagination and speculation alone? And if this is to be our answer, how is it possible to explain the fact that remarkably similar cataclysms distinguish the creation myths of other cultures far removed from ancient Egypt? The forcible separation of heaven and earth, for example, forms a recurring motif in creation myths around the globe as does the period of primeval darkness.[725] Is all this to be attributed to collective imagining?

The historical reconstruction offered here stands in stark contrast to the conventional story: It is our opinion that Egyptian cosmogonic myth has nothing whatsoever to do with the familiar experience of sunrise—that, in fact, it encodes a remarkably accurate memory of catastrophic planetary events. Creation, as we have documented here, is catastrophic from start to finish and recounts the glorious appearance ($ḥˁ$) of the Horus-star while in conjunction with the uraeus goddess, accompanied by the shaking of heaven and terrifying thunder-like sounds. Indeed, it is the

---

[725] See the comprehensive discussion in M. van der Sluijs, *Traditional Cosmology, Vol. One* (London, 2011), pp. 152-184. See also W. Staudacher, *Die Trennung von Himmel und Erde* (Darmstadt, 1968).

encircling of the Horus-star (Mars) with the comet-like headband (*sšd*) of the uraeus goddess (Venus) that inspired the mythological interpretation that the star-god had been akhified or transfigured.[726] Thus it is that, from the vantage point of the terrestrial skywatcher, the Horus-star was akhified *within* the body of Venus (Hathor, Wadjet, Nut, etc.). It is this decidedly catastrophic planetary conjunction which stands at the very heart of Egyptian funerary religion.

A pivotal episode in Creation saw the appearance of a heaven-spanning crescent, conceptualized as the god Thoth and credited with dispelling the storm that eclipsed the primordial cosmos. Ancient pictographs and cylinder seals depicting a crescent in conjunction with a star-like object encode this natural history, hitherto almost uniformly overlooked and misunderstood (see figure one).[727]

Figure 1

In addition to appearing alongside a heaven-spanning crescent, the prototypical epiphany of the Horus-star was accompanied by a Divine

---

[726] Hence K. Goebs, *Crowns in Egyptian Funerary Literature* (Oxford, 2008), p. 40 observes of the Eye of Horus: "The crown's equation with the Eye…demonstrates that in the funerary texts the crown is the symbol of the luminous outer appearance, which the deceased and reborn king acquires when he is transfigured as a star."

[727] Adapted from figure 80 from B. Teissier, *Egyptian Iconography on Syrian-Palestinian Cylinder Seals of the Middle Bronze Age* (Fribourg, 1996), p. 67.

Assembly (*ḥt*) in the sky, as depicted in figure two.⁷²⁸ The Imperishable Stars, like their stellar analogues the *ḥnmmt*, are to be understood as satellites revolving within the stellar entourage (*šnwt*) encircling the Horus-star. Thus it is that Horus is made to announce: "The Entourage is knit together about me by the Imperishable Stars."⁷²⁹

Figure 2

The universal acclamation and thunderous shouting (*nhm*) said to greet the prototypical sunrise, finally, is to be understood as the very real din that attended the explosive events in question as fiery extraterrestrial material was ejected from the immediate vicinity of the Horus-star (and Venus), whereupon it congealed into an entourage of "stars" or stellar material encircling the central "sun." The Egyptian tradition that the Eye-goddess scattered green stars about the celestial landscape at the Time of Beginning evidently refers to this catastrophic astronomical event. Recall again the passage quoted earlier: "O you who stride out greatly, strewing green-stone, malachite, turquoise of (?) the stars, if you are green, then the King will be green, (even as) living rush is green."⁷³⁰ Here, almost certainly, is the historical origin for the Egyptian *répandre l'or* ritual

---

⁷²⁸ Adapted from plate 26 in L. Werr, *Studies in the Chronology and Regional Style of Old Babylonian Cylinder Seals* (Malibu, 1988).
⁷²⁹ *CT* III:363.
⁷³⁰ *PT* 567.

alleged to reenact the Eye-goddess's scattering of green material about the land upon returning from wandering abroad.[731] The pictograph describing this scattering—☼—recalls the celestial landscape depicted in figure two and encodes an explosive scattering of turquoise material across the celestial landscape, an awe-inspiring display of stellar pyrotechnics that was everywhere remembered as an outburst of radiant "joy" and prosperity associated with Creation.[732]

It is our view that any hypothesis purporting to offer a scientific explanation for Egyptian cosmogonic myth that fails to explain these catastrophic elements should be rejected. According to the historical reconstruction outlined here, the Egyptian myth of creation is best understood as a relatively realistic account of catastrophic astronomical events, albeit from the perspective of a pre-scientific culture that interpreted these extraordinary events in mythopoeic fashion (i.e., as an apocalyptic struggle between a fire-breathing dragon and the prototypical sun, among countless other mythical images). Being firmly grounded in witnessed natural events at a particular historical juncture in time—events that were utterly terrifying and mesmerizing in nature—a *mysterium tremendum et fascinosum par excellence*, as it were, it stands to reason that the stellar agents participating in the events in question might well be deemed worthy of veneration and/or emulation.[733] Such, in essence, is our understanding of the astronomical roots of Egyptian religion.

---

[731] J.-C. Goyon, "Répandre l'or et éparpiller la verdure," in J. van Dijk, *Essays on Ancient Egypt in Honour of Herman te Velde* (Groningen, 1997), pp. 85-99.

[732] Words for joy in a number of languages also denote turquoise-green or radiance. The Sumerian giri$_{17}$-zal offers a case in point. See M. Cohen, *An Annotated Sumerian Dictionary* (University Park, 2023), p. 489. See also C. Andrews, *Amulets of Ancient Egypt* (London, 1994), p. 103: "In the Late Period the word for turquoise—*mfk3t* (*mefkat*)—was used as a synonym for 'joy' and 'delight'." See also D. Stanulewicz et al, "Axiological aspects of Polish Colour Vocabulary," in W. Anderson et al eds., *Colour Studies* (Amsterdam, 2014), p. 262.

[733] T. Jacobsen, *Treasures of Darkness* (New Haven, 1976), p. 3: "Basic to all religion—and so also to ancient Mesopotamian religion—is, we believe, a unique experience with power not of this world. Rudolph Otto called this confrontation 'Numinous' and analyzed it as the experience of *mysterium tremendum et fascinosum*, a confrontation with a 'Wholly Other' outside of normal experience and indescribable

## Conclusion

> "The most fortunate author is one who is able to say as an old man that all he had of life-giving, invigorating, uplifting, enlightening thoughts and feelings still lives on in his writings, and that he himself is only the gray ash, while the fire has been rescued and carried forth everywhere."[734]

It is now time to summarize our findings and throw down the gauntlet. A primary objective in writing this monograph was to document the importance of planetary agents in ancient Egyptian religion. When I first started out on this odyssey some 50 years ago, the idea that astral religion pervaded the earliest civilizations of Egypt and Mesopotamia was considered utterly fanciful, a sure sign that the author had fallen victim to the Pan-Babylonian heresy.[735] Today that idea is no longer considered quite so controversial and I am encouraged to see Egyptologists embracing the obvious.[736]

A second objective—and a recurring theme in all of my writings—was to marshall evidence that memories of planetary catastrophe are

---

in its terms: terrifying, ranging from sheer demonic dread through awe to sublime majesty; and fascinating, with its irresistible attraction, demanding unconditional allegiance. It is the positive human response to this experience in thought (myth and theology) and action (cult and worship) that constitutes religion."

[734] Friedrich Nietzsche, *Human All Too Human* (Lincoln, 1996), p. 125. Translated by Marion Faber and Stephen Lehmann.

[735] Typical is the pronouncement of an early correspondent of mine, Wolfgang Heimpel, "Mythologie A.1," in E. Ebeling & B. Meissner, *Reallexikon der Assyriologie, Vol. 8* (Berlin, 1993-1997), p. 539: "The plots of myths provide clear evidence that the primary concern of myth was with the great stages of human life, and that astral connections and allegorization cannot have shaped the myths in a fundamental way."

[736] J. Quack, "A Goddess Rising 10,000 Cubits into the Air," in J. Steele ed., *Under One Sky* (Münster, 2002), p. 291: "It is typical for the Egyptians that astronomical background is presupposed in religious texts." See also K. Goebs, "A Functional Approach to Egyptian Myth and Mythemes," *JANER* 2 (2002), p. 41: "We will need to get used to thinking in terms of stellar deities other than the sun and moon gods displaying certain mythical features."

encoded in the oldest Egyptian texts. At the outset of this inquiry we cited Jan Assmann:

"[Ideas of global catastrophe] are not specifically Late Period conceptions, but very old and very real anxieties based on multifarious historical and personal experiences (famine, epidemic, revolution, foreign rule etc.). The persistence of this theme in quite diverse areas of Egyptian literature reveals the obsessional nature of these anxieties."[737]

If there are indeed allusions to apocalyptic catastrophes at the Time of Beginning, as seems undeniable, how are we to explain that circumstance? Certainly not by reference to famine, epidemic, and the disruptions occasioned by foreign rule. The catastrophes in question, as clearly reported in the Egyptian texts, were celestial in nature and involved the most prominent planetary bodies.

On the rare occasion that Egyptologists have actually confronted the catastrophic traditions in the Egyptian texts, they have typically sought to interpret them by reference to mundane terrestrial matters. Christopher Eyre's explanation of the archaic tradition of Sakhmet's wading through human blood is typical: "The image of the goddess wading in blood might potentially be an image of wading in the inundation water; silt-bearing water—the good floodwater—was in modern times 'red' as opposed to 'white' water from artificial irrigation."[738] Seriously? Is this the best hypothesis modern science can offer on what amounts to a universal mythological theme?

Is it really possible to believe, with Eyre, Goebs, and the vast majority of Egyptologists, that the innumerable references to the raging of the Eye of Horus amidst apocalyptic storm and the attendant slaughter of mankind are to be explained as mere hyperbole on the part of Egyptian skywatchers—this from a culture otherwise known for their preference for literal, concrete imagery? At what point do all the ad hoc conjectures become simply too strained and superficial to maintain?

---

[737] J. Assmann, *Egyptian Solar Religion in the New Kingdom* (London, 1995), p. 54.
[738] C. Eyre, *The Cannibal Hymn* (Liverpool, 2002), p. 162.

What is most needed at this point in Egyptology is a return to a more concrete, evidence-based understanding of the Pyramid Texts and cosmogonic myth. Hymns speaking of the shaking of heaven and earth at the inaugural appearance of the Horus-star need to be understood as relatively faithful accounts of witnessed natural events, not only because the Egyptian mindset demands it but because the cosmogonic traditions of other cultures attest to the same basic idea. So, too, texts speaking of a "greening" associated with the prototypical sunrise are best understood as accurate memories of extraordinary astronomical events. Once this strategy is adopted, an entire new perspective opens up and the seemingly bizarre traditions surrounding the Eye, uraeus, Horus-star, *Akhet*, solar boat, and Divine Assembly suddenly begin to make sense and take their proper place within a coherent belief-system.

The very same argument applies to the earliest artworks featuring stellar objects and extraterrestrial structures. Pictographs and cylinder seals depicting the ancient "sun" as set atop a Primeval Hill and/or encircled by a giant crescent or assembly of stars point to a radically different solar system well within the memory of humankind. Properly understood, these archaic artworks serve to complement our findings derived from a comparative analysis of Egyptian cosmogonic myth. At the same time such artworks confirm our underlying thesis that the initial stimulus driving Egyptian cosmogonic myth and religion was astronomical in nature and had relatively little to do with speculation and/or projection onto the sky of human concerns. The sun was provided with a boat precisely because a giant boat-like structure formerly appeared in close proximity to the primordial sun. So, too, the sun was conceptualized as having a central "eye" precisely because a Venusian "eye" originally appeared in close proximity to the primordial sun. And what is true of the solar boat and Eye of Horus is also true of the uraeus-serpent, Divine Assembly, and dozens of other attributes affiliated with the primordial sun.

Simply put, there can be no proper understanding of ancient Egyptian civilization without coming to grips with the compelling evidence for astral religion and recent episodes of planetary catastrophism. It is the eyewitness testimony of prehistoric skywatchers that provides the long-sought Rosetta stone for deciphering Egyptian religion and cosmogonic myth. The end result is nothing less than a revolution in how we view the history of our planet and the origins of human civilization—not to mention the theoretical foundations of modern astronomy.

# Acknowledgments

I was initially introduced to the wonders of Egyptian religion and cosmogonic myth by David Talbott, whose *The Saturn Myth* and assorted writings formed a major inspiration for my own research. Dave and I collaborated for the better part of forty years, and his innumerable insights remain essential to my thinking. His formative influence is likely evident on every page of this manuscript.

Marinus van der Sluijs kindly consented to proofread the rough draft and provided countless corrections and learned commentary. *Egypt Under the Stars* is much improved thanks to his careful editorial eye and profound knowledge of ancient cosmogonic myth.

Eric Douma read an early draft of this work and offered some invaluable feedback and encouragement. In a perfect world, I would love to include these three fellows as co-authors on the byline as I have benefited immensely from their decades of friendship and camaraderie. That said, I remain sensitive to my mother's sage counsel regarding guilt by association.

# Bibliography

Abusch, T., *Essays on Babylonian and Biblical Literature and Religion* (Leiden, 2020).

Allen, J., *Genesis in Egypt* (New Haven, 1988).

Allen, J., "The Cosmology of the Pyramid Texts," in W. Simpson ed., *Religion and Philosophy in Ancient Egypt* (New Haven, 1989), pp. 1-28.

Allen, J., "Reading a Pyramid," in C. Berger et al eds., *Hommages à Jean Leclant I* (Cairo, 1994), pp. 5-28.

Allen, J., "The Celestial Realm," in D. Silverman ed., *Ancient Egypt* (Oxford, 1997), pp. 114-131.

Allen, J., *The Ancient Egyptian Pyramid Texts* (Atlanta, 2005).

Allen, J., *Middle Egyptian* (Cambridge, 2010).

Allen, J., *Grammar of the Ancient Egyptian Pyramid Texts, Volume 1: Unis* (Winona Lake, 2017).

Allen, T., *Horus in the Pyramid Texts* (Chicago, 1916).

Almansa-Villatoro, M., "The Cultural Indexicality of the N41 Sign for *bjꜣ*: The Metal of the Sky and the Sky of Metal," *Journal of Egyptian Archaeology* 105 (2020), pp. 73-81.

Altenmüller, H., "Djed-Pfeiler," *Lexikon der Ägyptologie 1* (Berlin, 1975), cols. 1100-1105.

Altenmüller, H., "Aspekte des Sonnenlaufes in den Pyramidentexten," in F. Daumas ed., *Hommages à Francoise Daumas* (Montpellier, 1986), pp. 1-15.

Amiet, P., *La glyptique mésopotamienne archaique* (Paris, 1961).

Andrews, C., *Amulets of Ancient Egypt* (London, 1994).

Anthes, R., "The Original Meaning of *mꜣꜥ ḫrw*," *JNES* 13 (1954), pp. 21-51.

Anthes, R., "Sonnenboote in den Pyramidentexten," *ZÄS* 82 (1957), pp. 77-89.

Anthes, R., "Egyptian Theology in the Third Millennium B.C.," *JNES* 18 (1959), pp. 169-212.

Anthes, R., "Das Sonnenauge in den Pyramidentexten," *ZÄS* 86 (1961), pp. 1-21.

Anthes, R., "Horus als Sirius in den Pyramidentexten," *ZÄS* 102 (1975), pp. 1-10.

Assmann, J., "Horizont," *Lexikon der Ägyptologie 3* (Berlin, 1977), cols. 3-7.

Assmann, J., "Schöpfung," *Lexikon der Ägyptologie 5* (Wiesbaden, 1984), cols. 677-690.

Assmann, J., "Sonnengott," *Lexikon der Ägyptologie 6* (Berlin, 1984), cols 1087-1094.

Assmann, J., "Death and Initiation in the Funerary Religion of Ancient Egypt," in W. Simpson ed., *Religion and Philosophy in Ancient Egypt* (New Haven, 1989), pp. 135-159.

Assmann, J., "Isis," in K. van der Toorn et al, *Dictionary of Deities and Demons in the Bible* (Leiden, 1999), cols. 456-458.

Assmann, J., *Egyptian Solar Religion in the New Kingdom* (London, 1995).

Assmann, J., *The Mind of Egypt* (Cambridge, 1996).

Assmann, J., *The Search for God in Ancient Egypt* (Ithaca, 2001).

Ayali-Darshan, N., "The Other Version of the Story of the Storm-god's Combat with the Sea…," *JANER* 15 (2015), pp. 20-51.

Badawy, A., "The Ideology of the Superstructure of the Mastaba-Tomb in Egypt," *JNES* 15 (1956), pp. 180-183.

Badawy, A., "The Stellar Destiny of Pharaoh and the So-Called Air-Shafts of Cheops' Pyramid," *MIO* 10 (1964), pp. 189-206.

Bagnall, R., & Dero, P., eds., *The Hellenistic Period* (Oxford, 2004).

Baines, J., "On the symbolic context of the principal hieroglyph for 'God'," in U. Verhoeven & E. Graefe eds., *Religion und Philosophie im alten Ägypten* (Leuven, 1991), pp. 29-46.

Baines, J., "Egyptian Myth and Discourse," *JNES* 50 (1991), pp. 81-105.

Baines, J., "Origins of Egyptian Kingship," in D. O'Connor & D. Silverman eds., *Ancient Egyptian Kingship* (Leiden, 1995), pp. 95-156.

Baines, J., "Sources of Egyptian Temple Cosmology," in D. Ragavan ed., *Heaven and Earth* (Chicago, 2013), pp. 395-424.

Barta, M., "The Ancient Egyptian Sky," in S. Vannini ed., *King Tut: The Journey Through the Underworld* (New York, 2020), pp. 244-254.

Barta, W., "Zur Bedeutung des Stirnbands-Diadems *sšd*," *Göttinger Miszellen* 72 (1984), pp. 7-8.

Begelsbacher-Fischer, B., *Untersuchungen zur Götterwelt des Alten Reiches im Spiegel der Privatgräber der IV. und V. Dynastie* (Fribourg, 1981).

Bell, L., "Luxor Temple and the Cult of the Royal Ka," *JNES* 44 (1985), pp. 251-294.

Belmonte, J., and Lull, J., *Astronomy of Ancient Egypt* (Cham, 2023).

Bergman, J., "Isis," in *Lexikon der Ägyptologie 3* (Berlin, 1980), cols. 183-203.

Berndt, R., "A 'Wonguri'-Mandeikai song cycle of the moon-bone," *Oceania* 19 (1948), pp. 16-50.

Betrò, M., *Hieroglyphics* (New York, 1996).

Beinlich, H., "Sterne," *Lexikon der Ägyptologie 6* (Wiesbaden, 1986), cols. 12-13.

Billing, N., *Performative Structure* (Copenhagen, 2018).

N. Billing, "Text and Tomb: Some spatial properties of Nut in the Pyramid Texts," in Z. Hawass et al eds., *Egyptology at the Dawn of the Twenty-first Century, Vol. 2* (Cairo, 2003), pp. 129-136.

Black, J., et al., *The Electronic Text Corpus of Sumerian Literature* (http://www-etcsl.orient.ox.ac.uk/) (Oxford, 1998).

Blackman, A., "The Stela of Nebipusenwosret," *JEA* 21 (1934), pp. 1-9.

Blackman, A., & Fairman, H., "The Myth of Horus at Edfu—III," *JEA* 29 (1943), pp. 2-36.

Boehmer, R., *Die entwicklung der Glyptik während der Akkad-Zeit* (Berlin, 1965).

Bolshakov, A. *Man and his Double in Egyptian ideology of the Old Kingdom* (Wiesbaden, 1997).

Boltz, W., *The Origin and Early Development of the Chinese Writing System* (New Haven, 1994).

Borghouts, J., *The Magical Texts of Papyrus Leiden I 348* (Leiden, 1971).

Borghouts, J., "The Evil Eye of Apophis," *JEA* 59 (1973), pp. 114-150.

Bosse-Griffiths, K., "The Great Enchantress in the Little Golden Shrine of Tut'Ankhamun," in J. Gwyn Griffiths ed., *Amarna Studies and Other Selected Papers* (Fribourg, 2001), pp. 111-123.

Boylan, P., *Thoth* (London, 1922).

Breasted, J., *Development of Religion and Thought in Ancient Egypt* (Philadelphia, 1912).

Briggs, R., "Astronomy," in S. Mercer, *The Pyramid Texts, Vol. IV* (New York, 1952), pp. 38-48.

Brown, D., *Mesopotamian Planetary Astronomy-Astrology* (Groningen, 2000).

Brugsch, H., *Religion und Mythologie der Alten Aegypter* (Leipzig, 1890).

Brunner-Traut, E., "Farben," *Lexikon der Ägyptologie 2* (Wiesbaden, 1977), cols. 117-128.

Budin, S., *Images of Woman and Child from the Bronze Age* (Cambridge, 2011).

Burkert, W., *The Orientalizing Revolution* (London, 1992).
Caminos, R., *The Chronicle of Prince Osorkon* (Rome, 1958).
Carrier, C., *Textes des Sarcophages du Moyen Empire Égyptien, Vol. II* (Paris, 2004).
Chamberlain, del V., *When Stars Came Down to Earth* (College Park, 1982).
Clark, R., *Myth and Symbol in Ancient Egypt* (London, 1959).
Cochrane, E., "Sothis and the Morning Star," *Aeon* 3:5 (1994), pp. 77-94.
Cochrane, E., *Martian Metamorphoses* (Ames, 1997).
Cochrane, E., "Aphrodite Urania," *Aeon* 5:2 (1998), pp. 43-62.

Cochrane, E., *The Many Faces of Venus* (Ames, 2001).
Cochrane, E., *Fossil Gods and Forgotten Worlds* (Ames, 2010).
Cochrane, E., *The Case of the Turquoise Sun* (Ames, 2024).
Collier, S., *The Crowns of Pharaoh* (Ph.D. Dissertation: University of California Los Angeles, 1996).
Cumont, F., *Astrology and Religion among the Greeks and Romans* (New York, 1960).
Darnell, J., "Hathor Returns to Medamud," *JEA* 22 (1995), pp. 47-94.
Darnell, J., "The Apotropaic Goddess in the Eye," *Studien zur Altägyptischen Kultur* 24 (1997), pp. 35-48.
Darnell, J., "A Midsummer Night's Succubus…," in S. Melville & A. Slotsky eds., *Opening the Tablet Box* (Leiden, 2010), pp. 99-140.
Depuydt, L., "The Function of the Ebers Calendar Concordance," *Orientalia* 65 (1996), pp. 61-88.
Depuydt, L., "Sothic Chronology and Old Kingdom," *Journal of the American Research Center in Egypt* 37 (2000), pp. 167-186.
Depuydt, L., "Ancient Chronology's Alpha and Egyptian Chronology's Debt to Babylon," in M. Ross ed., *From the Banks of the Euphrates* (Winona Lake, 2008), pp. 35-50.
de Young, G., "Egyptian astronomy," in H. Selin ed., *Encyclopaedia of the History of Science, Technology and Medicine in Non-Western Cultures* (Norwell, 1997), pp. 111-112.
Edwards, S., *The Symbolism of the Eye of Horus in the Pyramid Texts* (1995).
Edzard, D. O., "Deep-Rooted Skyscrapers and Bricks: Ancient Mesopotamian Architecture and its Imagery," in M. Mindlin et al eds., *Figurative Language in the Ancient Near East* (Jerusalem, 1987), pp. 13-22.
Eliade, M., *Myths, Rites, and Symbols* (New York, 1975).

Erman, A., *Hymnen an das Diadem der Pharaonen* (Berlin, 1911).
Eyre, C., *The Cannibal Hymn* (Liverpool, 2002).
Fairman, H., "The Myth of Horus at Edfu—I," *JEA* 21 (1935), pp. 26-36.
Faulkner, R., "The 'Cannibal Hymn' from the Pyramid Texts," *JEA* 10 (1924), pp. 97-103.
Faulkner, R., "The Bremner-Rhind Papyrus—II," *JEA* 23 (1937), pp. 10-16.
Faulkner, R., "The Bremner-Rhind Papyrus—IV," *JEA* 24 (1938), pp. 41-53.
Faulkner, R., "The King and the Star-Religion in the Pyramid Texts," *JNES* 25 (1966), pp. 153-161.
Faulkner, R., *The Ancient Egyptian Pyramid Texts* (Oxford, 1969).
Faulkner, R., "'The Pregnancy of Isis': A Rejoinder," *JEA* 59 (1973), pp. 218-219.
Faulkner, R., *The Ancient Egyptian Coffin Texts* (Warminster, 1973).
Faulkner, R., *The Egyptian Book of the Dead* (San Francisco, 1994).
Finnestad, R., *Image of the World and Symbol of the Creator* (Wiesbaden, 1985).
Firchow, O., "Königsschiff und Sonnenbarke," *WZKM* 54 (1957), pp. 34-42.
Fischer, H., "Hieroglyphen," *Lexikon der Ägyptologie 2* (Wiesbaden, 1977), cols. 1189-1199.
Foster, B., *Before the Muses* (Bethesda, 1993).
Frankfort, H., *Kingship and the Gods* (Chicago, 1948).
Frankfort, H. & H. A., "Myth and Reality," in H. Frankfort et al eds., *Intellectual Adventure of Ancient Man* (Chicago, 1946), pp. 3-30.
Frayne, D., *Old Babylonian Period* (2003-1595 BC) (Toronto, 1990).
Friedman, F., "The Root Meaning of $ȝḫ$: Effectiveness or Luminosity," *Serapis* 8 (1984/5), pp. 39-46.
Friedman, F., ed., *Gifts of the Nile: Ancient Egyptian Faience* (Leuven, 1992).
Gahlin, L., "Creation Myths," in T. Wilkinson ed., *The Egyptian World* (London, 2007), pp. 296-309.
Gardiner, A., "The Coronation of King Ḥaremḥab," *JEA* 39 (1953), pp. 13-31.
Gardiner, A., *Egyptian Grammar* (Oxford, 1957).
Giveon, R., "Soped in Sinai," *Festschrift für Westendorf, Vol. 2* (Göttingen, 1984), pp. 777-784.
Goebs, K., "A Functional Approach to Egyptian Myth and Mythemes," *JANER* 2 (2002), pp. 27-59.

Goebs, K., "*Niswt nḥḥ*—Kingship, Cosmos, and Time," in Z. Hawass ed., *Egyptology at the Dawn of the Twenty-first Century, Vol. 2* (Cairo, 2003), pp. 238-253.

Goebs, K., "Kingship," in T. Wilkinson ed., *The Egyptian World* (New York, 2007), pp. 275-295.

Goebs, K., *Crowns in Egyptian Funerary Literature* (Oxford, 2008).

Goebs, K., "King as God and God as King," in R. Gundlach & K. Spence eds., *Palace and Temple* (Wiesbaden, 2011), pp. 57-101.

Goebs, K., "Receive the Henu—that You May Shine Forth in it like Akhty," in F. Coppens, J. Janák & H. Vymazalová eds., *Royal versus Divine Authority* (Wiesbaden, 2015), pp. 145-175.

Goldwasser, O., *Prophets, Lovers and Giraffes* (Wiesbaden, 2002).

Goyon, J.-C., "Répandre l'or et éparpiller la verdure...," in J. van Dijk, *Essays on Ancient Egypt in Honour of Herman te Velde* (Groningen, 1997), pp. 85-100.

Grapow, H., "Die Welt vor der Schöpfung," *ZÄS* 67 (1931), pp. 34-38.

Griffiths, J. G., "Remarks on the Mythology of the Eyes of Horus," *Chronique d'Egypte* 33 (1958), pp. 182-193.

Griffiths, J. G., *The Conflict of Horus and Seth* (Chicago, 1969).

Griffiths, J. G., "Review of 'The Imperishable Stars of the Northern Sky in the Pyramid Texts'," *JEA* 80 (1994), pp. 231-232.

Guilhou, N., *La Vieillesse de Dieux* (Montpellier, 1989).

Gundel, W., "Sirius," in *RE 5* (Stuttgart, 1927), cols. 314-351.

Gunn, B., "Notes on the Aten and his names," *JEA* 9 (1923), p. 168.

Gunn, B., "Note," *JEA* 25 (1939), pp. 218-219.

Hall, H. R., "Review of *De Egyptische Voorstellingen betreffende den Oerheuvel*," *JEA* 10 (1924), pp. 185-187.

Hallo, W., & van Dijk, J., *The Exaltation of Inanna* (New Haven, 1968).

Hancock, J., et al, *Storks, Ibises and Spoonbills of the World* (London, 1992).

Hannig, R., *Ägyptisches Wörterbuch I* (Mainz, 2003).

Hawass, Z., *Mountains of the Pharaoh* (Cairo, 2006).

Haynes, R., "Aboriginal Astronomy," *Aust. J. Astr.* 4:3 (1992), pp. 127-141.

Heimpel, W., "A Catalog of Near Eastern Venus Deities," *Syro-Mesopotamian Studies* 4:3 (1982), pp. 9-22.

Heimpel, W., "The Sun at Night and the Doors of Heaven," *JCS* 38/2 (1986), pp. 127-151.

Heimpel, W., "Mythologie A.1," in E. Ebeling & B. Meissner, *Reallexikon der Assyriologie* 8 (Berlin, 1993-1997), pp. 537-564.

Helck, W., "Aphrodite," *Lexikon der Ägyptologie 1* (Wiesbaden, 1975), col. 337.

Hornung, E., "Chaotische Bereiche in der geordneten Welt," *ZÄS* 81 (1956), pp. 28-32.

Hornung, E., "Dat," *Lexikon der Ägyptologie 1* (Wiesbaden, 1975), cols. 994-995.

Hornung, E., *Der ägyptische Mythos von der Himmelskuh* (Freiburg, 1982).

Hornung, E., *Conceptions of God in Ancient Egypt* (Ithaca, 1982), p. 227.

Hornung, E., *Die Nachtfahrt der Sonne* (Zurich, 1990).

Hornung, E., *Idea Into Image* (Princeton, 1992).

Hornung, E., "Ancient Egyptian Religious Iconography," in J. Sasson ed., *Civilizations of the Ancient Near East, Vol. 3/4* (Farmington Hills, 1995), pp. 1711-1730.

Hornung, E., *The Ancient Egyptian Books of the Afterlife* (Ithaca, 1999).

Hruška, B., "Zum Zum heiligen Hügel in der altmesopotamischen Religion," *WKZM* 86 (1996), pp. 161-175.

Irby-Massie, G., & P. Keyser, P., *Greek Science of the Hellenistic Era* (London, 2002).

Jacobsen, T., *Treasures of Darkness* (New Haven, 1976).

Jamison, S., & J. Brereton, J., *The Rigveda* (Austin, 2014).

Jansen-Winkeln, K., "'Horizont und Verklärtheit': Zur Bedeutung der Wurzel ꜣḫ," *Studien zur altägyptischen Kultur* 23 (1996), pp. 201-215.

Johnson, S., *The Cobra Goddess of Ancient Egypt* (London, 1990).

Jorgensen, J., "Myths, Menarche and the *Return of the Goddess*," in R. Nyord & K. Ryholt eds., *Lotus and Laurel* (Copenhagen, 2015), pp. 131-164.

Joseph, A., "Divine Wrath in Ancient Egypt," *Études et Travaux* 31 (2018), pp. 27-65.

Junker, H., *Der Auszug der Hathor-Tefnut aus Nubien* (Berlin, 1911).

Kákosy, L., "Sothis," *Lexikon der Ägyptologie 5* (Berlin, 1984), pp. 1110-1117.

Kákosy, L., "Astral Mythology in Egypt," *Acta Antiqua* 40 (2000), pp. 213-216.

Katz, D., *The Image of the Netherworld in the Sumerian Sources* (Bethesda, 2003).

Kemp, B., *100 Hieroglyphs* (London, 2005).

Kern-Lileso, E., "Stirnband und Diademe," *Lexikon der Ägyptologie* 1 (Wiesbaden, 1975), cols. 45-49.

Kocklemann, H., "Ein neuer funerärer Spruch mit Anrufung der Mumienbinde," in B. Backes, Müller-Roth, M., & S. Stöhr, S. eds., *Ausgestattet mit den Schriften des Thot* (Wiesbaden, 2009), pp. 89-104.

Kramer, S., *From the Poetry of Sumer* (Berkeley, 1979).

Krauss, R., *Astronomische Konzepte und Jenseitsvorstellungen in den Pyramidentexten* (Wiesbaden, 1997).

Krauss, R., "The Eye of Horus and the Planet Venus," in J. Steele & A. Imhausen eds., *Under One Sky* (Munster, 2002), pp. 193-208.

Krauss, R., "Egyptian Sirius/Sothic Dates, and the Question of the Sothis-Based Lunar Calendar," in E. Hornung, R. Krauss, & D. Warburton eds., *Ancient Egyptian Chronology* (Leiden, 2006), pp. 439-457.

Krauss, R., "Stellar Power and Solar Components in Ancient Egyptian Mythology and Royal Ideology," in M. Rappenglück et al eds., *Astronomy and Power* (Oxford, 2016), pp. 137-142.

Krupp, E., *Beyond the Blue Horizon* (Oxford, 1991).

Kurth, D., *Den Himmel stützen* (Brussels, 1975).

Kurth, D., *Edfou VII: Übersetzungen* (Wiesbaden, 2004).

Lambert, W., "Lugal-IGI.DU-anna," *Reallexikon Assyriologie* 7 (Berlin, 1983), p. 142.

Lambert, W., *Babylonian Wisdom Literature* (Winona Lake, 1996).

Lapinkivi, P., *The Sumerian Sacred Marriage* (Helsinki, 2004).

Lehner, M., *The Complete Pyramids* (London, 1997).

Lesko, L., "Ancient Egyptian Cosmogonies and Cosmology," in B. Shafer ed., *Religion in Ancient Egypt* (Ithaca, 1991), pp. 88-122.

Lichtheim, M., *Ancient Egyptian Literature, Vol. 1* (Berkeley, 1975).

Lichtheim, M., *Ancient Egyptian Literature, Vol. II* (Berkeley, 1976).

Lieven, A. von, "The soul of the sun permeates the whole world," *Pandanus*10 (2010), pp. 29-60.

Lloyd, A., "Expeditions to the Wadi Hammamat," in J. Hill et al eds., *Experiencing Power, Generating Authority* (Philadelphia, 2013), pp. 361-382.

Lull, J., & Belmonte, J., "The Constellations of Ancient Egypt," in J. Belmonte & M. Shaltout eds., *In Search of Cosmic Order* (Cairo, 2009), pp. 155-194.

Mace, A., & H. Winlock, H., *The Tomb of Senebtisi at Lisht* (New York, 1916).

Macfarlane, A., *The God Min to the End of the Old Kingdom* (Sydney, 1995).

Majno, G., *The Healing Hand* (Cambridge, 1975).

Manassa, C., *The Late Egyptian Underworld* (Wiesbaden, 2007).
Maravelia, A., "The Function and Importance of Some Special Categories of Stars in the Ancient Egyptian Funerary Texts, 2," in A. Maravelia & N. Guilhou eds., *Environment and Religion in Ancient & Coptic Egypt* (Oxford, 2020), pp. 243-256.
Martin, K., "Urhügel," *Lexikon der Ägyptologie* 3 (Berlin, 1980), cols. 873-875.
Maul, S., "Die altorientalische Hauptstadt—Abbild und Nabel der Welt," in G. Wilhelm ed., *Die orientalische Stadt* (Halle, 1997), pp. 109-124.
D. Meeks, D., & Favard-Meeks, C., *Daily Life of the Egyptian Gods* (Ithaca, 1996).
Mercer, S., *The Pyramid Texts in Translation and Commentary, Vol. 2* (New York, 1952).
Milbrath, S., *Star Gods of the Maya* (Austin, 1999).
Miller, D., *Stars of the First People* (Boulder, 1997).
Muller-Winkler, C., "Schen-Ring," *Lexikon der Ägyptologie* 5 (Wiesbaden,1984), pp. 577-579.
Müller, W., "Egyptian Mythology," in L. Gray ed., *The Mythology of All Races, Vol.* 12 (Boston, 1918).
Nagy, G., *Greek Mythology and Poetics* (Ithaca, 1990).
Nelson, H., "Certain Reliefs at Karnak and Medinet Habu…," *JNES* 8 (1949), pp. 310-345.
Neugebauer, O., "Egyptian Planetary Texts," *Transactions of the American Philosophical Society* 32 (1942), pp. 209-250.
Neugebauer, O., & Parker, R., *Egyptian Astronomical Texts I: The Early Decans* (London, 1960).
Neugebauer, O., & Parker, R., *Egyptian Astronomical Texts, Vol. 3* (London, 1960).
Neugebauer, O., *A History of Ancient Mathematical Astronomy* (Heidelberg, 1975).
Neugebauer, O., *A History of Ancient Mathematical Astronomy, Vol. 2* (Berlin, 1975).
Nietzsche, F., *Human All Too Human* (Lincoln, 1996).
Nyord, R., *Breathing Flesh: Conceptions of the Body in the Ancient Egyptian Coffin Texts* (Copenhagen, 2009).
Onians, R., *The Origins of European Thought* (Cambridge, 1954).
Orwell, G., "Politics and the English Language," *The Orwell Reader* (New York, 1984), pp. 355-366.
Nicholson, P., & Shaw, I., *Ancient Egyptian Materials and Technology* (Cambridge, 2000).

Otto, E., "Dua," and "Duai," in W. Helck ed., *Lexikon der Ägyptologie I* (Wiesbaden, 1975), cols. 1147-1148.

Parker, R., "The Year in Ancient Egypt," *Journal of Calendar Reform* 25 (1955), pp. 81-83.

Parker, R., "Egyptian astronomy, astrology, and calendrical reckoning," in C. Gillispie ed., *Dictionary of Scientific Biography, Vol. 16* (New York, 1971-1980), pp. 706-727.

Parpola, S., "The Assyrian Tree of Life," *JNES* 52:3 (1993), pp. 161-208.

Potts, D. T., "Notes on Some Horned Buildings in Iran, Mesopotamia and Arabia," *RA* 84 (1990), pp. 33-40.

Puhvel, J., *Comparative Mythology* (Baltimore, 1987).

Quack, J., "A Goddess Rising 10,000 Cubits into the Air," in J. Steele & A. Imhausen eds., *Under One Sky* (Münster, 2002), pp. 283-294.

Quack, J., "The Planets in Ancient Egypt," in P. Read ed., *Oxford Research Encyclopedia of Planetary Science* (Oxford, 2019), pp. 1-35.

Quirke, S., *Ancient Egyptian Religion* (London, 1992).

Quirke, S., *Going out in Daylight* (London, 2013).

Rashed, M., "The Significance of the Hieroglyph [deleted] 'The Egg with the Young Bird Inside', in G. Miniaci eds., *The World of Middle Kingdom Egypt (2000-1500 BC)* (London, 2015), pp. 309-324.

Redford, D., "$Ḥꜥy$ and Its Derivatives," in D. Redford, *History and Chronology of the Eighteenth Dynasty of Egypt* (Toronto, 1967), pp. 3-27.

Redford, D., "Egypt and the World Beyond," in D. Silverman ed., *Ancient Egypt* (London, 1997), pp. 40-57.

Reiner, E., & Pingree, D., *Babylonian Planetary Omens, Part Three* (Groningen, 1998).

Richter, B., "On the Heels of the Wandering Goddess," in M. Dolinska &. H. Beinlich eds., *Ägyptologische Tempeltagung* (Wiesbaden, 2010), pp. 155-185.

Richter, B., *The Theology of Hathor of Dendera* (Atlanta, 2016).

Rikala, M., "Sacred Marriage in the New Kingdom of Ancient Egypt," in M. Nissinen & R. Uro eds., *Sacred Marriages* (Winona Lake, 2008), pp. 115-144.

Ritner, R., "Horus on the Crocodiles," in W. Simpson ed., *Religion and Philosophy in Ancient Egypt* (New Haven, 1989), pp. 103-116.

Roberts, A., *Hathor Rising* (Devon, 1995).

Roberson, J., "The Iconicity of the Vertical: Hieroglyphic Encoding and the *Akhet* in Royal Burial Chambers of Egypt's New Kingdom," in I. Zsolnay ed., *Seen Not Heard* (Chicago, 2023), pp. 31-62.

Rose, L., "Just Plainly Wrong: A Critique of Peter Huber," in L. Greenberg & W. Sizemore, eds., *Velikovsky and Establishment Science* (Glassboro, 1977), pp. 102-112.

Rossi, C., "Science and Technology: Pharaonic," in A. Lloyd ed., *A Companion to Ancient Egyptian, Vol. 1* (Oxford, 2010), pp. 390-408.

Rudnitzky, G., *Die Aussage über 'Das Auge des Horus'* (Copenhagen, 1956).

Schäfer, H., "Weltgebäude der alten Ägypter," *Die Antike* 3 (1927), pp. 91-127.

Schenkel, W., "Horus," *Lexikon der Ägyptologie* 3 (Berlin, 1980), cols. 14-25.

Schumacher, I., *Der Gott Sopdu der Herr der Fremdländer* (Göttingen, 1988).

Schunck, M., *Untersuchungen zum Wortstamm ḥr* (Bonn, 1985).

Sethe, K., *Zur Sage vom Sonnenauge* (Leipzig, 1912).

Sethe, K., "Altägyptische Vorstellungen vom Lauf der Sonne," *Sitzungsberichten der Preussischen Akademie der Wissenschaften* (Berlin, 1928), pp. 259-284.

Sethe, K., *Übersetzung und Kommentar zu den altägyptischen Pyramidentexten, Vol. III* (Glückstadt, 1962).

Shaw, I., "Introduction: Chronologies and Cultural Change in Egypt," in I. Shaw ed., *The Oxford History of Ancient Egypt* (Oxford, 2000), pp. 1-15.

Sherkova, T., "Solar Notions, Rituals and Images in Pre-Dynastic Egypt," in A. Maravelia ed., *In Quest of Light* (Montpellier, 2009), pp. 133-136.

Simons, S., "A Star's Year: The Annual Cycle in the Ancient Egyptian Sky," in J. Steele, *Calendars and Years* (Oxford, 2007), pp. 1-25.

Sjöberg, Å., & Bergmann, E., *The Collection of the Sumerian Temple Hymns* (Locust Valley, 1969),

Smith, M., *On the Primaeval Ocean* (Copenhagen, 2002).

Smith, M., "P. Carlsberg 462: A Fragmentary Account of a Rebellion Against the Sun God," in P. Frandsen & K. Ryholt eds., *A Miscellany of Demotic Texts and Studies* (Copenhagen, 2000), pp. 95-112.

Spalinger, A., "Notes on the ancient Egyptian calendars," *Orientalia* 64 (1995), pp. 17-32.

Spalinger, A., "The Destruction of Mankind…," *Studien zur Altägyptischen Kultur* 28 (2000), pp. 257-282.

Stanulewicz, D., et al, "Axiological aspects of Polish Colour Vocabulary," in W. Anderson et al eds., *Colour Studies* (Amsterdam, 2014), pp. 258-272.

Staudacher, W., *Die Trennung von Himmel und Erde* (Darmstadt, 1968).

Steele, J., *Ancient Astronomical Observations and the Study of the Moon's Motion (1691-1757)* (London, 2012).

Steinkeller, P., "Inanna's Archaic Symbol," in J. Braun et al eds., *Written on Clay and Stone* (Warsaw, 1998), pp. 87-100.

Steinkeller, P., "Early Semitic Literature and Third Millennium Seals," in P. Fronzaroli ed., *Literature and Literary Language at Ebla* (1992), pp. 245-275.

Steinkeller, P., "On Stars and Men…," in A. Gianto ed., *Biblical and Oriental Essays in Memory of William L. Moran* (Rome, 2005), pp. 11-47.

Stephens, F., "Prayer of Lamentation to Ishtar," in J. Pritchard, *Ancient Near Eastern Texts Relating to the Old Testament* (Princeton, 1969), pp. 383-384.

Stephens, S., *Seeing Double: Intercultural Poetics in Ptolemaic Alexandria* (Berkeley, 2003).

Stern, S., *Calendars in Antiquity* (Oxford, 2012).

Stewart, H., "Traditional Egyptian Sun Hymns of the New Kingdom," *Bull. Inst. Arch.* 6 (1967), pp. 29-74.

Stille, A., "Perils of the Sphinx," *New Yorker* (February 10, 1997), pp. 54-66.

Strudwick, N., *Texts From the Pyramid Age* (Atlanta, 2005).

Sugi, A., "The Iconographical Representation of the Sun God in New Kingdom Egypt," in Z. Hawass et al eds., *Egyptology at the Dawn of the Twenty-first Century, Vol. 2* (Cairo, 2003), pp. 514-521.

Talbott, D., *The Saturn Myth* (New York, 1980).

Talbott, D., "The Ship of Heaven," *Aeon* 1:3 (1988), pp. 57-96.

Talbott, D., "The Great Comet Venus," *Aeon* 3:5 (1994), pp. 5-51.

Teissier, B., *Egyptian Iconography on Syrian-Palestinian Cylinder Seals of the Middle Bronze Age* (Fribourg, 1996).

Thomas, E., "Solar Barks Prow to Prow," *JEA* 42 (1956), pp. 65-79.

Troy, L., "Mut Enthroned," in J. van Dijk ed., *Essays on Ancient Egypt in Honour of Herman te Velde* (Groningen, 1997), pp. 301-315.

van Buren, E. D., "The Sun-God Rising," *Revue d'Assyriologie* 49 (1955), pp. 1-14.

van der Molen, R., *A Hieroglyphic Dictionary of Egyptian Coffin Texts* (Leiden, 2000).
van der Sluijs, M., *Traditional Cosmology, Vol. One* (London, 2011).
van der Sluijs, M., *Traditional Cosmology, Vol. Three* (London, 2011).
Vanstsiphout, H., *Epics of Sumerian Kings* (Leiden, 2004).
Ventura, R., "Sun Rays in Ancient Egyptian Art," in A. Ovadiah ed., *Milestones in Art and Culture of Egypt* (Tel Aviv, 2000), pp. 15-38.
von Beckerath, J., "Bemerkungen zum ägyptischen Kalendar," *ZÄS* 120 (1993), pp. 7-22, 131-136.
von Dechend, H., "Bemerkungen zum Donnerkeil," *Prismata: Festschrift für Willy Hartner* (Wiesbaden, 1977), pp. 93-118.
von Weiher, E., *Der babylonische Gott Nergal* (Berlin, 1971).
Wainwright, G., "Letopolis," *JEA* 18 (1932), pp. 159-172.
Wainwright, G., "Some Celestial Associations of Min," *JEA* 21 (1935), pp. 152-170.
Waitkus, W., "Die Geburt des Harsomtus aus der Blüte," *Studien zur Altägyptischen Kultur* 30 (2002), pp. 373-394.
Wallin, P., *Celestial Cycles* (Uppsala, 2002).
Ward, W., *The Seal Cylinders of Western Asia* (Washington, 1910).
Watterson, B., *The Gods of Ancient Egypt* (London, 1984).
Werr, L., *Studies in the Chronology and Regional Style of Old Babylonian Cylinder Seals* (Malibu, 1988).
Westendorf, W., "Sonnenlauf," *Lexikon der Ägyptologie VI* (Berlin, 1984), cols 1100-1103.
Westendorf, W., *Altägyptische Darstellungen des Sonnenlaufs auf der abschüssigen Himmelsbahn* (Berlin, 1966).
Westendorf, W. "Horizont und Sonnenschiebe," *Studia Aegyptiaca* 1 (1974), pp. 389-398.
Westenholz, J., "King by Love of Inanna," *NIN* 1 (2000), pp. 75-89.
Westenholz, J., "Heaven and Earth," in *Gazing on the Deep* (Bethesda, 2010), pp. 293-326.
White, G., *The Religious Iconography of Cappadocian Glyptic in the Assyrian Colony Period and its Significance in the Hittite New Kingdom* (1993), a Dissertation submitted to the University of Chicago.
Wiebach-Koepke, S., "The Growth of Plants in the Light of the Sun-God," in A. Maravelia ed., *In Quest of Light* (Montpellier, 2009), pp. 51-70.
Wiggermann, F., "Nergal," *RlA* 9 (Berlin, 1999), pp. 215-223.
Wilkinson, R., *Reading Egyptian Art* (London, 1992).

Wilkinson, T., *Early Dynastic Egypt* (London, 1999).
Wilkinson, T., *The Rise and Fall of Ancient Egypt* (New York, 2010).
Willems, H., *The Coffin of Heqata* (Leiden, 1996).
Wilson, J., "Deliverance of Mankind from Destruction," in J. Pritchard ed., *The Ancient Near East* (Princeton, 1958), pp. 3-4.
Wilson, J., "Egypt," in H. Frankfort et al eds., *Before Philosophy* (Baltimore, 1946), pp. 31-124.
Woods, C., "Sons of the Sun: The Mythological Foundations of the First Dynasty of Uruk," *JANER* 12 (2012), pp. 78-96.
Woods, C., "At the Edge of the World: Cosmological Conceptions of the Eastern Horizon in Mesopotamia," *JANER* 9:2 (2019), pp. 183-239.
Woods, C., "The Sun-God Tablet of Nabû-apla-iddina Revisited," *JCS* 56 (2004), pp. 23-103.
Zabkar, L., *Hymns to Isis in Her Temple at Philae* (Hanover, 1988).
Zago, S., *A Journey through the Beyond* (Columbus, 2022).
Zandee, J., *Der Amunhymnus des Papyrus Leiden I 344, Verso, Vol. 1* (Leiden, 1992).
Zandee, J., "Prayers to the Sun-god from Theban Tombs," *Jaarbericht ex Orient Lux* 16 (1964), pp. 48-71.

www.ingramcontent.com/pod-product-compliance
Lightning Source LLC
Chambersburg PA
CBHW080323080526

44585CB00021B/2444